THE DAEMONIC IMAGINATION
Biblical Text and Secular Story

edited by
Robert Detweiler
William G. Doty

Scholars Press
Atlanta, Georgia

THE DAEMONIC IMAGINATION

edited by
Robert Detweiler
William G. Doty

© 1990
The American Academy of Religion

Library of Congress Cataloging in Publication Data

The Daemonic imagination / edited by Robert Detweiler, William G.
  Doty.
  p. cm. -- (AAR studies in religion ; no. 60)
  Papers presented at a colloquy held in Boston in 1987, sponsored
  by the American Academy of Religion.
  Includes index.
  ISBN 1-55540-530-4 (alk. paper). -- ISBN 1-55540-531-2 (pbk.)
  1. Demoniac possession--Congresses. 2. Demonology in literature-
-Congresses. 3. Bible. N.T. Gospels. Mark--Criticism.
Interpretation, etc.--Congresses. 4. Healing of the Gerasene
demoniac (Miracle)--Congresses. 5. Narration in the Bible-
Congresses. 6. Atwood, Margaret Eleanor, 1939- Sin eater-
-Congresses. I. Detweiler, Robert. II. Doty, William G., 1939- .
III. American Academy of Religion. IV. Title: Demonic
imagination. V. Series.
BS2585.6.D5D34   1990
809'.93382--dc20   90-47455
                                                CIP

Printed in the United States of America
on acid-free paper

The Daemonic Imagination

ÆR

American Academy of Religion
Studies in Religion

Editor
Lawrence S. Cunningham

Number 60
THE DAEMONIC IMAGINATION

edited by
Robert Detweiler
William G. Doty

ACKNOWLEDGMENTS

Permission has been granted by Simon and Schuster, Inc. to reprint "The Sin Eater" by Margaret Atwood from her collection *Dancing Girls and Other Stories.* Copyright © 1977, 1982 by O. W. Toad, Ltd.

Permission has been granted by The Johns Hopkins University Press to reprint "The Demons of Gerasa" by René Girard from his book *The Scapegoat.* Copyright © 1986 by The Johns Hopkins University Press. The chapter appears there without the subheadings added in this volume.

Permission has been granted by *Listening: Journal of Religion and Culture* to reprint "Narrative Identity and Religious Identity" by David Pellauer. The essay appears in *Listening*, 23/2 (Spring, 1988), 134-42 without the subheadings added in this volume.

An expanded version of "Biblical Exorcism and Reader Response to Ritual in Narrative" by Carol Schersten LaHurd appears in *Biblical Theology Bulletin.*

The editors wish to thank Gregory Salyer and June Mann of Emory University, and Darwin Melnyk and Dennis Ford of Scholars Press, for their work in preparing this volume for publication via camera ready copy.

CONTENTS

Contents

PREFACE
James B. Wiggins

Participation in the colloquy in 1987, which was the background occasion for the essays brought together here by Robert Detweiler and William G. Doty, was a memorable instance of the convergence of my interests and responsibilities during the past decade. Being simultaneously in the offices of the Executive Director of the American Academy of Religion, chair of the Board of Trustees of Scholars Press, chair of a department of religion and professor of religion has not always led to such convergences. But it was at an AAR meeting in 1973 that I first presented a paper on narrative and subsequently edited a book of essays that included several written by active AAR members. Thus, my participation in the consultation was continuous with my vocational commitments. When Professor Detweiler invited me to contribute a preface to a book to be published by Scholars Press, it seemed the appropriate culmination of the originary occasion's "effective history," as Hans-Georg Gadamer would have it.

The AAR colloquia in Boston and (in 1988) in Chicago were exciting and stimulating. These essays succeed remarkably in communicating the power and importance of the issues and the reflections upon them that were brought together into those conversations. There is a demonstration of imaginative inquiry and criticism assembled in this collection. That already marks the enterprise as distinctive, since imagination and critical rationality have been so forcefully sundered in Western thought since the Enlightenment.

The essays are dramatically "postmodern" in their taking-for-granted sense that we live in linguistically constructed worlds of which the poets (the supreme "wordsmiths" among us) are the oracles and harbingers. The essays are reflexive in demanding that those living in imaginatively generated communities of discourse take ethical responsibility for the world so imagined. Were more critics so inclined, perhaps the radical seriousness of the challenges set forth by literary artists (among others) would be more honestly recognized. In the climate of contemporary

American sensibilities, which includes some who would restrict artistic expression, there is already an ironic witness to the power of imagination to disrupt and challenge taken-for-granted systems of order, whether legal, political or moral. Some among us want undisruptive art, which is to say unimaginative art.

But the two narratives that focus the essays in this book, the story of the Gerasene demoniac in the Gospel according to Mark, and Margaret Atwood's short story "The Sin Eater," tell of other things than the conventional and the taken for granted. The critical reflections gathered in these essays wrestle with the imaginative constructs that intrude upon a sensitive reader of these disturbing stories.

That these narratives are poly-valent and plurisignificative is amply indicated by the diverse readings provoked by them. This diversity indicates how dramatically the shifts in critical practice have moved from seeking the one correct reading and understanding of a text, whether biblical or otherwise, to a deep appreciation of and respect for the difference that a story makes from one reader or community of readers to another. The imaginative language of the story arouses the imaginative reading of the critic. The conversation therein initiated by the story challenges both its teller/author and its hearer/reader with the question: do you take responsibility for a world so construed? Tomorrow, when different stories engage sensitive readers, the question will be far less whether yesterday's stories were "true" and today's "false," and much more whether responsibility will be taken for today's stories that will be the analogue to the responsibility taken by the radiations that were born from and sustained by yesterday's stories.

William Doty in his Afterword begins with the words of the novelist John Fowles: "You create out of what you lack. Not what you have." It is imagination that moves into the lack, the void, the chaos and speaks of what has never been but might yet be. Although the perfect symphony will never be composed, the flawless building never be built, the novel or poem that exhausts the genres never be written, the indomitable spirit that seeks to do those things leaves each generation with its valiant, if failed, expressions. Driven and lured by whatever it lacks, each new generation will create its own finite, failed expressions. Happily, much can be learned from these attempts, provided that the fantasy of success and perfection can be overcome. Doty, through Kafka's parable "Das Ziel," reminds the reader that "away from here" ("weg-von-hier") is humanity's aim. It is indeed fortunate that "it is truly an immense journey," since it is humankind's destiny.

The editors and essayists have done us the service of provisioning us for continuing the adventure. If it would be excessive to claim that sufficient provisions are herein offered for the entire immense journey, it is accurate to insist that food and drink more than sufficient for the evils of this day's reading and reflection are delectably provided. I invite you to the banquet. Let tomorrow's hunger and thirst await their own satisfactions.

FROM CHAOS TO LEGION TO CHANCE: THE DOUBLE PLAY OF APOCALYPTIC AND MIMESIS
Robert Detweiler

> When you have once seen the chaos, you must make
> some thing to set between yourself and that terrible
> sight; and so you make a mirror, thinking that in it
> shall be reflected the reality of the world; but then you
> understand that the mirror reflects only appearances,
> and that reality is somewhere else, off behind the
> mirror; and then you remember that behind the mirror
> there is only chaos.[1]

FROM CHAOS TO APOCALYPTIC

One story underlies and threatens all others in the short history of human expression, and it is the story that all others resist. Its substance is that the world is out of control. A basis of it is what Paul Ricoeur calls "the horror of the unformed," or what we know from the history of theology and philosophy as the *horror vacui*.[2] Chaos is the nightmare of the human race—worse even than suffering and death. If the world could have a plan, suffering and death might have meaning, but chaos is disorder, planlessness, and prevents meaning.

The story of chaos is seldom told, for as soon as it begins, it is modulated (some would say displaced) into narratives of order and control. Yet—and thus—the story of chaos haunts every tale of order. It is the repressed, spectral story, unnerving in its absence, that wants body but that forces in its stead articulation of the tales of order. It has, itself, only the extremities of beginning and end.

One could argue, of course, that a tale of chaos is an impossibility, a contradiction in terms, for the very dynamic of its telling imposes an order, however makeshift, that denies chaos, and in this sense all narration as indeed all rational discourse asserts order over chaos. But one could also argue that such imposition is only a superimposition, that the ordering story

1

merely covers over the terrifying blank of chaos, and hence we are compelled to tell stories again and again: as long as we do, we fill in the blank; we can believe that this modicum of control derives from, replicates, a natural orderliness of the cosmos.

Such belief is at the heart of religion and myth. All religions (at least all traditional religions) provide more or less extensive narratives—cosmogonies and theogonies—of how the overcoming of chaos initiates the beginning of the world. In many such mythologies chaos is a primordial absence, an emptiness sometimes imaged as an abyss or a primal unbounded force older than the gods and out of which they emerge. The word itself, identical with the Greek *chaos*, in

> Hesiod's *Theogony* (c. eighth century BCE) denoted a cosmogonic 'yawning gap, chasm, or void,' from which generated the successive worlds of the gods and mankind.   Hesiod, who drew upon earlier mythological sources, rather neutrally depicted the original chaos as merely the empty, dark space that allowed for the penetrating movement of erotic desire and for the appearance of Earth (Gaia) as the secure home for all subsequent created forms and beings. . . . The primal chaos is itself only the blind abyss necessary for the creation of the physical world, but *chaos* here [in *Theogony*] also refers to the mythic period—and by implication to a kind of 'chaos-order' or condition—of the pre-Olympian gods who struggle against the imposition of Zeus's all-encompassing rule.[3]

In Hesiod's writing Chaos is also the primeval goddess who spawns Night, Erebus (Darkness), Tartarus (Hell), and Eros; by the time of Orphic myth Chaos is projected as coexistent with Erebus and Night at the start; and still later, in Ovid's *Metamorphosis*, "Chaos had evolved from the Hesiodic nothingness into a confused mass from which all things were created by harmonizing the various parts."[4] One observes the human need to embody and personify chaos, to transform chaos into some order-shaping narrative, dramatically in the so-called

Babylonian Genesis myth, the Mesopotamian cosmogony *Enuma Elish*. Here Tiamat, mother of the gods, is portrayed as a primordial monster, a dragon who with her mate Apsu produces the gods but who is eventually destroyed by them, above all by her son Marduk, king of the gods, and her body cut up to create the world. One reason why Tiamat's children killed her may have been her prodigious fertility: she gave birth to so many gods that the establishing of order was impossible.[5] In the monotheistic creation story that begins the Hebrew Bible, on the other hand, chaos is simply *tohu wa vohu*, "the deep," "without form and void" (Genesis1:2), and the background or context out of which the presumably co-preexisting Yahweh fashions the world.[6]

Without taking too reckess a leap, we might go on to say that the attempted (re)claiming of the world from chaos occurs via two powerful concepts that influence the two major strands of narrativity in the Greco-Judeo-Christian tradition. One of these is the concept of apocalypse that permeates the Hebrew-Christian *Heilsgeschichte*, the story of the salvation of God's people. The other is the concept of mimesis from Aristotle's discussion of tragedy in his *Poetics*. Neither of these is present in the early stages of their respective Hebrew and Greek cultural contexts.[7] The earliest Hebrew apocalyptic impulses are found in the postexilic prophetic writings of the late sixth century BCE, considerably earlier than the "classical" Jewish apocalyptic texts such as 1 *Enoch*, Daniel, and 4 *Ezra*,[8] and do not inform the older texts of the Hebrew Bible—although the stories of the patriarchs, kings, judges, and prophets certainly are accounts of efforts to force order on a chaotic and hostile environment as Yahweh employs his chosen folk to subjugate the land's evil inhabitants. Similarly, the highly sophisticated literary criticism of Aristotle from the fourth century BCE is a giant step beyond the Dionysian rituals, out of which both classical tragedy and comedy evolved, and which sought to impose ecstatic order on unruly religious expression.

Both apocalyptic and mimesis actually attempt to overcome narrativity, the first by substituting the spectacle of cataclysm (again the influence of chaos) and the mystical revelatory message for plot, and the second by redirecting the drama of story into the systematizing language of rhetoric and logic.[9] But narrative has always managed to assert itself. The mystic-fantastic event nature of apocalyptic and the realistic-programmatic discourse nature of mimesis seem to need the embodiment of narrative to sustain them, to provide them with continuity and context that defend against the encroachment of disorder in ways that the discontinuity of apocalyptic (i.e., its dependence on the abrupt, visionary message and on divine intervention) and the categorizing of mimesis (i.e., its abstracting pull, its reduction of plots to series of formulas) cannot.

The crucial involvement of apocalyptic and mimesis with narrative enables them to thwart chaos while in the process of engaging it.[10] Both owe to a fear of chaos their obsession with overcoming it. Hence both stress conflict (a basic disorder), crisis (a decisive engagement with the forces of conflict), and resolution, but they do so in significantly different ways. For both of them the source of the conflict is, one way or another, in the relationship of the natural to the supernatural, the human to the divine. Whereas in the case of Judeo-Christian apocalyptic, the conflict comes to focus on various incarnations of evil in the supernatural and the natural realms (including humans), in Greek tragedy—which I will adopt for the time being as representing a mimesis functioning in temporal contrast to apocalyptic—the conflict is localized in human beings, although the gods may be behind it, and the driving force of *moira*, or fate, is not necessarily evil; it simply is. In the Book of Revelation, for example, the world-ending catastrophe is caused by the evil of Satan and his cosmic cohorts as well as by individual and collective human wickedness, but in *Oedipus* the king's sins of pride, incest, and murder are the result of bad luck and inner flaws and do not mirror a universal evil.

In apocalyptic the crisis is a climax of divine revelation, as for instance in the Book of Revelation, where Christ will return to end the conflict by subduing evil and revealing the new age and who those are who will enjoy it. In *Oedipus* that climax is merely the king's *anagnorisis*, his recognition of his wrongdoing and of the ironic chain of events leading up to this moment of insight. Revelation in apocalyptic is foundational and world transforming. In mimesis it is "merely" instructive for the unlucky hero of tragedy and for the audience absorbing the drama. Or we could say that whereas the *peripeteia* of Greek tragedy, the reversal of fortune that the hero experiences as he recognizes his sin and guilt, occurs *as* the moment of crisis, in apocalyptic the reversal happens after the crisis, as good triumphs over evil and initiates an era of blissful existence.

And finally, this resolution of conflict in apocalyptic is a universalized version of the *peregrinatio vitae*, the circling-back after profligate existence, qua the Prodigal Son, whereby "the blessedness at the end is conceived not simply to equal, but to exceed the innocence and happiness at the beginning."[11] In Greek tragedy, by contrast, the resolution is the ennobling suffering of the hero brought low and, above all, the affective transfer to the audience, whose members undergo catharsis and are empowered by this emotional, mimetic cleansing.[12]

THE PERSISTENCE OF APOCALYPTIC

If such comparison of apocalyptic and mimetic literature in terms of narrative form appears to be apples and oranges— inappropriate if not outright bizarre—it is because of an enduring misconception that believes the influence of apocalyptic to have steadily declined to the point of impotence as reason succeeded religion in Western culture and as, correspondingly, mimesis as the embodiment of realism (eventually a scientific realism) increasingly prevailed. I will argue that this is not the case, that apocalyptic for over two thousand years has remained in immensely valuable and determinative conflict with mimesis, and that in the late twentieth century—not inappropriately at the end of a millenium—the crisis of representation, which is the crisis of mimesis and realism, is in certain ways suffering "resolution" by apocalyptic.

Most of this introductory essay is, in fact, a sketch of selected moments in the history of Western culture showing apocalyptic asserting and reasserting itself against the momentum of mimesis. Since the essays following this one in this volume all, one way or another, assume the importance of apocalyptic in tension with mimesis in the Gerasene demoniac and sin eater narratives, yet do not comment on the history of that tension, it seemed worth-while to me to provide such background. We will see how apocalyptic and mimesis have influenced each other and how, today, the threatened destruction of the physical world, what has come to serve as the de-idealized model for representation, leads to a new apocalyptic consciousness. Against this background the essays on the Mark and Atwood texts take on a certain urgency that should, whenever possible, characterize literature and religion scholarship.

We recall that mimesis for Aristotle is a singular kind of imitation, an imitation of an ideal action—ideal referring to perfect, original forms that humans attempt to (re)produce in our imperfect world. Humans by their mimetic action thus participate in the creation of an ameliorating world, and their goal is the achievement of a perfected cosmos, the matching of the real to the ideal. Apocalyptic eschatology envisions the reverse. In spite of human efforts toward the good, the corruption of humans and nature dictates that evil produces an increasingly malignant world, one that becomes at last so degenerate that it must be destroyed and replaced by a new creation.

These two models of cosmic destiny have interacted throughout the history of Western culture. It is still a commonplace to think that because much of Greek culture, including Aristotle's works, was lost to the Western world until the Renaissance (and then in good part inspired the Renaissance), the Middle Ages were an era—and the last one—dominated by apocalyptic faith and imagination. Even this needs qualification. As the expectation of Christ's early return waned more and more in the years following the birth of the church, adjustments to the apocalyptic sense of time took place. As a result, the Christian Apocalypse was simultaneously spiritualized and historicized, above all by Augustine. The spiritualizing meant that the anticipated return of Christ literally to rule a new earth was now reinterpreted to refer to the qualitatively different lives of the redeemed in the present, to those enjoying and suffering the life of the church. The historicizing meant that God's plan of salvation was now seen to need an extended period of time, however long or short it might be, for its fulfillment.

Such an alignment of apocalyptic to the perceived exigencies of history is an invasion of a sort of mimesis not attributable to Aristotle, obviously—although when Aristotle was eventually rediscovered this sort of reality adjustment could easily be combined with his influence. As Marjorie Reeves puts it, "Thus Judeo-Christian apocalyptic thought moved the idea of the time-process on to a new plane and created the concept of history as the field of God's activity, revealing his hidden purposes as the *saeculum* moved towards its end."[13] Reeves goes on to describe how Augustine subscribed to a linearly conceived apocalyptic doctrine that expected an end of the world but "in the same breath . . . was teaching that the climax of history had already been reached and passed in the life and death of Jesus. God's purpose had been unveiled and there was no room for a new revelation within history."[14]

One could suggest that a Christianized entelechy has been effected here. It is not the imitation of an ideal action that moves the world along toward its fulfillment. Rather, Christ concentrates that action in himself and brings the realized ideal from the future into the present, so that the church can articulate—live out—that ideal. This is an early critical point in the relationship between apocalyptic and mimesis, but one that is never developed, as entelechy comes under the domination of history and Platonic idealism and is grasped either as linear progress or the model of immutable perfection. In late medievalism two figures illustrate the power of history that comes between apocalyptic and mimesis: the Cistercian Joachim of Fiore and the Franciscan Petrus Johannis Olivi.

Joachim's trinitarian theology of history taught, against Augustine, an interpretation of the Book of Revelation that anticipated an age of the Holy Spirit to follow the contemporary age of the Son (which had succeeded the age of the Father) and identified the Johannine apocalyptic tropes with specific world transforming historical events and persons. As Reeves says, "Joachimism gave historical happenings a unique importance, linking past, present and future moments of time with transcendental purpose. . . . [I]t opened up the prospect of new human agencies called to participate in the last decisive works of God in history."[15] Olivi radicalized Joachim's apocalyptic teaching to a point that he and his fellow Franciscan Spirituals viewed themselves as the only true church. Active in the second half of the thirteenth century, Olivi knew Aristotle's work and considered him both a positive and negative force: he could be utilized for philosophical reflection but was finally, as a pagan thinker, a destructive influence and connected to the Antichrist. Again the ambivalence.

Surprising, in light of our understanding of the Renaissance era as the flourishing of humanism, is that during those centuries apocalyptic remained a powerful force in cultural life generally and in narrative in particular. Ricoeur claims that by this time apocalyptic itself is undergoing significant change: "the invalidation of the prediction concerning the end of the world has given rise to a truly qualitative transformation of the apocalyptic model. . . . The Apocalypse, therefore, shifts its imagery from the last days, the days of terror, of decadence, of renovation, to become a myth of crisis."[16] Ricoeur, moreover, sees this shift as strongly influencing literary composition as well (beginning with Elizabethan tragedy), insofar as it changes the nature of literary endings (i.e., makes them "immanent" rather than "imminent") and erodes a key function of narrative fictions, which is to provide us with the "consolation" of a full and satisfying conclusion.[17]

I agree that this transformation happened, but Ricoeur may be precipitous in placing it this early and in suggesting that it was totally successful More accurate is that the greatest crisis in Western Christendom, the Protestant Reformation, helped to sustain an "imminent" apocalyptic at least for the reforming side. Bernard Capp writes that "During the first half of Elizabeth's reign there developed a general consensus that the pope was Antichrist and that the end of the world was at hand," then goes on to say that after the defeat of the Spanish Armada in 1588 a patriotic passion was added to the apocalyptic obsession that produced varieties of millenarianism.[18] Not the least of these was the militant reform of Cromwell and his army, carried out as a cleansing of Britain from the Antichrist forces of both the royalists and Scots Presbyterians—although after Cromwell became Protector "the millenial excitement was gone. Christ may come to rule, he [Cromwell] declared later, but only 'to set up His reign in our hearts.'"[19]

With the Restoration in 1660 came another expectation of the millenium, this one to be a new age of Establishment order. As Capp concludes his essay, "The millenial excitement of the civil wars marked the end of a chapter, not of the story. Apocalyptic belief with a clear political dimension was to remain part of the mainstream of thought down to the very end of the Stuart age."[20] The shift of apocalyptic expectations of the end into a "myth of crisis" may have occurred during the mid-seventeenth century, then, but even this transformation was, as we shall see, far from total.

Three writers from the northern European Renaissance and Reformation can serve to illustrate the interaction of apocalyptic and mimesis and the prominent influence of such interaction in that age: David Pareus, Edmund Spenser, and William Shakespeare. Pareus was a professor of both Old and New Testament at the University of Heidelberg around the turn of the century (from sixteenth to seventeenth) and an interpreter of the Book of Revelation according to the structure of classical drama. As Michael Murrin explains, Pareus considered the Book of Revelation a tragedy yet dealt with it according to the then-common aesthetic model of comedy and divided it into seven little plays demarcated by comic speeches.[21] The focus of the whole drama is on Antichrist—the suffering caused by the terrible beast, the cosmic conflict with it, and its final subjugation. Murrin shows that Pareus had to restructure various sequences of Revelation to make it work as classical drama and hence that his interpretation of the work presented in play form is internally inconsistent. I find it intriguing not only that Pareus in his time thought of this central apocalyptic text in dramatic terms but that he believed the author of the book to have *conceived* it as a drama. Here is evidence of how mimesis as an ordering force in the mind of a Protestant Renaissance theologian functions to channel the energy of chaos that continues to fuel apocalyptic.

Pareus was an influence on John Milton, and we could profitably explore the use of apocalyptic related to mimesis in *Paradise Lost*, but I will turn instead to the earlier, more inventive role of these in *The Faerie Queene*. Spenser's epic masterpiece (1590, 1596), although it is militant apocalyptic, is neither tragedy nor in any obvious sense Aristotelian—its metaphysical foundation is Christian-Neoplatonic—and thus one might ask how mimesis is pivotal in it. The answer is that mimesis can be deduced from the Christian humanism that also inheres Spenser's perspective and that sees the journey toward holiness—a major theme of *The Faerie Queene*—as a personal-communal entelechy, a natural self-realization made possible by the grace of God active in Christ. If Aristotle does not figure "mimetically" in Spenser's cosmology, in other words, he is present, however fugitively, in Spenser's ethics. Joseph Wittreich declares that

> Spenser in *The Faerie Queene* canonizes the apocalyptic myth as a literary convention—makes of it a weapon not for instigating but for averting catastrophe, employs it as a means for scrutinizing the interdependence of self and society and the meaning of history. . . . To read Spenser's poem within an apocalyptic framework is to behold a gradual withdrawal from the apocalyptic promise—is to witness a distancing of apocalypse into future history and, eventually, a pushing of that promise beyond history into eternity.[22]

This is undoubtedly so, but one needs to emphasize, as Florence Sandler does in her essay on *The Faerie Queene*, that Spenser and his readers attached a specific millenarian stress to contemporary political events that made a new kingdom of holiness imminent.[23] In this view the death of the Roman Catholic Queen Mary—a representative of the papal Antichrist—in 1558, for example, could be understood as the end of a period of apocalyptic suffering like that described in the Book of Revelation, and the ascendancy of the Protestant Elizabeth to the throne could be taken as the triumph of the Bride of Christ, "representing in her virginity the return of the True Church."[24] Insofar, then, as individuals followed the example of Spenser's Arthurian Knight of Holiness in striving toward lives of sanctification, they would also participate in the restoration of Una, the fulfillment of the church's mission.

Kermode says that "When tragedy established itself in England it did so in terms of plots and spectacle that had much more to do with medieval apocalypse than with the *mythos* and *opsis* of Aristotle."[25] If this is true, Shakeaspeare's *King Lear* (c. 1603-07), the greatest of Jacobean tragedies, merges those medieval elements with a complex mimeticism that, as Wittreich says, uses "apocalypse against itself, not to deny it as a possibility but to distance the consummation of history into the future."[26] *King Lear* reflects the preoccupation of James I with the Book of Revelation—a preoccupation by the monarch that led the nation to concern itself anew with the nature of apocalyptic in its time. Shakespeare's genius is, among other strategies, to feature in his play a king (whose story is drawn from history and legend) who experiences a classical tragic fall amidst apocalyptic trappings but is then purged by both tragedy and apocalypse in a redemptive personal resolution. In this manner Shakespeare can take advantage of his own ruler's apocalyptic interests but at the same time push beyond millenarian prediction to a more profound and frightening apocalyptic vision, one in which an elemental chaos is imaged in the evil and madness of creation, tempered by the formal constraints of tragedy, but then released again to project a remarkably modern landscape of disorder.

King Lear is the first work of apocalyptic and mimesis, at least in English-language literature, that carries through the sequence of my title—from chaos to legion to chance. Here an *ur*-disorder is organized into an orchestration of evil impulses directed by a Christian sense of ultimate control, but that assurance disintegrates towards the end, and one is left with a suspicion that all is hazard. It is a kind of drama sensationalized into spectacle and shock effect in so-called blood tragedy.

Kermode in the midst of an argument about the "as-if" nature of fiction compares "the consciously false apocalypse" of *King Lear* to that of the Third Reich: "If *King Lear* is an image of the promised end, so is Buchenwald; and both stand under the accusation of being horrible, rootless fantasies, the one no more true or more false than the other."[27] It is a jolting comparison, one that compels us to recognize our present-day reality of apocalyptic and mimesis intertwined that was presaged by Shakespeare: the apocalypse, mediated by the ordering mimeticism of the Nazis—their compulsion for total order provoked by the terror of chaos—has happened in our day. Moreover, it continues to happen via other forces, always fundamentalist in their need for absolute control, but it is an apocalypse that has lost its myth and thus coincides with sheer accident. Is this not the other side of chaos?

APOCALYPTIC AND THE RISE OF REALISM

It would not be difficult to document further the persistence of apocalyptic as Western culture moved toward the modern age, often asserting itself vigorously precisely at those moments when a realism-engendering mimesis seemed to prevail. One thinks, for example, of the enduring prophetic work of William Blake, his vision of heaven and hell and of the struggle between the armies of good and evil, at a time when Enlightenment thought was ascendant and Neoclassical artists such as Swift and Pope were mocking popular millenarian excesses.[28] Or one learns to revise the opinion that the Romantic and Victorian eras, the time of the rise of democracies and of rational individualism, were characterized by a lengthening distance from the Bible and by an accompanying apocalyptic that made representations of last things merely symbolic and metaphoric. Such revision is necessary because we now know, as Mary Wilson Carpenter and George P. Landow inform us, that "a dramatic—and until recently, almost completely unnoticed—revival of biblical prophecy, typology, and apocalyptics" marked the nineteenth century.[29]

I will limit myself to commentary on just two moments of apocalyptic assertion in the midst of mimesis on the way to the modern age, two moments that figure strongly in the rise of recent, "postmodern" fiction in its relation to texts of faith that is a central concern of this volume. One of these moments is the emergence of the modern novel genre. The other is the work of that archetypal Victorian realist George Eliot.

The modern English-language (to which we must limit ourselves) novel is said to begin around 1740 with the work of Samuel Richardson (e.g., *Pamela, Clarissa*), Henry Fielding (e.g., *Joseph Andrews,* a parody of *Pamela; The History of Tom Jones*), and Tobias Smollet (e.g., *Roderick Random, Peregrine Pickle*), but apocalyptic in league with mimesis strongly informs the work of immediate predecessors, above all that of Daniel Defoe. *The Adventures of Robinson Crusoe* —published in 1719, when Defoe was almost sixty—is a fiction masquerading as documentary (the story is loosely based on the shipwreck experience of the sailor Alexander Selkirk) that begins in chaos but then charts a practical transformation that is "a microcosm of the eighteenth century's triumph over nature."[30] It is, in other words, a nearly perfect example of an updated Aristotelian mimesis, of "creative imitation" in action, as Crusoe domesticates his island, subjugates the disordering, brute native inhabitants, and guides it toward an Enlightened entelechy.

That Defoe was not altogether taken in by his own depiction of utilitarian progress is suggested by his 1722 account, *The Journal of the Plague Year*. Here mimesis is turned back on itself and apocalyptic reappears. Defoe, methodically and with discipline— as in *Robinson Crusoe*—"reports" details of the suffering and death visited on the bewildered and terrified population of London by the bubonic plague. The narrator—a common saddler—is so absorbed in numbers (so many bodies, so many children stillborn or aborted) that his account seems like a rationalist quantifying version of apocalyptic numerology. Further, he is fascinated by the magical signs employed by those who believe that "the plague was not the hand of God, but a kind of possession of an evil spirit," and illustrates those signs, for example, by the word "Abracadabra" shaped as a triangle.[31] The saddler's Christian witness to these blasphemers is met only with "hellish, abominable raillery," and at last he flees them, "lest the hand of that Judgment which had visited the whole city should glorify His vengeance upon them, and all that were near them."[32] If Crusoe's island is a model of rational progress, London of Defoe's *Journal* is a miniature end of the world.

Diana Neill thinks that Defoe's writing represents "the Nonconformist age of English fiction. The old struggle between vice and virtue was still raging, but no longer on an abstract, imaginary plane. The vices were now subtly embodied in worldly temptations while the virtues that resisted them were precariously enclosed in the alloy of character."[33] More accurate, I think, is to say that Defoe and his middle-class (more or less) readers recognized the conflict as being played out both in nature and human behavior, that "good" nature might mitigate evil human acts just as human courage might make sense of natural catastrophe, and that in this interaction the Apocalypse might be, if not altogether averted, at least indefinitely postponed.

The mid-eighteenth century looks indeed to be the genesis of bourgeois realism in the novel. Even the epistolary form, imitating the constraining medium of communication by letters, dominated from the start, as with *Clarissa, Joseph Andrews*, and Smollett's *Humphrey Clinker*. Yet a portentous disorder also marks that beginning. One of the first novels is an anti-novel—a "postmodern" text that predates modernism. This is Lawrence Sterne's *The Life and Opinions of Tristram Shandy, Gentleman* (1760-67). The multi-volumed *Tristram Shandy* mocks the tradition of mimetic realism almost before the tradition begins. It is a bulky, ingenious narrative of discontinuity and digression, an antic diversion from the young tradition of the novel that tests and transgresses the limits of story yet manages nonetheless to be masterful storytelling.

Its first-person narrator, Tristram himself, tells the tale from the start although he is not born until the fourth volume, at which point he emerges with a badly smashed nose. Most of the novel is taken up with convoluted discussions and disquisitions among family members and friends, above all the senior Shandy, Tristram's father, and the redoubtable Uncle Toby, on subjects such as noses, names, significant battles, and the mysteries of sex, most of which borrow shamelessly from venerable texts or invent texts to be exploited. Sterne's iconoclasm extends to the novel's format and physical appearance. There are chapters of a few words, with no words at all, ending in asterisks, consisting of Latin, and containing squiggly lines that purport to graph the narrative progression. If Jorge Luis Borges had lived in eighteenth-century England, *Tristram Shandy* is the kind of fiction he might have written.

The novel is emphatically not apocalyptic, but it is, oxymoronically, a model of chaos. It made its clergyman-author famous amd suggests the appetite his countrymen and women had for the culturally perverse. It made moralists uneasy, shocked those who believed a vicar should not be sportive, and was purposefully ignored in the next century by the Victorians. In its subversion of mimesis by its selection of creative imitation as its subject matter, it anticipated the nihilistic metafictions of the late twentieth century that work toward and play with their own destruction.

Whatever exuberant demons possessed Sterne and his fiction of mischief found no welcome a century later from George Eliot, born Mary Ann Evans. Eliot was a stern rationalist and theologian, a resolute writer of realistic fiction whose novels in spite of their mimetic energy and density are deeply marked and moved by apocalyptic. Neill says of Eliot that "She was the first Victorian novelist to depict a character from the inside and to portray realistically the spectacle of deterioration in people who are not intrinsically evil;" and further that "Her sense of the tragedy in life is Aristotelian."[34] Yet Carpenter and Landow show persuasively that a vigorous apocalyptic strain permeates not only her "Italian Renaissance" novel *Romola* (1864) but earlier and later works of hers as well. They argue that *Romola* is

> a symbolic narrative in which elaborate patterns of myth and metaphor inform her characteristic realism, and the model for such a reading of history is to be found primarily not in classical mythology or other sources proposed by recent critics but in the Book of Revelation, which she had learned to read as a symbolic history of the Western world. . . . [L]ike so many other lapsed Evangelicals, such as Ruskin and Carlyle, she long retained the impress of her former faith. In particular, after she had lost the belief that served as the basis for certain basic evangelical attitudes, she still felt drawn to the Apocalyptic scheme as an imaginative structure.[35]

Carpenter and Landow demonstrate further that Eliot's interest in apocalypticism was part of a widespread movement of the mid-nineteenth century, although in her case it took the form of an earnest attempt to comprehend history, via a reading of the Book of Revelation, that would project for her era not a world cataclysm but a new reformation. Indeed, the plot of *Romola* features such reformation, and she intends it to be relevant for her own age.[36]

Eliot's realism, then, still draws on a biblical model of time's unfolding (time's denouement) in ways that mark not the end of belief expressed through fiction (the culmination of which is said to be Matthew Arnold's substitution of poetry for belief) but rather the deepening ambiguity of the faith and art relationship. It is not remotely as simple as one critic sketches the state of soul of Gothic novel authors such as Horace Walpole from the mid-eighteenth century: "Under the rationalist skin, a grinning skull, a hankering after chaos and old night."[37] Now, with the likes of Eliot, apocalyptic becomes a foundation for mimesis precisely because the belief in the literal Apocalypse has waned. The symbolic reading of history functions as a creative imitation that not only reflects the apocalyptic dynamic (its intense, *kairos*-oriented pattern of conflict, climax, and resolution) but helps to realize it. This is not Aristotelian entelechy, for that kind of self-fulfillment lacks a historical dimension, and the nineteenth century struggles above all with history. Thus Eliot accommodates realism by reading apocalyptic as symbolic history but immediately qualifies that realism by the very—perhaps reflexive—act of orienting history to a symbol system derived from the agonies of Christian origins.

AN APOCALYPTIC OF SURVIVAL

Eliot, Poe, Hawthorne, Melville, Hardy, Conrad, even Henry James, among others, all work one way or another under the long shadow of apocalyptic, which throughout the twentieth century becomes darker, more obtrusive, and more obsessive. In the modern to the postmodern age, what looks like the hegemony of realism and the absorption of mimesis into scientific objectivity (creative imitation is taken up into experimentation and disinterested observation) is revealed as another myth that needs to be interpreted—reread, as has been the myth of Apocalypse for generations. The hermeneutics of suspicion takes shape through Freud's formulation of a dominating unconscious; through the projections of class warfare; through the literal wars and the holocausts of genocide and material obliteration they produce; and finally through the late-century recognition that we are in the process of destroying our planet.

In all of these, apocalyptic takes shifting shape as that which is uncontrollable (indeed out of control), monstrous, and the result of chance. We are taught that the unconscious is the largely incomprehensible force that governs us, that forms our behavior patterns through the accidents of childhood, and that knows no limits to excess. We have seen class warfare change from what seems now to be the meta-apocalyptic vision of Marx to the challenge of desperate underclasses suppressed by the wealthy, in which struggle a randomness of violence and death is both a symptom and a weapon. Auschwitz and Hiroshima have become master metaphors of the human ability to design the mass destruction of races and places, yet their evocation makes it possible to ignore the genocide that continues in many parts of the world. The realization that global decay is happening through the very technology employed to "subdue" nature is a late *anagnorisis* that seems not to prompt *peripeteia,* for the moment of reversal may well be past in a world that has forgot the conditions of tragedy.

A recent issue of *Esquire* asks the question, on the cover, "Has American Writing Gone to Hell?"[38] The answer is, in terms of a renewed emphasis on apocalytic, that it has, as has the fiction of Great Britain, the European continent, Latin America, and—not surprisingly—Japan. Hoagland argues that a younger generation of writers lacks moral vision and commitment and hence composes less valuable fiction, and he relates their stance also to the global disaster upon us: "This fleeting assumption that God is either dead or a plaything helps explain why my reductive colleagues—and they are legion—both in their work and their public personae have shown no anguish at the holocaust that is quickly consuming the natural world, and thereby have countenanced it."[39] Hoagland's harsh—although defensible—judgment should not obscure the fact that a number of contemporary writers, also "legion" and including younger ones, have "gone to hell" in creative imitation of apocalyptic that tries to embody, metaphorize, dramatize the literary version of a hermeneutics of suspicion.

Some of these authors and their apocalyptic narratives are well known if not notorious: Masuji Ibuse and *Black Rain,* Thomas Pynchon and *Gravity's Rainbow,* J. G. Ballard and *The*

Atrocity Exhibition, Don DeLillo and *White Noise*, Margaret Atwood and *The Handmaid's Tale*, Günter Grass and *Die Rättin*. Others are lesser known and deserve better. Examples are Russell Hoban and *Riddley Walker*, Paul Auster and *The Country of Last Things*, Carolyn See and *Golden Days*, Maggie Gee and *Grace*. Joseph Dewey says that "What the twentieth century has so unnervingly fashioned and what these writers [of apocalyptic fiction] have finally faced is death on so large a scale that it discounts humanity."[40] Our era has started to realize, in all senses of the word, through technology what the believers in biblical apocalyptic from pretechnological ages could not even imagine: destruction of such magnitude that the human perspective is overwhelmed. It is a situation in which mimesis as creative imitation is threatened with its final loss of meaning, since helping the universe toward its self-fulfillment now seems to mean hastening its sorry end.

It is also a situation in which a heresy suggests itself: that writers and readers of fiction might worry less about keeping the lines clear between literature and belief and more about plotting metaphors and narratives of survival. Dewey refers to our apocalyptic "literature's bravest affirmation, its commitment to its community, its ministering to a critical moment in history, a moment when we stand about our own history, the sun shadowed black by stacks of corpses piled like cordwood—that is the history of this century."[41] If this sounds excessive (and it does), one can find the same sentiment offered in more sober, nonliterary context by a philosopher of the holocaust. Edith Wyschogrod concludes her book *Spirit in Ashes* with these words: "The social I demands that the whole human community, whose possible extinction is part of the formation of the I, persevere in existence. Postmodern selfhood must now be understood as living within the ambit of the tensions created by this demand."[42]

I believe that we can plot narratives of survival, minister to this critical moment in history, engage the social I to persevere in existence by chancing the use of literature in the cause of belief— as if we finally, on some level, ever did anything else with our literary texts. I do not mean that we should press literature into the service of dogma. I take my cue here rather from M. H. Abrams on apocalyptic: "This biblical paradigm has survived the biblical myth in which it was incorporated and has deeply informed Western views of the shape of history and the destiny of mankind and the world, whether in simple or sophisticated, in religious or secular renderings."[43] It is a paradigm often obscured throughout the rise of secularization and the favoring of mimesis, and one that has traded its traditional religious foundation for a basic desire to survive.

Such apocalyptic faith, to be articulated in our stories, is simply a belief, in the face of considerable contrary evidence, that we can survive, and can do so as intact communities that nurture dignity and affection. Writing and living that faith may be our last chance against chaos.

ATWOOD AND THE DEMONS

The foregoing may seem like too grim and weighty a preparation for the comparisons of a brief biblical passage and a short story that comprise the essays of this volume, but I think that it is justified in at least two ways. One is that the texts selected for comparison are themselves vivid examples of apocalyptic struggling with mimesis. This is manifest with the Gerasene demoniac narrative. The episode is immediately preceded by an account of Jesus preaching Kingdom of God parables, which kingdom the disciples expect to appear "mimetically," like other political regimes, whereas Jesus means it apocalyptically—as we learn in Mark 13, which consists of Jesus' lengthy depiction and warning of the end of the world. The center of the action, in fact, comprised of Jesus purging the Gerasene of his demons, could be read as a proleptic apocalyptic action representative of the great Apocalypse to come.

The interaction of apocalyptic and mimesis in "The Sin Eater" is less obvious but hardly any less forceful. It helps to know, first, that apocalyptic has been steadily on Atwood's mind and in her art—present in the atmosphere of diseased nature and environmental destruction as early as her second novel *Surfacing* (1972) and informing the plot directly in *The Handmaid's Tale* (1986). Further, the collection containing "The Sin Eater" includes a last-days-of-civilization story, "When It Happens," depicting a middle-aged Canadian farm woman pondering how to survive following what may be the nuclear destruction of cities to the south.[44] With this knowledge of Atwood's interest in mind, one can readily see at least apocalyptic overtones in the waste and death imagery of "The Sin Eater," and above all in the concluding airport dream—a setting for countless stories in which a plane takes off to deliver its just-deceased passengers to heaven or hell—which ends the narrative with a cosmic vision of "dark space. . . thousands of stars, thousands of moons." Yet the tale at the same time relies "creatively" on mimesis, for example in its use of the historical sin-eating folk practice to serve as symbolic referent for the action, and (balancing that old religious referent) in its dramatizing of the psychiatric, doctor-patient situation to stand for the secularized human condition.[45]

A second justification for introducing this volume with a discourse on apocalyptic and mimesis is that the essays in this collection exemplify how a late twentieth-century apocalyptically aware interpretive community might respond to its threatening and threatened environment. Our focus on these two brief texts, the attempt of most of us to read them "against" each other (and William Doty's effort in his Afterword to read the essays against each other), is among other things an act of fellowship that engages—as one must these days—a hermeneutics of suspicion, constantly reading between and behind the lines, in order to envision (it would be too much to say "to offer") hope.

Since Doty discusses all of the essays in his concluding summary-analysis, I will describe here only their genesis, how this volume came to be. Versions of some of the essays were first presented as papers at a consultation (a program unit meeting only once) of the annual American Academy of Religion meeting in Boston in 1987. My design then was to see, at a time when the signs of a rapprochement between biblical and literary scholarship were already quite strong, whether students from the two fields, as well as those working at the interstices, had valuable things to say to each other based on shared-text interpretation—and I chose the Gerasene demoniac and sin eater narratives as a pair that signalled similarities as well as deep differences. The session was lively and resonant, but I did not consider developing the papers into a volume for publication until a number of consultation participants—some who presented papers and some who did not—urged me to do so. At that point I met with Doty and agreed with him to co-edit an expanded volume. We requested revisions of the original papers, sought essays representing perspectives not illustrated in the consultation papers (e.g., Lowry's homily, Arnold's myth studies approach, Morey's feminist approach), and received permission to reprint Girard's "The Demons of Gerasa" chapter from his influential book *The Scapegoat* as well as the Atwood story.

The essays are arranged in a threefold pattern: first those that treat only the Mark 5 passage, then those that deal only with "The Sin Eater," and finally those, the majority, that discuss both. We want the essays to illustrate how the texts, biblical and secular, can be read productively in a variety of ways—e.g., linguistically, psychologically, reader-responsively—but we do not consider the interpretations to be exhaustive. We want them, rather, to be provocative and hope that they will inspire other ways of reading the texts (the possibilities are legion) and of undertaking other kinds of combined biblical and literary criticism.

Finally, a comment on our title. "The daemonic imagination" plays, of course, on "demon" and "daemon" (or, transliterated, "daimon"). As Frieden points out in his essay, the term "demon" has suffered a long transformation (one that the linguists call pejoration). In Classical Greece, as *daimōn*, it had positive denotation and meant a guiding or protecting spirit. J. Bruce Long says that "In the late Greco-Roman period, the term *daimōn* . . . like the Latin *genius*, was commonly employed in reference to lesser spirits or demigods, especially patron or guardian spirits that protect the homestead, family, and property of the suppliant. Still later, the word *daimonium* (transliterated into Latin as *daemonium*) was assigned to evil spirits that torment human beings, cause them physical and mental harm, inflict them with mental infirmities, and lead them into evil ways."[46]

We want our title to recover the ambiguity, even the ambivalence, of daemon/demon as a reminder that the imagination creating and responding to traditionally sacred and avowedly secular texts still works for good or for evil, that it is difficult to tell the difference, yet that it is the responsibility of the critic to tell the difference. Indeed, *telling* the difference may, at this late date, still help to make the difference.

NOTES

1. John Banville, *Doctor Copernicus* (Boston: David R. Godine, 1984), p. 209.

2. Paul Ricoeur, *Time and Narrative*, Vol. 2, Kathleen McLaughlin and David Pellauer, trs. (Chicago: University of Chicago Press, 1985), p. 28.

3. N. J. Girardot, entry on "chaos" in Mircea Eliade, ed. *The Encyclopedia of Religion* , Vol. 3 (New York: Macmillan, 1987), p. 213. I am much indebted to Girardot's article for my treatment of chaos.

4. Entry on "chaos" in Maria Leach, ed., *Funk and Wagnall Standard Dictionary of Folklore, Mythology, and Legend* (San Francisco: Harper & Row, 1972), p. 211.

5. See entry on "Tiamat" in Leach, ed., *Funk and Wagnall Dictionary*, p. 1112. Tiamat may also have been an embodiment of the Milky Way.

6. Ricoeur summarizing Northrop Frye's treatment of apocalypse in *Anatomy of Criticism* says that "apocalyptic imagery . . . turns upon the idea of reconciliation in unity. . . . .[T]his symbolism has its demonic side in the figures of Satan, the tyrant, the monster, the barren fig tree, and the 'primitive sea,' the symbol of 'chaos.' . . . [T]his polar structure is itself unified by the strength of the desire that configures both the infinitely desirable and its contrary, the infinitely detestable, at the same time. From an archetypal and anagogical perspective, all imagery is inadequate in relation to this apocalyptic imagery of fulfillment and yet at the same time is in search for it." (*Time and Narrative*, Vol. 2, pp. 18-19). In other words, the very sense of chaos that "demonic" apocalyptic imagery projects is actually an intense effort to create order.

7. Ricoeur also connects Apocalypse with Aristotle's *Poetics* in *Time and Narrative*, Vol. 2, p. 23: "At first sight, this set of repprochements seems incongruous. Is not the Apocalypse a model of the world, while Aristotle's *Poetics* proposes only the model of a verbal work? The passage from one plane to the other . . . finds some justification in the fact that the idea of the end of the world comes to us by means of the text that, in the biblical canon received in the Christian West, at least, concludes the Bible. Apocalypse can thus signify both the end of the world and the end of the book at the same time. . . . [T]he

eschatological myth and the Aristotelian muthos are joined together in their way of tying a beginning to an ending and proposing to the imagination the triumph of concordance over discordance. It is not so out of place, therefore, to link the Aristotelian peripeteia to the torments of the last days in the Apocalypse."

8. I take my information here largely from John J. Collins, *The Apocalyptic Imagination: An Introduction to the Jewish Matrix of Christianity* (New York: Crossroad, 1987).

9. I have decided to use the term "apocalyptic" as my basic designation throughout even though "More recent scholarship has abandoned the use of 'apocalyptic' as a noun and distinguishes between apocalypse as a literary genre, apocalypticism as a social ideology, and apocalyptic eschatology as a set of ideas and motifs that may also be found in other literary genres and settings" (Collins, *The Apocalyptic Imagination*, p. 2). It seemed to me that these distinctions would be more confusing than helpful in my essay, although I have adopted them at a few places where they did seem appropriate. On the other hand, I use "mimesis" rather than "mimetic" as a basic designation, since "mimetic" has come to mean an array of many more things than I want to suggest.

10. Aristotle, of course, describes mimesis in his *Poetics* in the context of tragedy rather than of narrative fiction. See Ricoeur, *Time and Narrative*, Vol. 1, pp. 32ff on the justification for using narrative in connection with mimesis.

11. M. H. Abrams, "Apocalypse: Theme and Variations," in C. A. Patrides and Joseph Wittreich, eds., *The Apocalypse in English Renaissance Thought and Literature* (Ithaca: Cornell University Press, 1984), p. 347. My reliance on a number of essays in this excellent volume will become obvious.

12. I am well aware that in this discussion I am allowing "literature and religion to become mixed or confused with each other" (Ricoeur, *Time and Narrative*, Vol. 2, p. 27), and wish that I had space to address and respond to Ricoeur's argument on this "confusion" as it relates to apocalyptic and literary fiction as "broken myth" (*Time and Narrative*, Vol. 2, p. 26). I can remark only that my essay arrives finally there where Ricoeur seems to at the conclusion of his chapter on "The Metamorphoses of the Plot" (*Time and Narrative*, Vol. 2, p. 29): one must have a faith in narrative that is more than a faith in a

literary genre in order to channel apocalyptic from despair and fatalism toward hope.

13. Marjorie Reeves, "The Development of Apocalyptic Thought: Medieval Attitudes," in Patrides and Wittreich, eds., *The Apocalypse*, p. 40.

14. Reeves, "The Development of Apocalyptic Thought," p. 41.

15. Reeves, "The Development of Apocalyptic Thought," p. 51. I am indebted to Reeves for my information on Joachim and Olivi.

16. Ricoeur, *Time and Narrative*, Vol. 2, p. 23.

17. Ricoeur, *Time and Narrative*, Vol. 2, pp. 23ff. I cannot do justice here to Ricoeur's argument, which also involves his reading of Frank Kermode's *The Sense of an Ending: Studies in the Theory of Fiction* (New York: Oxford University Press, 1967).

18. Bernard Capp, "The Political Dimension of Apocalyptic Thought," in Patrides and Wittreich, eds., *The Apocalypse*, p. 97.

19. Capp, "The Political Dimension," p. 115.

20. Capp, "The Political Dimension," p. 118.

21. Michael Murrin, "Revelation and Two Seventeenth Century Commentators," in Patrides and Wittreich, eds., *The Apocalypse*. I am indebted to Murrin's essay for my information on Pareus.

22. Joseph Wittreich, "'Image of that horror': The Apocalypse in *King Lear*," in Patrides and Wittreich, eds., *The Apocalypse*, p. 176.

23. Florence Sandler, "*The Faerie Queene*: An Elizabethan Apocalypse," in Patrides and Wittreich, eds., *The Apocalypse*.

24. Sandler, "*The Faerie Queene*," p. 163.

25. Frank Kermode, *The Sense of an Ending*, p. 30.

26. Wittreich, "'Image of that horror'," p. 184.

27. Kermode, *The Sense of an Ending*, p. 38.

28. Paul J. Korshin, "Queuing and Waiting: the Apocalypse in England, 1660-1750," in Patrides and Wittreich, eds., *The Apocalypse*, is very helpful on apocalyptic in the Enlightenment and Neoclassicism

29. Mary Wilson Carpenter and George P. Landow, "Ambiguous Revelations: the Apocalypse and Victorian Literature," in Patrides and Wittreich, eds., *The Apocalypse*, p. 299.

30. S. Diana Neill, *A Short History of the English Novel* (London: Collier-Macmillan Ltd., 1964), p. 50. I am indebted to Neill for much of my discussion of the rise of the novel.

31. Daniel Defoe, *A Journal of the Plague Year* (New York: New American Library/Signet, 1960), p. 40.

32. Defoe, *A Journal*, p. 71.

33. Neill, *A Short History*, p. 55.

34. Neill, *A Short History*, p. 217.

35. Carpenter and Landow, "Ambiguous Revelations," p. 303.

36. Carpenter and Landow, "Ambiguous Revelations," p. 311.

37. Marvin Mudrick, Introduction to Horace Walpole, *The Castle of Otranto* (New York: Collier Books, 1963), p. 9.

38. *Esquire* (July, 1990). The article itself is by Edward Hoagland and is titled "Shhh! Our Writers Are Sleeping!"

39. Hoagland, "Our Writers Are Sleeping," p. 62.

40. Joseph Dewey, *In a Dark Time: The Apocalyptic Temper in the American Novel of the Nuclear Age* (West Lafayette, Indiana: Purdue University Press, 1990), p. 236.

41. Dewey, *In a Dark Time*, p. 237. Some examples of how *not* to merge literature and religion are discussed by Robert Jay Lifton and Charles B. Strozier in "Waiting for Armageddon" in *The New York Times Book Review* (August 12, 1990), 1, 24-25. Fundamentalist apocalyptic fiction such as Frank E. Peretti's popular *This Present Darkness* (now

in its twenty-sixth printing, with over a million copies sold since its publication in 1986) blends inept writing and formulaic religious faith in ways that to my mind actually lessen rather than convey any sense of urgency about global survival.

42. Edith Wyschogrod, *Spirit in Ashes: Hegel, Heidegger, and Man-Made Mass Death* (New Haven: Yale University Press, 1985), p. 216.

43. Abrams, "Apocalypse: Theme and Variations," p. 344.

44. The collection is Margaret Atwood, *Dancing Girls and Other Stories* (New York: Simon and Schuster, 1977). The Canadian edition of "The Sin Eater" is published in a collection of Atwood's stories called *Bluebeard's Egg and Other Stories* (Toronto: McClelland and Stewart, 1983).

45. Atwood did not invent sin eaters. They existed in Wales (and versions of them in the Scottish Isles, Bavaria, India, and Africa) into the seventeenth century and functioned as Joseph describes them in the story. See James Hastings, ed., *Encyclopaedia of Religion and Ethics*, Vol. XI (New York: Charles Scribner's Sons, 1921), pp. 572-76.

46. J. Bruce Long, entry on "demons" in Eliade, ed., *The Encyclopedia of Religion*, Vol. 3, p. 282.

CRIES FROM THE GRAVEYARD: A SERMON
Eugene L. Lowry

TEXT: MARK 5:1-19

(Please read this sermon aloud)

It was an ordinary little gentile village by the lake's edge . . .
  indistinguishable from a dozen other little gentile
  villages, perhaps . . .
    except for at least one thing.

If you were to spend the night there, it's quite possible you
would lose some sleep.

  You would be awakened in the middle of the night with
some awful cries and moans from some undisclosed source . . .
  cries that sounded half human, half like a wild animal.

Were you to inquire the next morning someone would tell you
about that crazy man in town.

  He was beside himself,
    not in control of his faculties.

      In fact, folks said that he had unclean spirits.
      He had a demon.

They had tried to chain him up,
    but he was not only wild, but very strong . . .
      and would simply break the bonds . . .
        and continue to moan, and shriek and cry.

The town and the crazy man had developed a kind of uneasy
truce—that is, he would stay out there in the graveyard among
the tombs . . .

27

and they would stay in town.

He wasn't fit to be among the living . . .
     and so he lived among the dead.

          That's the way it was.

Before we become too critical of the way they handled their
     social problems, we need to remember,
          after all, he was crazy.

Every now and then they could get a glimpse of him and his
bruises.

     Sometimes he was bleeding from having pushed himself
     against the edges of the rocks.

          Remember, in those days they didn't have any
               psychiatrists to help out.
                    They didn't have any mental health societies.
                    They didn't even have any United Way.
          So, we ought not criticize too much.

Into this scene comes Jesus.

Now, we wonder how it was that the man knew it was Jesus.

     Had he perhaps been closer into town than they had
          thought, and had overheard some conversations
          about the coming of Jesus?
               We don't even know that the community knew
               that Jesus was coming.

All we know was that this little boat appeared,
     and Jesus and a couple friends came in toward the shore.

As Jesus was getting out of the boat,
    this crazy man ran out,
        and he fell down in front of Jesus.

The text says he worshipped Jesus . . .
    looked up into his eyes and said:
        "What do you have to do with me?"
            "Jesus, son of the most high God, Do not
            torment me!"

    Do you feel that ambivalence?

He is attracted to Jesus, and yet repulsed at the same time.

He wants desperately to be whole, to be sane—
    and also he wants not to have anybody tamper with the way
    things are.
        You may call that crazy.

        I call it familiar.

I remember one time when I had this horrible cold.

I was sick . . . and couldn't seem to get better with home remedies,
    so I called my doctor.
        He wasn't the Great Physician, you understand, but he
        was pretty good . . .
            and patients knew the worship order quite well.

    I mean, you walk into the office and the receptionist says:
        "Please be seated." That's the call to worship.

Then you wait for 45 minutes . . .
    call them moments of meditation.

Then you go in and you get the word.

On the way out you present your tithes and offerings.
It's an act of worship.

Well, I went to my doctor. He gave me the word all right.
He said: "You can't fight off any infection;
you don't eat anything but sugar.
Don't you know those bugs like sugar just as
much as you do? I'm taking you off all those
cookies and all those soft drinks you live on."

You know what I said to him?
I said: "Do not torment me!"

I wanted to get well, of course, but, but . . . well you
know.

Jesus asked: "What's your name?"

The man's answer is classic.

He said: "My name is Legion."

A legion? Why, a legion is a Roman army group numbering 6,000
soldiers.
"My name is Legion." Get it?

To paraphrase: "I feel like 6,000 soldiers inside me . . .
sometimes they all march left,
sometimes right . . .
sometimes in all different directions.
I'm pulled one way, then another.

There's an army inside me, and I think I'm losing the war."

Crazy?. . .

Really familiar.

And we cry out. Cry out for unity, for integrity, for wholeness.
We all would like to be one.

Well, Jesus gets to visiting with the demons.

I never quite understood this part of the story.
The text says they got to conversing . . .
and some of us may just begin wondering how
strange for folks in the days of Jesus to believe
in demons.

In case we presume to be "above" this sort of notion,
perhaps we ought to be reminded that we all talk about
having viruses.
Viruses?
What's a virus, anyway? Does anybody know?
Is it animal, mineral, vegetable?
Have you seen one lately?

What we mean when we speak of viruses, is that something
has hold of us—quite beyond our control.

Perhaps someday, another group of people will
look back on our era and exclaim with disbelief:
"You know what?
They believed in viruses."

Yes, we do. Well, they believed in demons—
which is to say, the man was out of his mind.
One might say: "possessed."
Well, yes they did.

About the time it becomes clear that because of Jesus, the demons
    are going to take leave of the man,
          the poor fellow yells out:

          "Don't send them too far . . . don't send them too far!"

          There's that ambivalence, again.

The demons seemed to like the idea of moving on to the pigs
close by, who presently are minding their own business.

          They attach themselves to the pigs, some 2,000
          pigs . . . which figures out to be three demons per pig.

              And the pigs get frightened with all those
                  demons, and go rushing down the steep
                      embankment into the sea, and are
                          all drowned.

The text says that word reached town very shortly of what had
happened.

    I have a hunch that it reached town immediately.

          I don't understand anything about pigs, you
              understand, except that we have a little place in
              the country.
                  We call it a ranch.
                      The farmer next to us calls it a plot.

      The farmer's house is about a quarter of a mile away,
          and right next to his house is the feed lot for
          his pigs.

              Every now and then one of his pigs gets hurt
              or upset or something.

I don't know exactly what goes on over there,
but I have learned the meaning of the phrase
about
     "squealing like a pig."
       I bet folks can hear his pigs in the
       next county.

Can you imagine what 2,000 squealing pigs sounded
like as they rushed down into the sea?

     Well, I don't think they had to send a
     messenger into town.

       That would be rather redundant, don't
       you think?

Everybody in town came right out to find the cause of the
commotion.
    And there they found the demoniac.

     Sitting there,
       clothed and in his right mind.

       Think of that.

   Standing beside him was Jesus.

Can you imagine how excited they must have been?

  How utterly delighted?

    How joyful to discover this man who had been such a
    problem to them for so long was now whole?

    He was well again—thank God.

No they didn't.

Turning to Jesus, whose powerful presence caused this miracle,
     they said:
               "Would you please leave our neighborhood?"

                         It does have a familiar ring down through the
                         centuries, doesn't it?

     You would think they would have given him the key
     to the city.
                    Instead they suggest a bus ticket out of town.

                         "Get out."

But, why?

     Why this kind of response, anyway?

               Is it because they had grown all too comfortable with
               handling their social problems a particular way, and
               didn't want the routine altered?
               "We've always done it this way."

               Or, was it that they didn't trust the healing?
                    "Just wait until tonight. He looks just fine all
                         dressed up now—but wait 'til you hear him
                         in the middle of the night!"

     Well, these possible reasons do have a ring of plausibility
     to them.
                    But, they won't do . . .
                         too small for the reaction to Jesus.

The reason the folks told Jesus to leave is simple.

Very simple.

You see, *they owned the pigs.*

That's right. They owned the pigs—some 2,000 of them now drowned in the lake.

And a bit of biblical research will back it up.
The town's people owned the pigs and hired the
herdsmen.
It was the herdsmen who went in to report
on the status of the flock—
and reported to the owners what had
happened.

I suppose we should have suspected it all along.

Nothing too strange here.

Any time any healing takes place,
somebody is going to pay a price—
one way or another.

Any time any person or group gets a freedom they never had
before, somebody else loses some pigs.

One person's freedom generally means somebody
else's loss of privilege.

Yes, we do like people "in their place."

You can't understand South Africa without understanding
the principle here.
One needs only to find out who owns the pigs.

Do we find our country's official policy toward Central America strange and confused?
    Well, who owns the pigs there, anyway?

> On the other hand, it is amazing how
> compassionate and just our foreign policy is toward
> deprived, hungry and powerless people the world
> over—

> > that is, when somebody else's pigs are at
> > stake.

Just outside Jackson, Missouri, and right on the banks of the Mississippi, there is a park called the Trail of Tears State Park.
    Lovely place.

In the middle of the park is a monument with this inscription:
> "Here lies Princess Otaka, daughter of Chief
> Bushyhead. One of several hundred Cherokee
> Indians who died in the winter crossing of the
> Mississippi River in the hard winter of 1838,
> in the forced march from Georgia to Tennessee
> and the Carolinas to the territory now known as
> Oklahoma."

When I read that inscription a number of years ago, I drew a blank.

> I had never been told of the Trail of Tears when I studied
> American history in school.

> I did not know then how it was that thousands of Cherokee
> Indians were forced to leave land white folks wanted.

I did not know then that the Cherokee Nation—
    with its code of law and constitution—
        was known as one of the most respected civilized
        states in the world.

I did not know then that their Chief of State had been all
    over the world visiting with other heads of state.

I did not know then that when their Chief corresponded
with the President of the United States—
    pleading for justice and protection—
        that his letters utilizing English as a second
        language exhibited a better command of the
        English language than those written by the
        President.

I did not know then that they won their case for protection
    in the Supreme Court of the United States—
        a victory mocked by President Andrew Jackson
        with the words:
            "Well, let them enforce it."

I did not then know these things.

    All I knew about the Cherokee Nation, was that on
        several trips during my childhood,
        I had been driven through reservations in
        Oklahoma,

        and saw people . . .
        mute . . .
          detached . . .
            sitting with a distant look
            in their eyes.

It was like a graveyard. . . it *was* a graveyard . . . of smashed hope, stolen dreams and broken promises.

They had met their match, all right . . . that once proud Cherokee Nation.

They had run up against some folks who owned all the pigs.

And now upon reflection I can't help but wonder . . .

Did we chain them up on the reservation because they had a demon . . .

or did they get the demon because we tied them up on the reservation?

Whenever Jesus comes to any town,
the first folks to meet him are not the members of the
welcoming team from the Chamber of Commerce.

The first folks to meet Jesus will come running from out of the
tombs . . .
the ones called crazy . . .
the ones tied in chains, one way or another.

Certainly, they are not the only ones in town who need the
transforming power of Jesus.

Somehow, they are the quickest to know their
need.

When Jesus left that village, the man asked to go with him,
but Jesus said
"No, go back to your friends."

Back to your "friends"?
What friends?

He didn't have any friends—
except the *new* kind which can be
bonded among former "chain-*ers*" and
"chain-*ees*,"

both freed by Jesus' visit.

"Go back to your friends,

and tell the world what the Lord has done."

Yes, indeed, tell the world.

But, sometimes it is hard for me to tell the world,

because my ears are still being bombarded . . .

ringing with cries from the night . . .
and from squeals in the day.

And I know . . .

I know . . . I have some deciding to do.

THE LANGUAGE OF DEMONIC POSSESSION: A KEY-WORD ANALYSIS

Ken Frieden

MARK 5:1-20

They came to the other side of the sea, to the country of the Gerasenes. And when he had come out of the boat, there met him out of the tombs a man with an unclean spirit (*pneumati akathartō*) who lived among the tombs; and no one could bind him any more, even with a chain; for he had often been bound with fetters and chains, but the chains he wrenched apart, and the fetters he broke in pieces; and no one had the strength to subdue him. Night and day among the tombs and on the mountains he was always crying out, and bruising himself with stones. And when he saw Jesus from afar, he ran and worshiped him; and crying out with a loud voice, he said, "What have you to do with me, Jesus, Son of the Most High God? I adjure you by God, do not torment me." For he had said to him, "Come out of the man, you unclean spirit (*to pneuma to akatharton*)." And Jesus asked him, "What is your name?" He replied, "My name is Legion; for we are many." And he begged him eagerly not to send them out of the country. Now a great herd of swine was feeding there on the hillside; and they begged him [, all the demons, *pantes oi daimones*—manuscript variant], "Send us to the swine, let us enter them." So he gave them leave. And the unclean spirits (*ta pneumata ta akatharta*) came out, and entered the swine; and the herd, numbering about two thousand, rushed down the steep bank into the sea, and were drowned in the sea.

41

The herdsmen fled, and told it in the city and in the country. And people came to see what it was that had happened. And they came to Jesus, and saw the demoniac (*daimonizomenon*) sitting there, clothed and in his right mind, the man who had had the legion; and they were afraid. And those who had seen it told what had happened to the demoniac (*daimonizomenō*) and to the swine. And they began to beg Jesus to depart from their neighborhood. And as he was getting into the boat, the man who had been possessed with demons (*ho daimonistheis*) begged him that he might be with him. But he refused, and said to him, "Go home to your friends, and tell them how much the Lord has done for you, and how he has had mercy on you." And he went away, and began to proclaim in the Decapolis how much Jesus had done for him; and all men marveled.[1]

DEMONIC POSSESSION AND LINGUISTIC HISTORY

The story of the demoniac in Mark 5:1-20, with its mystery and drama, invites close literary analysis. This extensive New Testament account of demonic possession and exorcism first startles us with its depiction of a wild man who cannot be bound; then it describes an extraordinary encounter between the man and Jesus. Subsequently the passage shows the casting out of unclean spirits, and concludes with the demoniac's recovery. These verses convey a supernatural aura, suggesting a direct meeting of evil spirits, humanity, and the divine. When Jesus performs a miracle that appears to span heaven and earth, it substantiates the claim that he is "the Lord," and the demoniac even addresses Jesus as "Son of the Most High God"—granting a kind of authorization from outside the mundane realm. Nevertheless, the meanings of the narrative extend far beyond this passage and the parallel accounts in Matthew 8:28-34 and Luke 8:26-39, because the story partakes of a wide-ranging linguistic, literary, historical, and theological milieu.

The present remarks focus on the linguistic dimension, examining the language used to describe demonic possession. What language does the demoniac speak? In what language is he cured? How should we understand the phenomenon and history of possession by demons? Prior Hebrew, Aramaic, Greek, and Latin traditions provide the background against which the text introduces its theological innovations.

In order to analyze the demoniac story from a linguistic perspective, one must know more about the language of the characters represented in the Greek Testament. As is well known, Aramaic phrases occur at critical moments in the gospels; for example, Jesus is quoted as saying *Talitha cumi* (Mark 5:41) and *Eloi, Eloi, lama sabachtani* (Mark 15:34). One scholar sums up the linguistic situation by asserting that Aramaic was then "the *most commonly* used language, but the defense of this thesis must reckon with the growing mass of evidence that both Greek and Hebrew were being used as well."[2] Following the advent of the Roman legions a century earlier, moreover, Latin became increasingly prevalent.[3] Although the New Testament is written in Greek, it reflects immense cross-linguistic influence; in some instances, a Greek phrase (such as "the Most High") is essentially a translation from Hebrew, which places it in a specific conceptual context. In other cases, the New Testament strives to free itself of influences, purging ancient Greek of part of its pagan heritage.

We need to examine the language of Mark 5:1-20, paying special attention to its *key words* or *Leitwörter*.[4] As the demoniac is possessed by spirits, so the text is inhabited by foreign presences. Even if we cannot exorcise these linguistic demons, at least we should be able to identify them and determine whence they come. Specifically at issue are the words variously translated by "spirit," "demon," "demons," "devils," "demoniac," and "possessed." Returning to the New Testament Greek, we find that "spirit" is roughly equivalent to *pneuma*; in different contexts *pneuma* may refer to wind, to the human spirit, to an evil spirit, or to the Holy Spirit of God.[5] The other words cited ultimately derive from the Greek noun *daimōn*: the plural "demons" or "devils" are *daimones* (or *daimonia* in Luke 8:27-38), while the "demoniac" is, more literally, one who is demon-possessed (*daimonizomenon* or *daimonistheis*). Thus the demoniac's "legion" of demons may at first be reduced to a more manageable pair: demons (*daimones*) and spirit (*pneuma*).

Having ascertained that *daimones* and *pneuma* are key words in the story of the demoniac, we should delimit their range of meanings. Yet it is impossible to rely exclusively on dictionary definitions, because these words underwent semantic drift over the course of time. Dictionaries best convey the systematic meanings of language at a given time, and have little place for unconventional usage. Every language is subject to flux, however, and has a diachronic aspect that constantly develops; its syntax and semantics are variable. Hence a key-word analysis may function either synchronically or diachronically. It may examine the recurrence of a particular expression during a specific period, in a given body of literature, or it may trace the shifting significance of the phrase through linguistic and literary history.

The language of demonic possession stands in an intricate relationship to linguistic history. The demoniac's "demons" (*daimones*; elsewhere *daimonia*) have their earliest origins in Homeric and Hesiodic traditions; in Homer's epics, *daimōn* sometimes names a divine agency or mysterious higher power.[6] Hesiod and Heraclitus both refer to plural *daimones* as guardian spirits that watch over mortal beings.[7] The word *daimones*—not yet demons, and closer to divine spirits—also occurs in Plato's dialogues. Even more significant is Plato's use of the related word *daimonion*. Socrates was accused of "not believing in the gods whom the state supports, but in other new divinities" (*kaina daimonia*).[8] One possible reason for this accusation was Socrates' repeated reference to a *daimonion*, a divine voice or sign that prevented him from taking false steps (see, for example, *Euthydemus* 272e, *Phaedrus* 242b, *Theaetetus* 151a and *Euthyphro* 3b). There has been much debate over the exact nature of this *daimonion*. In the present context it is relevant that nineteenth-century Christian interpreters generally understood Socrates' daimonion as a guardian spirit; for them it represented Plato's rationalistic advance beyond the earlier *daimōn* and *daimones*, giving Socrates a singular divine guide that is both similar to the

Latin concept of a guardian *genius* and compatible with the notion of conscience.

Philo states that prior Greek philosophers called *daimonas* what the Septuagint refers to as "angels" (*angelous*).[9] The Septuagint itself employs the word *angelos* to translate from the Hebrew *malakh*. The Pentateuch originally refers to angels (*malakhim*) as divine messengers; no individual possesses a constant personal guide in the form of an angel. In contrast, Greek and Latin traditions developed a notion of the guardian angel or spirit, called an *angelos* or a *genius*.[10] While the Hebrew Bible, in accordance with strict monotheism, emphasizes that angels are always subordinate to God, later Greek and Latin writers retain polytheistic tendencies, indicating that the multiplicity of angels may not be reducible to a single divine force. Moreover, possibly under the influence of Persian dualism, writers in late antiquity increasingly suggest that good and evil angels act autonomously.[11] Demonic powers of darkness led by Satan, in particular, constitute a threat to divine providence.

The Septuagint was the decisive link in the linguistic process of cultural transfer. Since the early Christians relied on this translation, it necessarily influenced their religious terminology. For example, in translating the Hebrew word *satan* from the Book of Job, the Septuagint often employs *diabolus*, which formerly had a limited usage in the Greek language. Less frequently, the Septuagint directly transliterates the Hebrew words, producing the loanwords *satan* and *satanas*.[12] In other contexts, to designate foreign gods or spirits with a negative connotation, the Septuagint utilizes the pre-existing Greek substantatives *daimōn* and *daimonion*.[13] *Daimones* and *duimonia* in the New Testament depend on the negative meaning assumed by *daimonion* in the Septuagint. This illustrates one way in which Christianity brought together Hebrew and Greek precedents. By transforming Hebrew words into approximate Greek equivalents, the Septuagint exerts direct influence on religious history. The gospels then institute a substantial linguistic and theological novelty by employing the words *daimones* and *pneumata* to denote independent evil spirits, rather than false gods worshiped by idolaters.

New Testament demons and spirits also derive from prior Hebraic and Aramaic traditions. The Hebrew Bible contains several words that refer to supernatural beings. Foremost is *satan*, God's prosecuting angel (Job 1:6-2:7 and Zech. 3:1-2); this adversary does not have the autonomous status of Satan in the gospels, but acts only in conjunction with God. In addition, the demoniac's unclean spirit (*pneuma to akatharton*) alludes to the Greek of the Septuagint, which refers to an evil spirit (*pneuma poneron*) in the story of Saul. In the original Hebrew passage, in turn, "spirit" corresponds to Hebrew *ruah*: "the spirit of God (*ruah YHWH*) departed from Saul, and an evil spirit from God (*ruah raᶜa me'et YHWH*) troubled him" (1 Samuel 16:14). While this text distinguishes between the divine spirit and an evil spirit, it emphasizes that even the latter comes from God, and is subordinate to Him. Lesser fiends and demons occur under a variety of names including *seᶜirim* (Isaiah 13:21), *shedim* (Deut. 32:17), and *mazzikin* (Babylonian Talmud). All of the Hebrew and Aramaic background plays some indefinite role in the demoniac's plight. Consequently, when Jesus comes to cure the demoniac, he begins with the question: "What is your name?" Before proceeding, he tries to situate the demon linguistically, and thus gain power over it. The demonic retinue evades his inquiry and emphasizes its elusive multiplicity by answering: "Legion" (Mark 5:9)—that is, as numerous and mighty as the Roman legions that had infiltrated Palestine.

In their reference to the key words *daimones* and *pneuma*, then, early Christian writers necessarily rely on Greek and Hebraic expressions concerning divinity. Because of their commitment to monotheism, they dismiss the earlier notion that daimones could be separate divine guides. Such plural divinities would pose a serious threat, potentially undermining God's oneness. Hence Christianity excludes the positive connotations of Greek *daimōn*, *daimonion*, and *daimones*, instead turning them into evil demons. This occurs in the gospels and, afterward, in the writings of Chariton and Augustine.[14] What had formerly been a minor divinity became a demon or evil spirit.[15] In order to secure the monotheistic foundations of their new religion, ancient Christian writers had to transform the language in which they wrote.

FROM DAIMONES TO DEMONS

We should now interpret the language of Mark 5:1-20 in its linguistic context. At first sight, in the country of the Gerasenes, the demoniac appears as "a man with an unclean spirit (*pneumati akathartō*)" (Mark 5:2). The Gospel of Mark is, at this stage, more cautious in its language than are Matthew and Luke. Matthew 8:28 refers to "two demoniacs (*daimonizomenoi*)," whereas Luke 8:27 mentions a man who "had demons (*daimonia*)." In the original Greek of Mark 5:15-18, the demoniac is called demonically-possessed; only a textual variant to Mark 5:12 indicates that he had demons (*daimones.*).[16] At issue is the status of these supernatural spirits, which are otherwise mentioned and exorcised in Mark 1:32-34, 1:39, 7:26-40, and elsewhere. When Jesus cures the demoniac, he calls: "Come out of the man, you unclean spirit" (Mark 5:8; compare Luke 8:29). Thus the Gospel of Mark reveals a terminological wavering between "unclean spirits" and "demons." In addition, the story of the demoniac contains a discrepancy in number: at one point he has a single unclean spirit, while at another stage thousands of unclean spirits leave him. It may be that the initial description in the singular applies to the man's damaged psyche, while the following narrative explains his condition by referring to demonic possession by innumerble spirits. In any event, the parallel accounts in Matthew and Luke unify the language by referring more uniformly to plural demons as *daimones* or *daimonia*.

Another seminal passage concerning demons in the synoptic gospels sheds light on the theological system that was linked to demonic possession, exorcism, and Satan. Mark 3:22-30 hints at both the political strife and the metaphysical battles associated with the rise of the Christian sect. Some Jerusalem scribes criticize Jesus, saying "He is possessed by Beelzebul, and by the prince of the demons he casts out demons" (3:22). In other words, since they do not recognize him as the Messiah, they identify him with an evil force that opposes God. If he successfully casts out demons, they charge, this is only because he is their leader. In response, Jesus speaks in parables:

How can Satan cast out Satan? If a kingdom
is divided against itself, that kingdom cannot
stand. . . . And if Satan has risen up against
himself, and is divided, he cannot stand, but is
coming to an end. But no one can enter a strong
man's house and plunder his goods, unless he
first binds the strong man; then indeed he may
plunder his house. Truly I say to you, all sins will
be forgiven the sons of men, and whatever
blasphemies they utter, but whoever blasphemes
against the Holy Spirit never has forgiveness,
but is guilty of an eternal sin—for they [the
scribes] had said, "He has an unclean spirit."
(Mark 3:23-30)

Demons and demoniacs participate in a theological drama. The
text fully accepts the dualism between good and evil, God and
Satan; it sets up a direct opposition between the Holy Spirit and
unclean spirits. Jesus stakes his claim as a divine representative
on his ability to counter evil beings.

"Demons" and "unclean spirits" have multiple significance in
the synoptic gospels. First and foremost in the Gospel of Mark,
they serve to identify Jesus. One unclean spirit in the Capernaum
synagogue cries out: "What have you to do with us, Jesus of
Nazareth? Have you come to destroy us? I know who you are,
the Holy One of God" (Mark 1:24; compare Luke 4:41). Second,
they show Jesus' ability to control forces of the world and beyond
it. In the previous scene, during a storm on the Sea of Galilee
Jesus commands the forces of nature, calming a physical wind
(*pneuma*). Now he expels supernatural forces of evil, thus allying
him with the power of good. Third, his casting out of unclean
spirits underscores the dichotomy between unclean spirits and the
Holy Spirit. Fourth, Satan or Beelzebul as head of the demons
acts as the tempter of Jesus, further sharpening the metaphysical
opposition (Mark 1:12-13, Matthew 4:1-11, and Luke 4:1-14).
Here Satan has become the quintessential figure of evil rather
than one of many evil spirits.

This background gives new meaning to the demoniac story. In
fact, its placement immediately following a chapter of parables

(Mark 4) may encourage interpretation along allegorical lines. The exorcism story does not merely recount an event, but bears myriad potential meanings. It suggests the effort of Christianity to drive out foreign, especially pagan influences, epitomized by the multiple *daimones* that had become unacceptable to a nascent monotheistic system. As represented in the gospels, Jesus appears to exorcise the Greek language of its demons; he reasserts the unity of God by showing that other supposed deities are merely evil demons. In the course of his travels, he shows his ability to rid Palestine of its evil demons and its competing polytheistic systems; he dispenses with the long Greek tradition that spoke of *daimones* in positive terms. Furthermore, the story of his successful exorcism might be understood as an indirect political statement. We know that Roman legions were prominent in first-century Palestine, and that there were numerous rebellions by the local population, ultimately leading to the destruction of the Second Temple in Jerusalem. Since the demoniac says his name is "Legion," this could suggest a disguised, subversive meaning: as Jesus drives out a legion of demons into the swine, so his contemporaries might rely on him to drive out the Tenth Legion of Roman conquerors. His views are sometimes more explicit, as when he proclaims: "Render to Caesar the things that are Caesar's, and to God the things that are God's" (Mark 12:17).

Although we can read the Greek gospels in any number of more or less scholarly English editions, the problems of translation are not so readily solved. The meaning of this text frequently depends on its precise attempt to reappropriate and transform Judaic and Hellenistic thought. No English rendition can retain the exact verbal components that embody this textual revolution. From a modern point of view, we might be inclined to see the demoniac as a man suffering from psychosis. Yet ancient authors seldom believed that such disorders could be explained as purely individual conditions. Instead, they assumed that the disturbances were caused by the intervention of supernatural beings.

Contrary to the common opinion that language and literature give expression to underlying cultural and historical trends, key-word analysis of the kind exemplified here shows that the opposite is sometimes the case: linguistic drift influences and contributes to intellectual history. Christianity could not have arisen as it did without the Greek language and, more specifically, without the late Greek of the Septuagint. From this standpoint, the gospels both inherit and embody a radical linguistic innovation in relation to prior Greek literature. Through the pliant medium of Greek, a polytheistic system of thought was transformed into a dualism that emphasized God's perpetual conquest over Satan.

With the advent of Christianity, *daimones* became demons and took on purely negative connotations. Christian writers gradually accepted the notion that Satan, Beelzebul, or the Devil is a metaphysical antithesis to God.[17] Hence, in a related way, Luther's German rendition of the New Testament often refers to "devils" (*Teufel*).[18] This linguistic usage assumes a kind of dualism, separating good and evil as two opposing cosmic forces. The synoptic gospels, placing special weight on demonic possession and on Jesus' ability to exorcise demons, introduce a dramatic struggle between good and evil; to cure a demoniac is to expel a threatening presence. Palestine appears overrun by evil beings that emerge at the intersection of psychological, linguistic, political, and theological realms.

Mark 5:1-20 thus presents a scene of dualism—between holy and unclean spirits—and overcomes it, showing the greater power of good. This seminal Christian narrative illustrates the syncretistic impulse to appropriate prior thought, and to create an amalgam that reconciles multilingual sources. Only by transforming *daimones* into demons and expanding the role of Satan do the gospels achieve their theological swerve away from Judaism and Greek religion.

NOTES

1.   This and subsequent English translations of the gospels are quoted from the revised standard version in *The Oxford Annotated Bible* (New York: Oxford University Press, 1962). Parenthetical key words and manuscript variants in the Greek original are drawn from the *Griechisches Neues Testament: Text mit kurzem Apparat*, Hermann von Soden, ed. (Göttingen: Vandenhoeck & Ruprecht, 1913).

2.   J. A. Fitzmyer, "The Languages of Palestine in the First Century A.D.,"
     Catholic Biblical Quarterly 32 (1970), 518.

3.   Fitzmyer, "The Languages of Palestine," 507.

4.   The present discussion of key words and *Leitwörter* has been
     influenced by a passage in Martin Buber's essay "Zu einer neuen
     Verdeutschung der Schrift," supplement to the Buber-Rosenzweig
     translation of the Pentateuch (Darmstadt: Wissenschaftliche
     Buchgesellschaft, 1984).   Buber defines the *Leitwort* as "a word or a
     word-root . . . that significantly recurs in a text, a textual sequence, or
     textual context" (15; this passage is also contained in Buber's Werke
     [Munich: Kösel, 1964], Vol. 2, p. 1131).   Compare the discussion by
     Robert Alter in *The Art of Biblical Narrative* (New York: Basic Books,
     1981), pp. 92-94.

5.   See entry for *pneuma* in *A   Greek-English   Lexicon   of   the   New
     Testament and Other Early Christian Literature*, William F. Arndt
     and F. Wilbur Gingrich, eds. (Chicago: University of Chicago Press,
     1957), pp. 680-85.

6.   This is a simplified, synchronic definition.   For a more extensive
     discussion see my *Genius and Monologue* (Ithaca: Cornell University
     Press, 1985), pp. 33-38.

7.   See Hesiod, *The Works and Days, in The Homeric Hymns and
     Homerica* (Cambridge, MA: Harvard University Press, 1982), lines
     121-25 and 140-42, and   Heraclitus in *Die Fragmente der
     Vorsokratiker*, Vol. 1, B63,   Hermann Diels and Walther Kranz, eds.
     (Berlin: Weidmann, 1951).

8.   See Plato's *Apology* 24b.

9.   *De somniis*, Book 1, Chapter 22.

10. See my *Genius and Monologue*, pp. 49-53.

11. See the Manual of Discipline, in *The Dead Sea Scriptures*, Theodor H.
     Gaster, tr. (New York: Doubleday, 1956), p. 43.

12. See the Septuagint, III Kings 11:14; here *satan* refers to a human
     adversary which God raises up against Solomon.

13.   See the Septuagint, Deut. 32:17, Ps. 90:6 (91:6), 95:5 (96:6), Isaiah 13:21, 65:11. Compare Edwin Hatch and Henry A. Redpath, *A Concordance to the Septuagint and the Other Greek Versions of the Old Testament (Including the Apocryhal Books)*, Vol. 1 (Oxford: Clarendon Press, 1897), p. 283.

14.   Chariton, *Chaereas and Callirhoe*, VI, 2, 9; St. Augustine, *De civitate dei*, VIII, 14 and X, 9.

15.   See entry for *daimōn* in *A Greek-English Lexicon of the New Testament and Other Early Christian Literature*, p. 168.

16.   See *Griechisches Neues Testament*, von Soden, ed., p. 71.

17.   Concerning the battle between Jesus and Satan, see P. André Lefèvre, "Ange ou bête? Le puissance du mal dans l'Ancien Testament," in the volume *Satan*, in *Etudes Carmélitaines* 27 (1948), 13: "It is difficult to believe in Christ the Redeemer without at the same time believing in his antagonist, the Devil."

18.   See Martin Luther, *Die Gantze Heilige Schrifft Deutsch* (Wittenberg, 1545), reprinted and ed. Hans Volz (Munich: Rogner & Bernhard, 1972), e.g. in Matthew 8:31, Mark 5:12, and Luke 8:27.

BIBLICAL EXORCISM AND READER RESPONSE TO RITUAL IN NARRATIVE
Carol Schersten LaHurd

A METHODOLOGICAL INTRODUCTION

In the dialogue between literary critics and biblical scholars there is often disagreement about how much attention to focus upon the "text itself" and how much to consider information, especially historical and theological, outside the text. This discussion of Mark 5:1-20 proposes to join these concerns in a reading that combines the methodologies of rhetorical criticism and reader response criticism with more "traditional" modes of biblical interpretation and models from ritual studies. From literary critics such as Wayne Booth, Walter Ong and Peter Rabinowitz come the notions that signals in the text help the reading audience to constitute itself and that literary features control distance between the narrator and reader, author and narrator, and so on. Reader response critics such as Stanley Fish, Wolfgang Iser and Hans-Robert Jauss have contributed the theory that meaning results from the interaction between the text and the reader's experience of it. Finally, ritual studies practitioners such as Victor Turner and Ronald Grimes have provided models from field observations of performed rituals that have application to ritual elements in narrative texts.

Acknowledging that concepts of implied author and implied audience are not objective realities so much as constructs based upon textual evidence, this analysis examines Mark 5:1-20 in light of the audience's possible "horizon of expectations,"[1] that is, the previous experience with literature and religious life that the first-century readers might have brought to their encounter with the text. The "author" referred to here is the one implied by the text. For the sake of brevity he is referred to as "Mark," but that designation makes no assumptions about the identity of the actual historical author. The audiences are divided into the *actual* (the historical readers, about whom we can only speculate), the *narrative* (the audience addressed by the story tellers of individual

53

episodes), and the *implied* (that imagined by the implied author of the entire Markan text).

Because part of the audiences' (both the actual and the implied) "horizon of expectations" is past experience of ritual, this analysis attends to the potential impact of ritual features in the Markan text. Ritual content in literature can occur as description of ritual enactments (the spoken words of an exorcism formula), inclusion of ritual elements (the liminal journeying of Jesus and the disciples in Mark 4-5), and recreation of ritual experience in which the reading or listening audience participates to some extent (the repetition of "commissioning" endings for healing and exorcism events). Indeed, many narrative features have the potential for creating ritual impact: descriptions of space and objects, sound and language, roles of participants.

Predicting how these features might influence audience response to Mark 5:1-20 requires some educated speculation about possible readers and their "horizon of expectations." The Markan gospel is thought to have been composed for Roman Christians,[2] presumably both Jews and gentiles (a mixture implied by references in Acts and Romans). Regardless of their ethnic background, these readers would have had some familiarity with demon exorcism, a common practice in the Greco-Roman world[3] and one that continued well into the patristic era.[4] Also pertinent for any discussion of Mark 5 are the possible readers' notions of clean and unclean. From attention to this issue elsewhere in the New Testament it is reasonable to assume that at least some of Mark's readers brought to the text the belief from ancient Judaism that God's people must be holy (i.e., "clean") because God is holy.[5] Such concepts make up part of the external material that can contribute to an analysis of the Markan text.

A READING OF MARK 5:1-20 AND ITS RITUAL ELEMENTS

To assess how the text of Mark 5:1-20 guides reader response, this analysis focuses on the context for the narrative within Mark 1-5, the gradual release of information to the implied audience, challenges to audience expectations and the potential impact of ritual elements. Mark's story of Jesus' public ministry begins with Jesus' preaching about the coming Kingdom of God (1:14-15) and with the exorcism of an unclean spirit (1:23-28). Indeed, in the four chapters preceding the Gerasene demoniac episode, Mark's narrative alternates between brief accounts of Jesus' encounters with demons (as well as of healings) and his Kingdom of God teachings. Exorcism scenes in 1:23-28, 1:34, and 3:11 all contain elements which point ahead to the extended account in Mark 5. And in 3:22 and 3:30 observers are said to view Jesus himself as possessed by an unclean spirit.

The immediate context for the Gerasene demoniac episode is a chapter of detailed teaching in parables to sympathetic crowds and in more direct manner to the disciples alone (4:33-34). As evening arrives, Jesus and the disciples set across the sea in a boat. In the midst of a violent storm Jesus must be awakened by his companions, who marvel at his ability to command the wind to cease (4:35-41). Jesus' deliverance of the demoniac then comes as an extended interlude before he and the disciples return to the boat and cross back to the other side for more teaching. At this point, rather than continuing the Kingdom of God *kerygma*, Mark narrates two interwoven healing events: Jairus' daughter and the woman with a continuous flow of blood.

Mark's story of Jesus does not contain the elaborate network of parallel scenes and repetition and variation characteristic of Luke's gospel; nevertheless, the sequence just described prepares the reader for the demoniac episode and influences its potential interpretation. The features this event shares with previous exorcism scenes and the interwoven Kingdom of God teachings work together to release insight gradually to the implied audience—permitting that audience a more informed interpretation than is possible for the narrative audience of the Mark 5:1-20 exorcism report. In two earlier exorcism scenes (1:23 and 3:11), the demons or their victims are said to cry out (*kradzō*). The same word appears in 5:5,7. In each scene the demon or unclean spirit identifies Jesus and acknowledges his power:

> "What have you to do with us, Jesus of Nazareth?
> Have you come to destroy us? I know who you are,
> the Holy One of God." (1:24)

And whenever the unclean spirits beheld him, they fell down before him and cried out, "You are the Son of God." (3:11)

Similarly, in each account Jesus rebukes the demons and demands silence. In addition to these exorcism references there is a comparable summary in 1:34: "And he healed many who were sick with various diseases, and cast out many demons; and he would not permit the demons to speak, because they knew him." The unclean spirits' ready acknowledgement of Jesus' identity is one clue to the theological significance of these exorcism stories. But the verb used for Jesus' rebuke of the demons also reveals that these are more than miraculous examples of Jesus' power. In 1:25 for *rebuking* demons, and again in 4:39, for the wind ("he . . . rebuked the wind"), the verb is *epitimaō* a word that implies not just "reproach but rather the defeat of the forces of God's enemies."[6]

Although *epitimaō* does not appear in the Mark 5 account, that word choice is one of the several textual clues to the significance of Jesus' actions with regard to demons and natural forces. Another is the interweaving of exorcism scenes with Kingdom of God teaching, teaching which links exorcism with the arrival of a new age. Passages such as Mark 4:26-29 and 30-32 reveal to the reader that the Kingdom is "present, but hidden" and soon to come in fullness.[7] While such teachings in Mark often appear to be misunderstood by the disciples, the reader has the advantage of interpreting them in the context of Jesus' eschatological actions, such as the ousting of unclean spirits and commanding of chaotic forces. As Kee argues, "Mark's strategy is that of evoking a response dialectically from his reader rather than simple, direct assertions, about Jesus as Lord."[8]

The Markan text not only influences its own interpretation through such guidance of reader response; it also provides challenges to reader expectations.[9] Reversals of expected outcomes abound in the Mark 5 narrative. Several that involve the text's ritual elements are the atypical use of exorcism formulae, the outcome of the exorcism itself (the destruction of a herd of pigs and the behavior of the cured demoniac), and the treatment of the concepts of cleanness and uncleanness. Neither the exorcism in 1:25 nor that in 5:1-20 makes use of typical formulae for such a ritual. The usual combination of the name of a god and the words "I adjure" comes instead from the voices of the demons. In 1:24 the demons use both Jesus' and God's names, and in 5:7 they unsuccessfully apply an exorcism formula to Jesus: "I adjure you by God, do not torment me."[10] Such a reversal of roles in Mark 5 is foreshadowed in Mark 3, where Jesus is seen as possessed by Beelzebul (v. 22) and an "unclean spirit" (v. 30).[11]

The Mark 5 demons' use of exorcism formula phrases to address Jesus is one unexpected detail. Also notable is Jesus' apparent failure to exorcise the spirits on the first try (5:8), a development which leads to an extended conversation between Jesus and the demons. This conversation yields additional clues to reader interpretation of the final outcome. The phrase, "My name is Legion; for we are many," has the double impact of recalling the unpleasant experience of Roman military occupation and of revealing what a difficult task exorcism will be, with so many spirits to command. Jesus' granting of the demons' wish to enter the nearby herd of pigs and the pigs' immediate destruction in the sea have been viewed by some as an example of the motif of "the devil being deceived."[12] Wherever this narrative detail originated, it evokes reader response as an unexpected ending for an exorcism story. In 1:28 Jesus' removal of an unclean spirit has resulted in his reputation extending "throughout all the surrounding region of Galilee." The Mark 5 exorcism also expands Jesus' fame, but in an unfavorable way when the demoniac's neighbors react in fear to the news of the pigs' destruction (5:15-17). Much scholarly speculation has been focused on this outcome. The drowning pigs have been likened to Pharoah's soldiers perishing in the midst of their pursuit of Moses and the people of Israel.[13] And their death has been viewed as a conclusive sign for the demoniac that the exorcism has been successful.[14] In light of the preceding discussion of Mark 5 in its narrative and theological context, a more defensible theory is that the pigs' destruction serves as convincing evidence for Jesus' eschatological victory over the forces of Satan and chaos.[15] After Mark 5's unusual exorcism account and previous depiction of Jesus as possessed and casting out demons in the name of Satan (3:21-30), the spirits' defeat as drowned swine symbolizes Jesus' power and authority and negates the earlier implications of his effectiveness and possible link with Satan.

Many of Mark 5's ritual elements have already been referred to in the analysis of the exorcism itself. However, a number of other narrative details in the Gerasene demoniac episode have the potential for impact on the reading audience. In a 1984 study Mark McVann describes the cycle of episodes in Mark 5 as a "ritual mini-drama."[16] Applying models from Victor Turner, McVann examines the liminal status and roles of various characters and of Jesus himself and relates them to functions within the early church. For McVann the characters undergo "a real ontological change" as a result of their liminal circumstances and encounters with Jesus.[17]

Such an analysis of the presence of liminality can extend as well to the readers' situations and their response to particular features of the Gerasene demoniac narrative. As has been noted, this episode takes Jesus and the disciples (and the implied audience) away from the crowds of followers and on a sea journey to a place of tombs and demoniacs outside of society's structure (and as Jesus and the disciples are already engaged in a visit to a semi-gentile region, they are further removed from their own social setting). The night-time storm experience at sea and the encounter with the chaotic and violent behavior of the demoniac further intensify their sense of being on the margins of social stability and personal safety.

One aspect of the liminality motif as it appears in Mark 5 is the movement between clean and unclean states. Not only is the man who Jesus and the disciples encounter possessed by a legion of unclean spirits; he has also been cast out by his community into the place of the dead—a further move into uncleanness. The man's return to cleanness includes the evicting of his demons into animals viewed as inherently unclean, the elimination of both the demons and the swine in the sea, and the man's restoration to a "clothed" and "right mind" state. This scene's potential impact on Mark's readers thus depends to some extent on those readers' notions of clean and unclean. Elsewhere in the New Testament literature, for example in Romans 14, I Corinthians 8 and Acts 10 and 15, there is evidence of concern for the categories of clean and unclean and how they were to be dealt with in the new Christian community. Mark's text also reveals some ambivalence about these categories. When Jesus heals a leper in 1:40-45, the verb for the healing is *katharidzō* or "cleanse." But the gospel's only other use of that verb refers to cleansing food (7:19). When Jesus heals the woman with a continuous flow of blood—presumably also an unclean condition in ancient Jewish understanding (see Leviticus 15:25)—the verb is not *katharidzō* but *iaomai*, "cure," and she is healed of a disease, *mastigos*, not uncleanness. The related term *akatharta*, "unclean," is used by Mark when referring to unclean spirits in 1:23, 26, 27; 3:11, 30 and 5:2, 8, 13. The vocabulary in 5:25-34, Jesus' public mingling with sinners (2:15) and his preaching about defilement (7:14-23), all serve as evidence that, with the coming of the Kingdom of God in Mark's gospel, long-held notions about clean and unclean are being challenged.

Given Jewish and Jewish-Christian ideas about ritual and moral uncleanness and apparent ambiguity about the concept in Mark's narrative, what can be said about the potential audience impact of Mark 5:1-20? If the inhabitants of the demoniac's home area are gentile,[18] then of course they could be expected to view the destruction of the pigs (not unclean for them) as potentially more threatening than the presence of one ostracized demoniac. Hollenbach suggests another reason why the neighbors in the narrative greet Jesus' action with distress. In light of sociological studies of life under colonialism, it is possible to view demon possession as a sort of social coping mechanism in colonial Palestine. Jesus' dramatic removal of that condition not only disrupted existing social patterns for dealing with demoniacs, but it might also have been seen as a threat to an accepted mode of containing open hostility toward the Roman oppressors.[19]

Considering the ritual experience of Mark's readers, however, there are at least two other ways this story within its Markan context might have affected them. First, the destruction of the herd of swine might have been viewed both as a victory for Jesus against the forces of chaos and Satan—and as an atoning sacrifice. One explanation for the Hebrew classification of swine as unclean is that the Israelites wanted to distance themselves from the use of pigs in Canaanite sacrifices, sacrifices that were inherently unclean from the Hebrew perspective.[20] But if Mark's text is questioning prevailing notions of clean and unclean, then it is possible to view this outcome as a challenge to reader expectations, a challenge to accept the mass destruction of the swine as a sacrifice in the mode of Leviticus 16.

The second potential impact of Mark 5:1-20 also relates to unexpected outcomes. Once the demoniac has been restored to cleanness (v. 15), he is commissioned by Jesus to witness to his friends. Such instructions represent a surprising departure from Jesus' usual demand for silence after healings and exorcisms.[21] But the commissioning of the former demoniac "to proclaim in the Decapolis" is not inconsistent with the long tradition of commissionings in Hebrew scripture or with some other episodes in Mark. Jesus' first healing in Mark is that of Simon's mother-in-law. Her healing is followed immediately by the words, "and she served them" (1:31). Such an outcome may appear to be one more example of first-century sexism—or it may be seen as a commissioning. When Jesus restores persons to wholeness, they are empowered to serve. Just as Isaiah of Jerusalem is cleansed by a burning coal and thus enabled to accept God's commission as a prophet (Isaiah 6), so too is the Gerasene demoniac restored to humanness and wholeness and inspired to share his good news.

Attention to ritual elements in the Markan text supports the claim that the Markan audience's familiarity with exorcism and commissioning rituals and with ideas of clean and unclean must have influenced their responses to the story of the Gerasene demoniac. First, the narrative positioning of this story within the Markan text and atypical features of its exorcism performance combine to guide the implied audience toward the episode's eschatalogical significance.[22] Second, the readers' participation in the liminality experienced by Jesus, the disciples and the demoniac, and their reception of the text's challenges to attitudes about uncleanness engage the readers in the transforming potential of ritual. To that extent, this text encourages the reading/listening audience to respond itself to commissioning opportunities as did the Gerasene demoniac.

NOTES

1. Hans-Robert Jauss, as quoted in Susan R. Suleiman and Inge Crosman, eds., *The Reader in the Text: Essays on Audience and Interpretation* (Princeton: Princeton University Press, 1980), pp. 35-37. Especially pertinent for New Testament critics is Jauss' view that the critic must reconstruct this horizon of expectations from information both inside and outside the text.

2. Vincent Taylor, *The Gospel According to Mark* (Grand Rapids: Baker Book House, 1966), p. 32.

3. J. M. Hull, "Exorcism in the New Testament," *Interpreter's Dictionary of the Bible*, Supplementary Volume (Nashville: Abingdon Press, 1962), p. 313.

4. Stephen Benko, "Early Christian Magical Practices," *SBL Seminar Papers* 21 (1982), 10-11.

5. L. E. Toombs, "Clean and Unclean," *Interpreter's Dictionary of the Bible* , Vol. 1 (Nashville: Abingdon Press, 1962), p. 647.

6. H. C. Kee, "The Terminology of Mark's Exorcism Stories," *New Testament Studies* 14 (1966), 232-46.

7. Elizabeth Schüssler Fiorenza, "Eschatology of the New Testament," *Interpreter's Dictionary of the Bible*, Supplementary Volume, p. 273.

8. Kee, "Mark's Exorcism Stories," 244.

9. One could argue that such apparent discrepancies have resulted from the chance combinations of traditional material or from the organic growth of narrative that inevitably yields a degree of "opacity," as is claimed by Frank Kermode in *The Genesis of Secrecy* (Cambridge: Harvard University Press, 1979). However, it seems unnecessary to choose between such alternatives and the elusive factor of authorial intention in order to make statements about the text's potential impact on an implied audience.

10. Everett Ferguson, *Demonology of the Early Christian World* (New York: Edwin Mellen Press, 1984), pp. 9-10.

11.   Rudolf Bultmann also notes that Jesus is addressed as a demon in the 1:21-28 episode, as well as in 5:7. See *The History of the Synoptic Tradition*, John March, tr. (New York: Harper & Row, 1963), p. 210.

12.   Bultmann, p. 210. Eduard Schweizer suggests the possibility that Mark 5 has combined a folk story about the devil and two thousand pigs with the basic exorcism account. See *The Good News According to Mark*, Donald H. Madvig, tr. (Atlanta: John Knox Press, 1970), p. 112.

13.   C. H. Cave, "The Obedience of Unclean Spirits," *New Testament Studies* 11 (1964), 97.

14.   William Barclay, *The Gospel of Mark* (Philadelphia: Westminster Press, 1975), p. 120.

15.   S. Vernon McCasland points to the Jewish apocalyptic notion that one activity of the Messiah will be the expulsion of demons. See *By the Finger of God: Demon Possession and Exorcism in Early Christianity in the Light of Modern Views of Mental Illness* (New York: Macmillan, 1951), p. 133.

16.   Mark McVann, *Dwelling Among the Tombs: Discourse, Discipleship, and the Gospel of Mark 4:35-5:43*, unpublished Ph.D. dissertation (Emory University, 1984), p. 150.

17.   McVann, pp. 4-5, 193.

18.   Scholars have long debated the question of the actual geographic location of the Gerasene demoniac episode (Taylor, p. 278). However, there is general agreement that the area was "semi-gentile" and under Roman control (see Schweizer, p. 113).

19.   Paul W. Hollenbach, "Jesus, Demoniacs, and Public Authorities: A Socio-Historical Study." *Journal of the American Academy of Religion* 49 (December, 1981), 576-81. Such an interpretation might profitably be examined from the perspective of Mary Douglas' views about social pollution and about ritual control of danger by segregating persons during transitional phases (e.g., birth, death, puberty). See *Purity and Danger: An Analysis of the Concepts of Pollution and Taboo* (London: Routledge & Kegan Paul, 1966; ARK Edition, 1984), especially pp. 96, 122.

20. Toombs, *Interpreter's Dictionary of the Bible*, Vol. 1, p. 643.

21. Vincent Taylor suggests that this exception may relate to the man's living in a region beyond Galilee. See *The Gospel According to Mark*, p. 285.

22. Kee explains that many Hellenistic exorcism stories simply served to "glorify the wonder-worker" and carried no deeper meaning (241).

SIDING WITH THE SWINE:
A MORAL PROBLEM FOR NARRATIVE
David Jasper

TWO HORIZONS OF INTERPRETATION

Literary critics have got themselves in a tangle in their reading of the Bible. In an essay on the Gospel of Mark, Kenneth R.R. Gros Louis promises that "as [a] means of demonstrating the literary achievements of the gospel we will consider what the story might mean to us as twentieth century students of *literature*."[1] In their anxiety to criticize the shortcomings of historical methods of scriptural interpretation, such critics have been drawn into obsessively ahistorical encounters with the text, making assumptions about its unity and its literary or fictional rather than its historical reality. Like Meir Sternberg, in the first chapter of his book *The Poetics of Biblical Narrative*, I want immediately to express unease in the face of such antihistorical bias. In Sternberg's words:

> All that needs emphasizing is that for literary
> analysts to deal responsibly with a compositional issue
> par excellence they must engage in a poetic valuation
> of a whole range of so-called extrinsic evidence: from
> the art of the Oriental tradition through the premises
> of monotheistic theology to the dating of the biblical
> canon. Milieu, world view, history of formation—all
> untouchables prove indispensable to literary study as
> such.[2]

Sternberg has himself been heavily criticized by Mieke Bal for his "ideological commitment to the text and his use of poetics to support it, if not to impose it."[3] His method turns him, according to Bal, from the literary scholar he claims to be into a theologian.

Heaven forbid! The point is, I think, that the Bible actually requires us to be both, not confusing the one with the other nor abandoning the one enterprise in an obsession with the other. In

65

more senses than one there are two "horizons" shaping the
interpreter's task: the horizons of the literary critic and the
theologian, and the horizons of the historical distinction between
text and interpreter. While we may aspire in the hermeneutic
endeavor, with Hans-Georg Gadamer, to a "fusion" of horizons,
in fact the two horizons, in either sense, can never become
identical. However close, they remain separate.[4]

The danger of making ahistorical literary assumptions about a
scriptural text may be illustrated from the curious fiction of
Wolfgang Iser's "implied reader" (suspended in the "virtuality of
the work"[5] above the particularities of personhood, place or time)
which is generated by the interaction of the text—the marks on
the page—with an historical reader. Within the text,
interpretation is threatened by areas of indeterminacy, shifting
perspectives and "gaps" which demand that the reader work
things out for himself in an imaginative reaching towards textual
realization.

The most notorious gap in the Gospel of Mark is at the end
("And they said nothing to anyone, for they were afraid," 16:8,
Revised Standard Version), with its lack of any conclusion to the
women's wordless fear. But, in fact, only insofar as the text is
abstracted above the particularities of its religious, cultural and
historical foundations does the textual problem really arise,
described in terms of a "structured blank." The problem of Mark
16:8 can, of course, be argued in many ways, denying or
supporting the integrity of the text. Was the gospel left
unfinished, was it damaged, was it intended as a riddle? But why
should it be seen as a *problem*, a "literary debate,"[6] or a structured
blank?

It is clear that the New Testament writers relied heavily upon
biblical typology and allusion and apparently could expect a high
degree of literate response from their readers. The birth and
infancy narratives of the Gospel of Matthew, for example, are a
patchwork of Old Testament allusion intended to identify Jesus'
messianic calling. We might then, following Austin Farrer,
propose that the conclusion to Mark's gospel was intended to be
read in the light of the Joseph story in Genesis. Joseph is lost,

dead to his brethren, and rediscovered in awesome circumstances in Egypt. His brothers, on recognizing him, react significantly: "His brethren could not answer him, for they were afraid" (Genesis 45:3); while the women at the end of Mark say nothing to anybody, for they, too, are afraid. Quite apart from the significance of the verb "to fear" throughout the gospel, employed at moments of insight in Jesus' presence (e.g., 9:32), we might assume that readers or listeners would readily engage with the familiar Joseph/Jesus typology and respond to the text's conclusion accordingly. Joseph's forgiveness and comforting of his wayward brothers were well known (Genesis 45:4ff), and there was nothing more to be said. The text of the gospel is quite explicit enough and nothing further need be spelled out.[7]

I have, of course, made a huge assumption about the history of the formation of this writing, on the basis, one might say, of pure guesswork. But Iser, one may say, has made no less an assumption in pursuing his ahistorical literary strategy. And if I *am* correct, and he is wrong, then something like the textual prehistory I have suggested is indispensable to literary understanding. Furthermore, while Iser proposes textual power in what is left implicit, the blanks to be filled in by the reader, my own proposal no less requires the resolution of indeterminacies, the filling in of gaps, the expectation of implicature. But the gaps will be *different* gaps, more subtle, and less prone to appear at points where the modern reader is simply frankly puzzled by the mysterious assumptions of a two-thousand year-old text.

THE HISTORY AND THEOLOGY OF MARK 5:1-20

As a literary critic I want to assume the unity of the text which narrates the healing of the Gerasene demoniac (Mark 5:1-20). But as a theologian and student of New Testament Greek, I find that that presents a problem. For I have to conclude that, historically, this narrative developed and grew for specific theological reasons. Its unity is historically complex.

The story begins baldly, interrupted by vv. 3-5, quite different in style from the rest of 1-12 and found only in the Markan version.

The curious succession of perfect infinitives in v. 4 is colloquial, almost racy, and typical of a style peculiar to the author of this gospel. With v. 6 we return to the sparser style of the opening of the narrative. The narrative proceeds without a further break (except possibly v. 8, largely peculiar to Mark) until v. 12. There are good reasons for thinking that vv. 12-13 are an addition to the original story.[8] Not only is the figure of two thousand peculiar to this version, but the style of the Greek again changes: e.g., the phrase translated as "let us enter them" (12b), is a typical Markan Hebraism. With v. 14, the tone again returns to its original pitch, broken for the last time in vv. 18-20. There again we see a modulation to Markan vocabulary and style: the loose genitive absolute (18), the compressed colloquialisms of Jesus' speech (18), and so on. Moreover, within the context of the gospel's "secrecy," the verses pose problems regarding the apparent willingness of Jesus to allow the man to preach (the "and" of v. 20 indicates the man's ready obedience) and his denial of the request that he might join Jesus' disciples.

I see two broad elements in this one narrative. The first is the basic healing story (1-2, 6-11 [possibly omitting 8], 14-17). The second, the Markan interpolations (3-5, [8], 12-13, 18-20). The main point of the healing story is made quite independently of the secondary interpolations. Juxtaposed with the stilling of the storm on the lake (Mark 4:35-41), the miracles are a sign of divine power in the precise Old Testament terms of Psalm 65:7-8. In the Greek Septuagint, which is the normal source for Old Testament references in Mark's gospel, we read: "who troubles the depths of the sea, the sounds of its waves [Hebrew adds: "and the madness of the peoples"]. The nations shall be troubled, and they that inhabit the ends of the earth shall be afraid of your signs" (my translation).[9] Here the word for nations/peoples refers specifically to the non-Jewish, gentile world, and the linking of such divine effects with the gentile context of Mark 5:1-20 prompts the development of the Markan interpolations, stressing the significance of Jesus' non-Jewish mission.

(1) Vv. 3-5: In Septuagint, Psalm 68:6, reference is made to God's mercy shown to "those who provoke," "who dwell among tombs." For Jews, of course, tombs were unclean, and their undesirability is highlighted by the man's condition as described in these verses.[10]

(2) Vv. 12-13: The swine also are unclean to a Jew (who was not even allowed to keep them), and unfit for food, their presence a further indication of gentile country. As the man is cleansed and leaves the tombs, so is the land cleansed of this uncleanness.

(3) Vv. 18-20: Jesus' presence having banished uncleanness from the land, its conversion is provided for by the proclamation of the man, now healed of his madness. He goes out to preach the gospel in the Decapolis.

The interpolations, therefore, are theologically weighted in a specific way linked with Jewish laws of uncleanness—a matter without relevance to the basic healing story—and with the gentile mission in mind. The second Markan element in the narrative has a purpose quite distinct, therefore, from the basic healing miracle which illustrates, in the light of the question asked in 4:41, Jesus' power over demonic forces. This complexity in the narrative structure of the story is all too easily overlooked by critics anxious to stress the unity of the text and the preconditioned response which the text calls forth with regard to the matter of uncleanness. Such critics ignore the fact that a) the matter of uncleanness is raised only in the Markan interpolations and not in the text as a whole, and b), given the theological and evangelistic purpose of these interpolations, they do not so much invite a questioning of traditional Jewish concepts of purity, but actually confirm those concepts in the cleansing of the land in readiness for its Christianizing. The interpolations are "Jewish," it seems, within the context of an apparently "gentile" narrative.

THE NARRATIVE UNITY OF MARK 5:1-20

However, having thus analyzed the story in the history of its formation and its specific *theological* purposes in that history, one needs also on the other hand to affirm the integrity of the text as we now read it against the grain of these diverse historical circumstances. I want to suggest the narrative difficulty which is exposed by the pull of explanatory parable or story against the reality of the textual sequence which is immediately experienced.[11] Abandoning historical complexities of textual interpolation, we need also to reaffirm the literary principle of the unity of the narrative of Mark 5:1-20. I begin now from that assumption.

Wolfgang Iser asserts that the literary work is identical neither with the text, nor with the realization of the text accomplished by the reader, but lies midway between the two.[12] Furthermore, this convergence can never be precisely pinpointed, but remains "virtual," and it is this virtuality of the work which gives rise to its dynamic nature. As Iser puts it, "if the reader were given the whole story, and there were nothing left for him to do, then his imagination would never enter the field, the result would be the boredom which inevitably arises when everything is laid out cut and dried before us."[13]

I have already criticized Iser's proposal for the literary work as the convergence of text and reader from the perspective of the complex historical formation of the biblical narrative as a necessary literary element in the process of interpretation. The argument must, however, be developed more subtly, drawing in part upon Paul de Man's essay "The Resistance to Theory."[14] De Man criticizes Iser insofar as he does "not allow for the problematization of the phenomenalism of reading," or to put it more simply, that at the very heart of writing, writing itself is put in question; a resistance to reading.

The application of Iser's theory of aesthetic response rooted in the text seems to me a) to tend towards a style of reading which is technically predictable, and b), by over-stressing *reading* as a theoretical problem, to de-emphasize the problem which arises from the *production* of texts. Once the historical virtue and complexity of the text are reasserted, not only is the nature of Iser's "implied reader" radically altered, but reading itself becomes a different problem caught between critical modes deriving ultimately, on the one hand, from structural linguistics, and on the other from historical perceptions of meaning and value.

Affirming the (by no means self-evident) necessity of reading implies for de Man two things:

> First of all, it implies that literature is not a transparent message in which it can be taken for granted that the distinction between the message and the means of communication is clearly established. Second, and more problematically, it implies that the grammatical decoding of a text leaves a residue of indetermination *that has to be, but cannot be,* resolved by grammatical means, however extensively conceived. (my italics)

First, then, there is a problem of distinguishing between the "message" (historical meaning and value inherent, or at least potential, in the text) and the modalities of production and reception. For a literary critic to isolate himself from the former is to pretend that all the stylistic and vocabular complexities of the Greek text of Mark 5:1-20 either do not exist or have no bearing upon interpretation. Second, the indetermination suggested by de Man is far more radical than the virtuality proposed by Iser. It is, by nature, irreducible—a gap not simply presented to the imagination or as a means to force us to question assumptions, but an indetermination forced upon us with the utmost seriousness by the very nature of textuality. In more religious terms—dare I say?—we are brought to the brink of mystery.

The tendency of literary theory in the face of the instability of the reading process is to replace a hermeneutical by a semiotic mode of interpretation. Busy in their task of decoding, such theorists can imagine that they are shedding the ideological and circumstantial problems which seem to befuddle the business of textuality and reading. In fact, as I have suggested, the example of Iser seems actually to threaten a new totalitarian tendency, heedless of the hermeneutical relationship to three areas in reflection upon the interpretation of ancient biblical texts—the historical, the theological and the linguistic.

MARK 5:1-20 AS NARRATIVE ART

I have offered one kind of reading of Mark 5:1-20. Let me suggest another, assuming, as I have said, narrative unity, the integrity of the text as we have it regardless of how it originally came to be. In his *The Peaceable Kingdom*, Stanley Hauerwas describes casuistry as a "narrative art." The basic point is simple. Hauerwas rejects the assumption "that we start out with a set of basic moral convictions from which we learn that certain kinds of behavior are right or wrong." [15] The problem is not so much with the basic principles themselves as with the attempt to demonstrate the rightness or wrongness of actions *abstracted from their narrative context.* From narratives which, in Hauerwas' terms, "comprise a living tradition," we learn the conditions of truth, and as narratives are tested against our ongoing, historical experience, so they are challenged and renewed within the context of each new generation of readers. Mindful of the cultural relativism which is necessarily a part of the study of biblical texts, I conclude with Hauerwas: "We cannot learn the story by doing exactly what others did, for we cannot do exactly what they did. Rather, we must let their lives imaginatively challenge our own, so that we may learn how to embody the virtues which determined not only what they did, but how they did it." [16]

As I return, therefore, to the text of the story in Mark's gospel, regardless of its Jewish or theological origins, the narrative faces me directly with certain moral difficulties by its "virtuality." I am perplexed by what seems to me to be a rather nasty story of Jesus, endowed with divine power to heal and restore, deliberately bringing about the destruction of two thousand innocent swine (unclean only to a Jew, and anyway see Acts 11:9 on cleanness) to the offense of the swineherds who cannot get rid of Jesus quickly enough—Mark 5:17. Certainly, in Hauerwas' term, I find this at least an imaginative challenge.

But at this point I come to my final criticism of Wolfgang Iser's phenomenological approach to the reading process. In his reading of the narrative, questions are forced upon the reader by the gaps strategically managed by the text to the undermining of our habitual ideological "repertoire."[17] Such gaps are realized within a particular strategy of reading under whose auspices is promoted a curious confusion of semiotic, ideological and historical challenges to the reader, all perceived within a single critical perspective. In response to this I have proposed two readings of the Markan story. The first focuses on the text itself, not its historical or textual backgrounds, assuming textual unity and a narrativity which poses a problem for me from within the connection between the story and felt moral commitments correlative with the story. My second reading regards the text from its historical reality, from a linguistic sensitivity to Greek style and the context of Jewish laws of cleanliness as a preparation for the Christianizing of the gentile Decapolis region.

In pursuing the linguistics of literariness, I appreciate how "literary approaches" to biblical narratives have unmasked the temptations to which much biblical criticism has been prone: its undue historicism, its ideological underpinnings and its failure to expand the ontological and epistemological bases of enquiry. However, I want to expand the framework within which textual control over the response of the reader is exercised, to the dialectic between my two strategies of reading, two horizons never identical, separate but close. Virtuality or indetermination is the result of an endless reciprocation between the theologial/historical and the literary/ethical, between an inescapable pattern of assumption and predetermination in the text and in criticism, and a persistent apprehensiveness about the predetermining intentionality in all human exchange, discourse and narrativity. Gaps and indeterminacies there are, in the hermeneutic problem of historical distance and the textual problem of complex resistance in the reader to the manifold dimensions of language. Within its Jewish framework, theology proposes, pushing towards absoluteness and definition (Jesus the worker of miracles against demonic powers, the cleanser of the land and provider of mission in the person of the cured man), while in a living tradition the energetic "virtue"[18] of the story undercuts, for us, the image and the illusion of dogmatic tendency. It arouses our compassion and our uncertainty, iconoclastic while refusing the destructive dictates of iconoclasm by promoting the possibility of new conditions of truth, new possibilities for theology from its own wreck.

The challenge is far more radical than anything proposed by Iser, not simply revisionist in a questioning of assumptions, but profoundly respectful of a theological text which provides a tightly coded pattern both prone to the upsetting immediacies of its own literariness and yet powerful to replenish the truth in the conditions of its narrative integrity.

NOTES

1. Kenneth R.R. Gros Louis, James S. Ackerman, Thayer S. Warshaw, eds., *Literary Interpretations of Biblical Narratives* (Nashville: Abingdon Press, 1974), p. 296.

2. Meir Sternberg, *The Poetics of Biblical Narrative, Ideological Literature and the Drama of Reading* (Bloomington: Indiana University Press, 1985), p. 13.

3. Mieke Bal, "The Bible as Literature: A Critical Escape." *Diacritics* 16/4 (1986), 72.

4. Anthony C. Thiselton, *The Two Horizons: New Testament Hermeneutics and Philosophical Descriptions* (Exeter: Paternoster Press, 1980), xix ff.

5. See Wolfgang Iser, *The Implied Reader: Patterns in Communication in Prose Fiction from Bunyan to Beckett* (Baltimore: Johns Hopkins University Press, 1984), pp. 274-94.

6. Austin Farrer, *The Glass of Vision* (Westminster: Dacre Press, 1948), p. 138. Farrer argues in terms of the "poetic pattern of the book," sidestepping the historical issues.

7. Compare Norman Petersen, "When Is the End not the End? Literary Reflections on the Ending of Mark's Narrative," *Interpretation* 34 (1980), 151-66, on implications in the text which stimulate expectations.

8. See further D.E. Nineham, *The Gospel of St. Mark*. The Pelican New Testament Commentaries (Harmondsworth: Faber and Faber, 1958), pp. 86 ff.

10. See also C.E.B. Cranfield, *The Gospel According to St. Mark*. The Cambridge Greek Testament Commentary (Cambridge: Cambridge University Press, 1972), p. 177.

11. See Warner Berthoff, *Literature and the Continuances of Virtue* (Princeton: Princeton University Press, 1986), p. 198.

12. Iser, *The Implied Reader*, pp. 274-75.

13. Iser, *The Implied Reader*, p. 275.

14. Paul de Man, *The Resistance to Theory* (Manchester: Manchester University Press, 1986), pp. 3-20.

15. Stanley Hauerwas, *The Peaceable Kingdom: A Primer in Christian Ethics*. (London: SCM Press, 1984), Ch. 7, "Casuistry as a Narrative Art," pp. 116-34.

16. Hauerwas, *The Peaceable Kingdom*, p. 118.

17. See Wolfgang Iser. *The Act of Reading: A Theory of Aesthetic Response*. (London: Routledge, 1978), p. 35.

18. See Berthoff, *Literature and the Continuances of Virtue*, pp. 279-80.

THE DEMONS OF GERASA
René Girard

MIMETICISM AND THE DEMONIC

The Gospels reveal all kinds of human relationships that at first seem incomprehensible and fundamentally irrational. These can and must ultimately be reduced to a single unifying factor: mimeticism. Mimeticism is the original source of all man's troubles, desires, and rivalries, his tragic and grotesque misunderstandings, the source of all disorder and therefore equally of all order through the mediation of scapegoats. These victims are the spontaneous agents of reconciliation, since, in the final paroxysm of mimeticism, they unite in opposition to themselves those who were organized in opposition to each other by the effects of a previous weaker mimeticism.

These are the underlying dynamics of all mythological and religious beginnings, dynamics that other religions succeed in concealing from themselves and from us by suppressing or disguising collective murders and minimizing or eliminating the stereotypes of persecution in a hundred different ways. The Gospels, on the other hand, expose these same dynamics with an unequaled severity and strength.

Peter's denial, the murder of John the Baptist, and, above all, the Passion itself, the true heart and center of this revelation, delineate the lines of force with an almost didactic insistence. It is a question of forcing people who from time immemorial have been imprisoned by mythological representations of persecution to accept certain decisive truths that would prevent them from making their own victims sacred and thereby free them.

Each of the Gospel stories reveals a religious origin that must remain hidden if mythology and ritual are to be the result. This origin is based on the unanimous belief in the victim's guilt, a belief that the Gospels destroy forever. There is no common ground between what happens in the Gospels and what happens in myths, particularly the more developed myths. Later religions diminish, minimize, soften, and even totally eliminate sacred guilt

77

as well as any trace of violence; but these are minor dissimulations and bear no relation to the system of representing persecution. This system collapses in the world of the Gospels. There is no longer any question of softening or sublimation. Rather, a return to truth is made possible by a process which, in our lack of understanding, we consider primitive simply because it reproduces the violent origin once more, this time in order to reveal it and thus make it inoperative.

The texts we have just read [e.g., on Peter's denial, the murder of John the Baptist] are all examples of this process. They correspond perfectly to the way in which Jesus himself, and after him Paul in the Epistles, defines the effect of disintegration that the Crucifixion had on the forces of this world. The Passion reveals the scapegoat mechanism, i.e., that which should remain invisible if these forces are to maintain themselves. By revealing that mechanism and the surrounding mimeticism, the Gospels set in motion the only textual mechanism that can put an end to humanity's imprisonment in the system of mythological representation based on the false transcendence of a victim who is made sacred because of the unanimous verdict of guilt.

This transcendence is mentioned directly in the Gospels and the New Testament. It is even given many names, but the main one is Satan, who would not be considered simultaneously *murderer from the beginning, father of lies, and prince of this world* were he not identified with the false transcendence of violence. Nor is it by chance that, of all Satan's faults, envy and jealousy are the most in evidence. Satan could be said to incarnate mimetic desire were that desire not, by definition, disincarnate. It empties all people, all things, and all texts of their substance.

When the false transcendence is envisaged in its fundamental unity, the Gospels call it the devil or Satan, but when it is envisaged in its multiplicity then the mention is always of demons or demonic forces. The word *demon* can obviously be a synonym for Satan, but it is mostly applied to inferior forms of the "power of this world,' to the degraded manifestations that we would call psychopathological. By the very fact that transcendence appears in multiple and fragmented form, it loses its strength and dissolves into pure mimetic disorder. Thus, unlike Satan, who is seen as principle of both order and disorder, the demonic forces are invoked at times when disorder predominates.

Since the Gospels give to these "forces" names that come from religious tradition and magic belief they would still appear to recognize them as autonomous, spiritual entities, endowed with individual personality. On every page of the Gospels we see demons speaking, questioning Jesus, begging him to leave them in peace. In the great temptation-in-the-desert scene Satan appears *in person* to seduce the Son of God with false promises and divert him from his mission.

Far from destroying magic superstitions and vulgar forms of religious beliefs the Gospels seem to reintroduce this type of belief in a particularly pernicious form. The witch-hunters of the late Middle Ages, after all, based the justification for their activities on the demonology and satanism of the Gospels. For many people, especially today, the swarms of demons "obscure the luminous aspect of the Gospels," and Jesus' miraculous cures are hard to distinguish from the traditional exorcisms of primitive societies. None of the miracles appears in my commentaries so far. Some critics have remarked on this and suggested, naturally, that I am avoiding an encounter that would not support my thesis; by choosing my texts with extreme care in order to avoid all the others, I confer a false probability on perspectives that are too contrary to good sense to be taken seriously.

In order to provide as conclusive a proof as possible I will once more refer to Mark. Of the four evangelists Mark is most fond of miracles, devotes the most time to them, and presents them in the fashion that is most contrary to modern sensibility. Perhaps the most spectacular of all the miraculous cures to be found in Mark is the episode of the *demons of Gerasa*. The text is long enough and contains enough concrete details to provide commentators with a grasp that is lacking in the shorter episodes.

Gerasa is one of those texts that is always alluded to with terms such as "wild," "primitive," "backward," "superstitious," and all the typical adjectives which positivists apply to religion in general, no matter what the origin, but which, because they are considered too pejorative for the non-Christian religions, will in the future be reserved for Christianity. My analysis will focus on Mark, but I will refer to Luke and Matthew each time their version provides interesting variants. After crossing the sea of Galilee, Jesus lands on the west bank, in heathen territory, in the country of Decapolis:

> And no sooner had he left the boat than a man with an unclean spirit came out from the tombs toward him. The man lived in the tombs and no one could secure him any more, even with a chain; because he had often been secured with fetters and chains but had snapped the chains and broken the fetters, and no one had the strength to control him. All night and all day, among the tombs and in the mountains, he would howl and gash himself with stones. Catching sight of Jesus from a distance, he ran up and fell at his feet and shouted at the top of his voice, "What do you want with me, Jesus, son of the Most High God? Swear by God you will not torture me!"—For Jesus had been saying to him, "Come out of the man, unclean spirit." "What is your name?" Jesus asked. "My name is Legion," he answered, "for there are many of us." And he begged him earnestly not to send them out of the district. Now there was there on the mountainside a great herd of pigs feeding, and the unclean spirits begged him, "Send us to the pigs, let us go into them." So he gave them leave. With that, the unclean spirits came out and went into the pigs, and the herd of about two thousand pigs charged down the cliff into the lake, and there they were drowned. The swineherds ran off and told their story in the town and in the country around about, and the people came to see what had really happened. They came to Jesus and saw the demoniac sitting there, clothed and in his full senses—the very man who had had the legion in him before—and they were afraid. And those who had witnessed it reported what had happened to the demoniac and what had become of the pigs. Then they began to implore Jesus to leave the neighborhood. (Mark 5:1-17)

The possessed lived among the tombs. This fact impressed Mark, and he repeats it three times. The wretched man, night and day, was always among the tombs. He comes out of the tombs to meet Jesus. He is freer than any other man since he has broken all the chains, despised all rules, and even, according to Luke, wears no clothes, yet he is possessed, a prisoner of his own madness. This man is a living corpse. His state can be recognized as one of the phenomena of the mimetic crisis that leads to the loss of differentiation and to persecution. There is no longer any difference between life and death, freedom and captivity. Yet existence in the tombs, far from human habitation, is not a permanent phenomenon, the result of a single and definitive break between the possessed and the community. Mark's text suggests that the Gerasenes and their demoniac have been settled for some time in a sort of cyclical pathology. Luke gives it even greater emphasis when he presents the possessed as a *man from the town* and tells us that a demon *had driven him into the wilds* only during his bad spells. Demonic possession abolishes a difference between life within and without the city, a difference that is not unimportant since it is mentioned again later in the text.

Luke's description implies intermittent spells, with periods of remission, during which the sick man returns to the city. "It was a devil that had seized on him a great many times, and then they used to secure him with chains and fetters to restrain him, but he would always break the fastenings, and the devil would drive him out into the wilds" (Luke 8:29-30). The Gerasenes and their demoniac periodically repeat the same crisis in more or less the same fashion. When the men of the city suspect that another departure is at hand, they try to prevent it by binding their fellow citizen with chains and fetters. They do this to *restrain him,* we are told. Why do they want to *restrain him?* The reason seems quite clear. Curing a sick man requires removal of the symptoms of his sickness. In this case the chief symptom is the wandering in the mountains and the tombs. This is what the Gerasenes are trying to prevent with their chains. The sickness is so terrible they have no hesitation in resorting to violence. But clearly this is not the best method: each time their victim overcomes every effort to hold him back. Recourse to violence only increases his desire for solitude and the strength of that desire, so that the unfortunate man becomes truly indomitable. "And no one had the strength to subdue him," Mark tells us.

The repetitive character of these phenomena is somewhat ritualistic. All the actors know exactly what is going to happen in each episode and behave appropriately so that in fact everything happens as it did before. It is difficult to believe that the Gerasenes cannot find chains and fetters strong enough to hold their prisoner. Perhaps they are ashamed of their violence and do not exert the energy needed to make it effective. Whatever the reason, they seem to behave like sick men whose every action fosters rather than decreases the disease. All rituals tend to be transformed into theatrical performances in which the actors play their parts with all the more exuberance for having played them *so many times before.* This does not mean that the participants do not experience real suffering. The drama would not be as effective as it obviously is if there were not moments of real suffering for the city and its surroundings, in other words for the community. The Gerasenes are consternated at the idea of their being deprived of the suffering. They must gain some enjoyment from this drama and even feel the need of it since they beg Jesus to leave immediately and stop interfering in their affairs. Their request is paradoxical, given that Jesus had just succeeded, without any violence, in obtaining the result which they had professed to be aiming at with their chains and fetters but which, in reality, they did not want at all: the complete cure of the possessed man. In this episode, as always, Jesus' presence reveals the truth of the hidden desires. Simeon's prophesy is once more confirmed. "You see this child: he is destined . . . to be a sign that is rejected . . . so that the secret thoughts of many may be laid bare."

But what is the meaning of this drama, what is its role on the symbolic plane? The sick man runs among the tombs and on the mountains, Mark tells us, always crying out and *bruising himself with stones.* In Jean Starobinski's remarkable commentary on this text he gives a perfect definition for this strange conduct: *autolapidation.*[1] But why would anyone want to stone himself? Why would one be obsessed with stoning? When the possessed breaks his bonds and escapes from the community he must expect to be pursued by those who tried to chain him. Such may actually be the case. He is fleeing from the stones that his pursuers may be throwing at him. The unfortunate Job was followed and stoned by the inhabitants of his village. Nothing similar is mentioned in the story of Gerasa. Perhaps because he never does become the object of stoning, the demoniac wounds himself with stones. In mythical fashion he maintains the peril with which he believes himself to be threatened.

Has he been the object of real threats, has he survived an aborted attempt at stoning like the adulterous woman in the Gospel of John, or is it, in this case, a purely imaginary fear, a simple *phantasm*? If it is a phantasm then I must ask the psychoanalyst whether the phantasm is the same among societies that practice stoning as among those that do not. Perhaps the possessed said to his fellow citizens: "Look, there's no need to treat me the way you wish, there's no need to stone me; I will carry out your sentence on myself. The punishment I will inflict on myself will be far more horrible than any you would dream of inflicting on me."

Notice the mimetic character of this behavior. As if he is trying to avoid being expelled and stoned in reality, the possessed brings about his own expulsion and stoning; he provides a spectacular mime of all the stages of punishment that Middle Eastern societies inflict on criminals whom they consider completely defiled and irredeemable. First, the man is hunted, then stoned, and finally he is killed; this is why the possessed lived among the tombs. The Gerasenes must have some understanding of why they are reproached or they would not respond as they do. Their mitigated violence is an ineffective protest. Their answer is: "No, we do not want to stone you because we want *to keep you* near us. No ostracism hangs over you." Unfortunately, like anyone who feels wrongfully yet feasibly accused, the Gerasenes protest violently, they protest their good faith with violence, thereby reinforcing the terror of the possessed. Proof of their awareness of their own contradiction lies in the fact that the chains are never strong enough to convince their victim of their good intentions toward him.

The violence of the Gerasenes is hardly reassuring for the possessed. Reciprocally, the violence of the possessed disturbs the Gerasenes. As always, each one tries to end violence with a violence that should be definitive but instead perpetuates the circularity of the process. A symmetry can be seen in all these extremes, the self-laceration and the running among the tombs on the one hand, the grandiloquent chains on the other. There is a sort of conspiracy between the victim and his torturers to keep the balance in the game because it is obviously necessary to keep the balance of the Gerasene community.

MIMETIC DOUBLES

The possessed does violence to himself as a reproach to the Gerasenes for their violence. The Gerasenes return his reproach with a violence that reinforces his own and somehow verifies the accusation and counteraccusation that circulate endlessly within the system. The possessed imitates these Gerasenes who stone their victims, but the Gerasenes in return imitate the possessed. A mirror relationship of doubles links the persecutors who are persecuted and the persecuted who persecutes. This is an example of the reciprocal relationship of mimetic rivalry. It is not a relationship of the stoned with those who stone him, but it is almost the same thing since, on the one hand, there is a violent parody of stoning and, on the other, the no-less-violent denial. This is a variant of violent expulsion that has the same aim as the other variants, including stoning.

If I am mistaken in my identification of mimetic doubles in the context of the demons of Gerasa, the mistake is not mine alone. It is shared in at least one of the Gospels, Matthew, when there is mention at the end of the miracle of a significant variant. Matthew substitutes for the single demoniac in Mark and Luke two identical possessed beings and has them speak for themselves instead of the demon—two demons—who are supposed to possess them. There is nothing to suggest a source different from Mark's. Rather it is an attempt to explicate (I wanted to say demystify) the demonic theme in general. In texts like the Gerasa text Matthew is often different from Mark, either in his suppression of a detail he considers worthless or in the explanatory twist he gives to the themes he retains, so that they are both the themes and his own explication. We saw one example in the murder of John the Baptist. Matthew substitutes the expression "prompted by her mother" for the exchange of questions and answers which, in Mark, suggests somewhat enigmatically the mimetic transmission of desire between mother and daughter.

Matthew is doing much the same thing here but much more audaciously. He wants to suggest what we ourselves have learned during our readings. Possession is not an individual phenomenon; it is the result of aggravated mimeticism. There are always at least two beings who possess each other reciprocally, each is the other's scandal, his model-obstacle. Each is the other's demon; that is why in the first part of Matthew's account the demons are not distinct from those they possess:

> When he reached the country of the Gadarenes on the other side, two demoniacs came toward him out of the tombs—creatures so fierce that no one could pass that way. They stood there shouting, "What do you want with us, Son of God? Have you come here to torture us before the time?" (Matt. 8:28)

The proof that Matthew considers the possession to be a function of the mimeticism of doubles and of the stumbling block lies in the fact that what he adds can be found neither in Mark's nor in Luke's text: those that came to meet Jesus, he tells us, were "so fierce that no one could pass that way." In other words these are essentially people who bar the way, like Peter with Jesus when he advised against the Passion. These are people who are each other's and their neighbors' scandal. Scandal is always contagious; those who are scandalized are likely to communicate their desire to you, or, in other words, drag you along their same path so that they become your model-obstacle and in turn scandalize you. Every reference in the Gospels to the way that is barred, the insurmountable obstacle, the stone too heavy to be raised, is an allusion to the whole concomitant system of scandal.

In order to explain possession through the mimeticism of scandal, Matthew turns to the minimal mimetic relationship, to what might be called its basic unit. He endeavors to return to the source of the evil. This movement is not generally understood since it reverses the mythological practice of today's psychology and psychoanalysis. The latter interiorize the double; they have need of an imaginary demon within consciousness or the unconscious. Matthew exteriorizes the demon in a real mimetic relationship between two real individuals.

Matthew improves the account of the miracle on this one major point or, rather, he prepares an analysis of it. He teaches us that duality cannot help but be present at the very outset of mimetic play. What is interesting is that, precisely because he introduces duality at the very beginning of his account, this writer then finds himself in difficulty in trying to introduce the multiplicity that is indispensable for the unfolding of the miracle. He has to eliminate Mark's key sentence: "My name is Legion; for there are many of us" which contributes so much to the fame of the text with its strange transition from singular to plural. This break is again found in the following sentence, which repeats indirectly the sequel to the proposals the demon is supposed to have made to Jesus: "and he begged him earnestly not to send them out of the district."

Nowhere in Matthew, or in Luke who is closer to Mark, do we find the one essential detail that the demon is actually many although he speaks as a single person, and, in a way, is only one person. By not including the crowd of demons Matthew loses the justification for the drowning of the herd of swine, yet he retains that action. In fact, he ultimately loses more than he gains. He seems to be aware of his failure and cuts the miracle short. Like all Mark's strokes of genius, such as Salome's question to her mother: "What shall I ask?," this juxtaposition of singular and plural in the same sentence may seem like a clumsy inclusion that has been eliminated by Luke who is generally more skillful and correct than Mark in his manipulation of the language. "'Legion,' he said—because many devils had gone into him. And these pleaded with him not to order them to depart into the Abyss" (Luke 8:30-31).

In his commentary on Mark, Jean Starobinski clearly shows the negative connotations of the word *Legion*. It indicates "the warlike mob, the hostile troop, the occupying army, the Roman invader, and perhaps even those who crucified Christ."[2] The critic rightly observes the important role played by the crowd not only in the history of the demoniac but also in the immediately preceding and succeeding texts. The healing in itself is portrayed as a single combat between Jesus and the demon, but before and after there is always a crowd around Jesus. First there was the crowd of Galileans whom the disciples sent away in order to get into the boat with Jesus. As soon as he returns the crowd is there again. At Gerasa there is not only the crowd of demons and the crowd of swine but there are also the Gerasenes who came running to him in crowds from the city and the country. Quoting Kierkegaard, "the mob is the lie," Starobinski notes that evil in the Gospels is always on the side of plurality and the crowd.

There is, nevertheless, a remarkable difference between the behavior of the Galileans and the behavior of the Gerasenes. Like the crowds in Jerusalem, the Galileans are not afraid of miracles. They could turn against the thaumaturge in an instant, but for the moment they cling to him as a savior. The sick gather from all quarters. In Jewish territory everyone is greedy for miracles and signs, wanting either to benefit personally or to have others benefit, or quite simply to be a spectator and participate in the unusual event as in a play that is more extraordinary than enlightening.

DEMONS AND GERASENES

The Gerasenes have a different reaction. When they see the demoniac "sitting there, clothed and in his full senses, the very man who had the legion in him before," they are afraid. They have the herdsmen explain to them "what had happened to the demoniac and what had become of the pigs." Instead of calming their fears and arousing their enthusiasm or at least their curiosity, the account increases their anxiety. The inhabitants demand Jesus' departure. And Jesus gives them that satisfaction without saying a word. The man he has cured wants to follow him, but he urges him to remain with his own people. He embarks in silence to return to Jewish territory.

There has been no sermon or any real exchange, not even a hostile one, with these people. We are given the impression that the entire local population demands his departure and that these Gerasenes arrive in an orderly fashion, unlike the flock without a shepherd that rouses Jesus' pity. The community is differentiated, since the inhabitants from the country can be distinguished from the inhabitants from the city. They ask for information calmly and make a thoughtful decision, which they then present to Jesus when they ask him to depart. They do not respond to the miracle with either hysterical adulation or passionate hate, but without hesitation they determine not to accept it. They want nothing to do with Jesus and what he represents.

The Gerasenes are not upset at the disappearance of their herd for mercenary reasons. Clearly, the drowning of their pigs disturbs them less than the drowning of their demons. If this is to be understood, it must be recognized that the attachment of the Gerasenes to their demons has its counterpart in the demons' attachment to the Gerasenes. Legion was not too fearful provided he was permitted to remain in his country. "And he begged him earnestly not to send them out of the district." Since the demons cannot survive without a living habitation they need to possess someone else, preferably a human being but, if not, then an animal, in this case the herd of swine. The reasonable request shows that the demons have no illusions. They ask as a favor the right to enter these loathsome animals: so they are obviously in a difficult position. They know they are dealing with someone powerful. They decide they are more likely to be tolerated if they are content with less. It is essential for them not to be *completely and definitively* expelled.

The reciprocal bond between the demons and the Gerasenes reproduces on a different level the relationship between the possessed and these same Gerasenes observed in our analysis. They cannot do without him or he without them. This conjunction of both ritual and cyclical pathology is not peculiar. As it degenerates ritual loses its precision. The expulsion is not permanent or absolute, and the scapegoat—the possessed— returns to the city between crises. Everything blends, nothing ever ends. The rite tends to relapse into its original state; the relationships of mimetic doubles provoke the crisis of indifferentiation. Physical violence gives way to the violence of psychopathological relationships that is not fatal but is never resolved or ended. The total lack of differentiation is never reached. There remains enough difference between the voluntary exile and the Gerasenes who refuse to expel him, enough real drama in each repetition to achieve a certain catharsis. A total disintegration is in process but has not yet taken place. The Gerasene society is therefore still somewhat structured, more so than the crowds from Galilee or Jerusalem. There are still differences within the system, between city and country for example, and these are manifested by the calmly negative reaction to Jesus' therapeutic success.

This society is not exactly in splendid shape; in fact it is quite disintegrated but not quite desperate, and the Gerasenes are able to preserve their fragile status quo. They still form a community in the accepted sense. As far as we can tell this system is perpetuated, for better or worse, by very degenerate sacrificial procedures that are nevertheless precious and irreplaceable since they have apparently reached the limit.

All the commentators say that Jesus heals the possessed by the classical methods of the shamans. For example, in this passage, he makes the impure spirit name himself, thereby acquiring over him the power that is so often associated in primitive societies with the manipulation of proper names. There is nothing very exceptional in this, and it is not what the text is trying to suggest to us. If there were nothing extraordinary in what Jesus did, there would have been no reason for the Gerasenes to be afraid. They certainly had their own healers who worked with the same methods critics attribute to Jesus. If Jesus were just another more successful *medicine man*, these good people would have been delighted rather than afraid. They would have begged Jesus to stay instead of going away.

Can the Gerasenes' fear be accounted for by rhetorical exaggeration? Is it lacking in substance and intended merely to make the Messiah's prowess more impressive? I do not think so. The destruction of the herd of pigs possessed by the demons is described in the same way in all three Gospels. "And the herd . . . charged down the cliff into the lake." The steep bank appears also in Matthew and Luke; therefore the pigs had to have been on a kind of promontory. Mark and Luke are aware of this, and to prepare the way for the cliff they place the animals *on a mountain*. Matthew does not mention a mountain but he does retain the cliff which means it was the cliff that caught the attention of the evangelists. It increased the height of the fall. The further the pigs fell, the more striking the scene. But the Gospels are not concerned with the picturesque, and it is not for the visual effect that they all speak of a cliff. A functional reason could be urged. The distance covered in free fall before hitting the surface of the lake guaranteed the definitive disappearance of the herd of pigs. There is no risk that they may escape, they will not swim back to the bank. All this is true; the cliff is necessitated by the realistic economy of the scene, but the Gospels were not particularly concerned with the realism either. There is something else much more essential.

Those who are used to reading mythological and religious texts will or should recognize immediately this theme of the cliff. Just like stoning, falling from a high cliff has collective, ritual, and penal connotations. This was a widespread practice among both ancient and primitive societies. It is a kind of sacrificial immolation that is distinct from the later practice of beheading. Rome had its Tarpeian rock. In the Greek universe the ritual *Pharmakos* was periodically put to death in the same way, especially in Marseille. The unfortunate man was made to throw himself into the sea from such a height that death was inevitable.

Two of the great ritualistic methods of execution figure explicitly in our text: stoning and falling from a high cliff. There are resemblances. All the members of the community can and should throw stones at the victim. All the members of the community can and should advance on the condemned person together and force him to the edge of the cliff so that there is no alternative but death. The resemblances are not limited to the collective nature of the execution. Everyone participates in the destruction of the anathema but no one enters into direct physical contact with him. No one risks contamination. The group alone is responsible. Individuals share the same degree of innocence and responsibility. It can be said that this is equally true of all other traditional forms of execution, especially any form of exposure, of which crucifixion is one variant. The superstitious fear of physical contact with the victim should not blind us to the fact that these techniques of execution resolve an essential problem for societies with weak or nonexistent judicial systems, societies still impregnated with the spirit of private revenge so that they were frequently exposed to the threat of endless violence at the heart of the community.

These methods of execution do not feed the appetite for vengeance since they eliminate any difference in individual roles. The persecutors all behave in the same way. Anyone who dreams of vengeance must take it from the whole collectivity. It is as if the power of the state, nonexistent in this type of society, comes into temporary but nevertheless real rather than symbolic existence in these violent forms of unanimity.

These collective modes of capital execution correspond so closely to the defined need that at first it is difficult to imagine that they occur spontaneously in human communities. So well adapted are they to their purpose it seems impossible that they were not conceived prior to their realization. This is always either the modern illusion of functionalism that believes that need creates the means or the ancient illusion of religious traditions that always point to a kind of primordial legislator, a being of superhuman wisdom and authority who endowed the community with all its basic institutions.

In reality things happen differently. It is absurd to think that such a problem is first posed in theory before it is resolved in practice. But as long as one does not accept that the solution might precede the problem or consider what type of solution might precede the problem, then the absurdity cannot be avoided. Obviously, this is one of the spontaneous effects of a scapegoat. In a crisis of mimetic conflict, the polarization on a single victim can become so powerful that all members of the group are forced to participate in his murder. This type of collective violence automatically prefigures the unanimous forms of execution that are egalitarian and performed at a distance, as we have noted.

This does not mean that the great primordial legislators claimed by so many religious traditions never existed. Primitive traditions, especially those that resemble each other, should always be taken seriously. Great legislators existed, but they never promulgated legislation in *their lifetimes.* It is obvious that they are identical with scapegoats whose murder is scrupulously imitated, repeated, and perfected in ritual because of its effects on reconciliation. The effect is real because this murder already resembles the type of execution that is derived from it and that reproduces the same effect of putting an end to vengeance. It would therefore seem to be derived from greater than human wisdom and can only be attributed to the sacred scapegoat, like all institutions whose origin lies in the mechanism of a victim. The supreme legislator is the very essence of a scapegoat who has been made sacred.

Moses is one example of the scapegoat-legislator. His stammer is the sign of a victim. We find traces in him of mythical guilt: the murder of the Egyptian, the transgression that causes him to be forbidden entrance into the Promised Land, his responsibility for the ten plagues of Egypt which are diseases that remove all differences. All the stereotypes of persecution are present except collective murder, which can be found on the fringe of official tradition, just as for Romulus. Freud was not wrong when he took seriously this hint of collective murder.

But, to return to the demons of Gerasa, is it reasonable to take into consideration the stoning and the cliff-top execution when interpreting this text? The context invites us to associate these two forms of execution. Stoning appears frequently in the Gospels and in the Acts: the adulterous woman saved by Jesus; Stephen, the first martyr; even the Passion is preceded by several attempts at stoning. There is also a significant attempt to push Jesus off a cliff that failed. The scene takes place in Nazareth. Jesus is received poorly in the city of his childhood; he cannot accomplish miracles there. His preaching in the synagogue scandalizes his listeners. He leaves without any disturbance, except in Luke, where the following happens:

> When they heard this everyone in the synagogue was enraged. They sprang to their feet and hustled him out of the town, and they took him up to the brow of the hill their town was built on, intending to throw him down the cliff, but he slipped through the crowd and walked away. (Luke 4:28-30)

This episode should be seen as a preliminary sketch and therefore an announcement of the Passion. Its presence indicates that Luke, and certainly the other evangelists, considered falling from a cliff-top and stoning as equivalents of the Crucifixion.

They understood what made such an equivalence interesting. All forms of collective murder have the same significance, and that significance is revealed by Jesus in his Passion. It is this revelation that is important, not the location of a particular cliff-top. If you listen to people who know Nazareth, the town and its immediate surroundings do not fit the role Luke gives them. There is no cliff.

Unfortunately, critics who have noticed this geographic inaccuracy were never curious enough to discover why Luke endowed the town of Nazareth with a nonexistent cliff. The Gospels are too interested in the diverse forms of collective death to be interested in the topography of Nazareth. Their real concern is with the demon's self-lapidation and the fall of the herd of pigs from the cliff. But in these cases it is not the scapegoat who goes over the cliff, neither is it a single victim nor a small number of victims, but a whole crowd of demons, two thousand swine possessed by demons. Normal relationships are reversed. The crowd should remain on top of the cliff and the victim fall over; instead, in this case, the crowd plunges and the victim is saved.

THE INVERSION OF VIOLENCE

The miracle of Gerasa reverses the universal schema of violence fundamental to all societies of the world. The inversion appears in certain myths but not with the same characters; it always ends in the restoration of the system that had been destroyed or in the establishment of a new system. In this case the result is quite different. The drowning of the swine has a definitive character; it is an event without a future, except for the person cured by the miracle. This text suggests a difference not of degree but of nature between Jesus' miracle and the usual healings. This difference of nature corresponds in actuality to a whole group of concordant details. Modern critics have failed to notice them. The fantastic aspects of the miracle seem too gratuitous to attract attention for very long. The request the demons make of Jesus, their disorderly withdrawal into the swine, and the downfall of the latter all seem like familiar old stories; whereas in fact the treatment of these themes is extraordinary. It corresponds strictly to what is demanded at this point by the revelation of the victim's mimeticism, even though the whole style remains demonological.

If need be, the demons will tolerate being expelled provided they are not expelled *from their country*. This would seem to mean that ordinary exorcisms are always only local displacements, exchanges, and substitutions which can always be produced within a structure without causing any appreciable change or compromising the continuation of the whole society. Traditional cures have a real but limited action to the degree that they only improve the condition of individual X at the expense of another individual, Y, or vice versa. In the language of demonology, this means that the demons of X have left him to take possession of Y. The healers modify certain mimetic relationships, but their little manipulations do not compromise the balance of the system, which remains unchanged. The system remains and should be defined as a system not of men only but of men and their demons.

This total system is threatened by the cure of the possessed and the concomitant drowning of the Legion. Because the Gerasenes suspect this they are uneasy. The demons have an even clearer understanding. They appear more lucid than the humans in this case which does not prevent them from being blind in other areas and easy to deceive. These themes are far richer in meaning than people have supposed. The qualities attributed to the demons correspond strictly to the true characteristics of this strange reality they are made to incarnate in the Gospels, the mimetic *disincarnation. As* desire becomes more frantic and demonic, it becomes more aware of its own laws, but this awareness does not prevent enslavement. Great writers appreciate this paradox and display it in their work. Dostoyevsky borrowed from the demons of Gerasa not only the title for his novel *The Demons* but also the system of relationships between characters and the dynamics of the abyss that sweeps the system away.

The demons try to "negotiate" with Jesus, as they do with the local healers. They deal as equal to equal with those whose power or lack of power is scarcely different from their own. The negotiation with Jesus is more apparent than real. This traveler is not initiated in any local cult; he is not sent by anyone in the community. He does not need to make concessions in order for the demons to leave the possessed. The permission he gives them to possess the swine has no consequence because it has no lasting effect. It is enough for Jesus to appear somewhere to put a stop to demons and challenge the inevitably demonic order of all society. Demons cannot exist in his presence. They become extremely agitated, have short periods of convulsion, and then tend to disintegrate completely. This inevitable course of events is indicated by the miracle's moment of crisis.

In every great defeat the finest maneuvers become the perfect instrument for the downfall. Our text succeeds in conferring that double significance on the bargaining between the miracle worker and the demons. The theme is borrowed from the practices of the shamans and other healers, but here it is merely a vehicle for the meanings that transcend it. The only hope of the demons in the presence of Jesus is to remain on the edges of the universe where they formerly held sway in its most evil-smelling corners. The demons turn to him willingly for shelter from the abyss that threatens them. Panic-stricken, they decide in haste, and for lack of a better choice, they *become pigs.* This is strangely similar to what happens everywhere. Even becoming pigs, like Ulysses' companions, the demons cannot survive. Drowning is final perdition. It realizes the worst fears of the supernatural herd, *expulsion from their own country.* This is Mark's remarkable expression; it takes note of the social nature of the game, of the demoniac's role in what some call the "symbolic." Luke's text is also instructive. In showing us the demons begging Jesus not to send them forever *into the abyss,* he clearly articulates the definitive annihilation of the demoniac that is the major significance of the text and explains the reaction of the Gerasenes themselves. These unfortunate people fear that their precarious balance depends on the demoniac, on the activities they share periodically and on the kind of local celebrity their possessed citizen had become.

There is nothing in the possession that does not result from frantic mimeticism. Hence the variant in Matthew that substitutes two possessed beings that are indistinguishable, and therefore mimetic, for the solitary demoniac of the other two Gospels. Mark's text expresses basically the same thing, less obviously but therefore more essentially, by presenting his single person possessed by a demon that is both one and multiple, both singular and plural. This implies that the possessed is possessed not by only one other, as Matthew suggests, but by all the others inasmuch as they are both one and many, or in other words inasmuch as they form a society in the human sense of the term. This is also the demonic sense, if one prefers, in that it is a society based on the collective expulsion. This is precisely what the possessed is imitating. The demons are in the image of the human group; they are the *imago* of this group because they are its *imitatio*. Like the society of the Gerasenes at the end of our text, the society of demons at the beginning possesses a structure, a kind of organization; it is the unity of the multiple: "My name is Legion; for there are many of us." Just as one voice is raised at the end to speak in the name of all the Gerasenes, one voice is raised at the beginning to speak in the name of all the demons. These two voices say the same thing. Since all coexistence between Jesus and the demons is impossible, to beg him not to chase away the demons, when one is a demon is the same as begging him to depart, if one is from Gerasa.

The essential proof of my thesis that the demons and Gerasenes are identical is the behavior of the possessed insofar as he is the possessed of these demons. The Gerasenes stone their victims and the demons force theirs to stone themselves, which amounts to the same thing. This archetypal possessed mimics the most basic social practice that literally engenders society by transforming mimetic multiplicity in its most atomized form into the strongest social unity which is the unanimity of the original murder. In describing the unity of the multiple, the Legion symbolizes the social principle itself, the type of organization that rests not on the final expulsion of the demons but on the sort of equivocal and mitigated expulsions that are illustrated by our possessed, expulsions which ultimately end in the coexistence of men and demons.

I have said that Legion symbolizes the multiple unity of society and that is true, but in the rightly famous sentence "My name is Legion; for there are many of us," it symbolizes that unity in the process of disintegration since it is the inverse of social development that prevails. The singular is irresistibly transformed into a plural, within the same single sentence; it marks the falling back of unity into mimetic multiplicity which is the first disintegrating effect of Jesus' presence. This is almost like modern art. *Je est un autre,* says Matthew. *Je* is all the others, says Mark.

THE CROWD MENTALITY

It is legitimate to identify the herd of pigs with the crowd of lynchers since the reference is explicit in at least one Gospel, that of Matthew. I am referring to a very significant aphorism that appears not far from the account of Gerasa. "Do not throw your pearls in front of pigs or they may trample them and then turn on you and tear you to pieces" (Matt. 7:6).

Yet in the account of Gerasa the lynchers experience the treatment "normally" reserved for the victim. They are not stoned like the possessed, but they go over the steep bank, which amounts to the same thing. If we are to recognize how revolutionary this inversion is we must transport it to classical Greek or Roman antiquity, which is more respected than the Judaic world of the Bible. Imagine the *Pharmakos* forcing the inhabitants of a Greek city, philosophers and mathematicians alike, over a precipice. Instead of the outcast being toppled from the height of the Tarpeian rock it is the majestic consuls, virtuous Cato, solemn juriconsults, the procurators of Judea, and all the rest of the *senatus populusque romanus.* All of them disappear into the abyss while the ex-victim, "clothed and in his full senses" calmly observes from above the astounding sight.

The miracle's conclusion satisfies a certain appetite for revenge, but can it be justified within the framework of my hypothesis? Does the element of revenge compromise my thesis that the spirit of revenge is absent in the Gospels? What is the force that drives the pigs into the sea of Galilee if not our desire to see them fall or the violence of Jesus himself? What can motivate a whole herd of pigs to destroy themselves without being forced by someone? The answer is obvious. It is the crowd mentality, that which makes the herd precisely a herd—in other words, the irresistible tendency to mimeticism. One pig accidentally falling into the sea, or the convulsions provoked by the demonic invasion, is enough to cause a stupid panic in which all the others follow.

The frantic following fits well with the proverbial stubbornness of the species. Beyond a certain mimetic threshold, the same that defined possession earlier, the whole herd immediately repeats any conduct that seems out of the ordinary, like fashions in modern society.

If just one animal were to stumble, accidentally, it would immediately start a new fashion of rushing headlong—*the plunge into the abyss*—whlch would carry the last little pig eagerly away. The slightest mimetic incitement can agitate a close-knit crowd. The weaker the purpose, the more futile and fatal, then the more mysterious it will appear and the more desire it will inspire. All the swine are scandalized and have therefore lost their balance. They are bound to be interested and even electrified by a sudden, more radical, loss of balance. Everyone is groping for that beautiful gesture, the gesture *that cannot be undone.* They rush headlong after the "bold innovator."

Whenever Jesus speaks he usually puts the mimeticism of the scandalized in the place of the works of the devil. If we do the same thing in this context the mystery evaporates. These pigs are truly possessed in that they are mimeticized up to their ears. We should not look in manuals of demonology for references other than those in the Gospels. We should turn instead to a more joyful, deeper literature. The suicidal demons of Gerasa are Panurge's supersheep who do not even need a Dindenneau to throw themselves into the sea. There is always a mimetic answer to the questions posed in our text, and that answer is always the best.

NOTES

1.   Jean Starobinski, "La Démoniaque de Gerasa," in *Analyse structurale a exégèse biblique* (Neuchatel: LABOR FIDES, 1971), pp. 63-94.

2.   Starobinski, "La Démoniaque de Gerasa."

NARRATIVE IDENTITY AND RELIGIOUS IDENTITY
David Pellauer

STORY AND SELF-DISCOVERY

The concluding remarks of Paul Ricoeur's remarkable three-volume study of time and narrative, which are more a self-critical retrospective look at what he has accomplished and its limits than a summary of what has gone before, quite unexpectedly introduce the notion of personal identity, as an individual or as a community, in relation to narrative discourse.[1] He places this discussion under the title of narrative identity, and I want to take up this particular problematic in light of Margaret Atwood's "The Sin Eater." Do Ricoeur's philosophical reflections on narrative and narrative identity help us to make sense of this text? More particularly, do his comments on the specific problem of narrative identity apply to this story; more importantly, do they help us in any way to make sense of the question of religious identity as a specific form of personal or communal identity?

One reason Ricoeur takes up this theme is his belief that insofar as the identity that is at issue here is a means of answering the question "who?" it must have a narrative form, because narrative is not just a way of making sense of the time and the temporality of our existence; it is also a way of rendering intelligible human action and its consequences, anticipated and unanticipated; a realm of our lives characterized by change, not by static identity. Hence the identity at stake here is better characterized in terms of a concept of "self-constancy" than in terms of one of unchanging "sameness."

The link of this notion of identity as self-constancy to narrative is constituted first of all by the fact that the temporal structure underlying this type of identity is closer to (if not identical with) the dynamic identity that occurs in the poetic composition of a narrative text than it is to cosmological time (conceived of as a series of point-like nows) or even to purely subjective time (with its emphasis on a difficult-to-unify experience of the past, the present, and the future). What is more, this link to the narrative

99

identity of a text, which may be said to mediate personal identity, indicates that such identity has to include changes, where these changes (or even reversals in fortune) are unified in terms of something like the point of view of a lived present within the context of the story of a life or the history of a people. This kind of dynamic unity, therefore, cannot be expressed simply in terms of a series of points where the ideas of before and after are applicable; it also requires the notion of "now" as a lived present. It is this experienced now that helps us to see how both past and future are connected to a lived-through present, one that retains its immediate past and anticipates its impending future. And with its ability to change point of view temporally as well as spatially, through memory and imagination, identity so conceived allows us to explore the more distant past and the long range future in the light of our lived-through present or that analogy of it which is the present of the narrative voice. In effect, then, one implication of Ricoeur's work is that we make sense of who we are by telling or at least by being able to tell the stories of our lives.

Furthermore, because such a close tie exists between narrative forms of discourse (and these may be either fictional or historical; that is, they may claim to tell us what happened or what could have happened or what could happen), insofar as such discourse configures and refigures human action at the level of lived experience, it can also refigure the identity of the person or community that hears or reads, and thereby imaginatively appropriates, this discourse. To be more precise we might say that individuals or communities that can be referred to in response to the question "who?" discover or tell who they are both in telling and in listening to or reading narratives. As Ricoeur puts it, life itself is "a cloth woven of stories told."

The self of this form of identity, then, is not the epistemological subject of modern theories of knowledge, who is everyone (as the atemporal potential "knower who knows a known"), hence no one (if by someone we mean an actually existing, embodied, finite, temporal individual capable of action and irreducible to just cognition). Rather, insofar as this subject is a self, or in the case of social forms something like a self, this self is the fruit of an examined life in the Socratic sense, a life purged by the catharsis that narrative can effect. This potentially liberating cathartic effect is surely one reason why stories are so important to us, both individually and communally, and why we so love and need to tell and hear them. But, of course, as psychoanalysis and the critique of ideologies teach us, often our stories are misleading in ways we cannot predict or control, and in ways that are destructive to us and to others as well. So our stories must check and correct one another, something they do when the process of storytelling is complemented by the process of reading and hearing. In this sense, we might even say that historians who correct misreadings and misleading memories of the past are like therapists who help us deal with misreadings and misleading memories of our own lives. Similarly, writers of fiction help us to see ourselves and our world in different ways; more specifically, they help us to see ourselves, others, and our situation in terms of a world that we might inhabit. In either case, history or fiction, through hearing and reading narratives we are enabled to see others and ourselves as "characters" in a tale that makes sense of our lives, our past, our present, and our possible future. And to extend the metaphor, seeing and understanding ourselves as characters in a story or a history enables us to have character in our daily lives.

RELIGIOUS IDENTITY AND EMPLOTMENT

What has all this to do with religious identity, a concept Ricoeur himself does not directly address, although he does use the example of the importance of the narrative of God's promises and acts to the identity of the Hebrew people as his leading example for narrative identity at the communal level? Three things, I think. First, it suggests that at least in some important ways religious identity too is linked to narrative discourse, and this on both the individual and the communal levels. For Christians, the story of the gospel tells us who we were, who we are, and who we will be, with strong overtones of an imperative regarding who we ought to be; that is, how we ought to act.

Second, and here I will follow another notion of Ricoeur's, it gives us a clue as to how narratives function more specifically as regards religious identity. I am thinking of Ricoeur's suggestion that religious discourse, which here includes more than narrative discourse, "names God."[2] It is in this sense that specifically religious language goes beyond merely poetic language with its power of redescribing reality. In the process of describing and redescribing reality, religious discourse, including its narrative forms, names God.[3] So for the question before us, which is the question about the relation of narrative theory and religion, one implication is to look for how, if at all, narrative texts can be said implicitly or explicitly to name God.

Third, there is the implication that religious identity is not just something we get from reading or hearing narratives. It is also a story that we tell and that it almost seems we must tell if we are to know who we are on this level of our existence. To put it more sharply, having a religious identity means being able to tell stories, not just the stories of our own lives as individuals and communities with histories and traditions, but also other stories, stories of who and what we might become, which stories all in different ways may name God. In this sense, narrative is one of the ways in which we name and pass on the name of the god who has been named to us.

What, if anything, has this to do with Atwood's story, with the religious category "sin" looming in its title? Again three things, I think, which can be brought together under the rubric of one way of reading this story.[4] These three things have to do with the plot, the time, and the action of "The Sin Eater." By applying them to our text, we are in effect making use of the broader theory in *Time and Narrative*, with the twist that the emphasis is on how this applies specifically to the idea of religious identity.

Interestingly, what Ricoeur has to say about time in relation to narrative depends on a peculiar feature of all narrative in his interpretation of this mode of discourse, namely that it has a plot, or to put it a better way: all narrative is configured by a plot, a process we may speak of as emplotment. Emplotment here does not refer to the story line (the linear sequence of the events in a narrative, or the reconstruction of that sequence); rather it refers to that aspect of any narrative, linked to its mimesis of action, that makes it what Ricoeur calls a "synthesis of the heterogeneous," a configuration that finally comes down to a discordant concordance embracing everything that happens in the narrative, at least if it is well-formed. Through its emplotment narrative redescribes, or better configures and refigures, human action which is already present on the level of mimesis$_1$.[5] This refiguration, as we shall see further below, first occurs in the configuration of the plot, then it is appropriated and perhaps applied in our lives through the process of reading (or hearing) the text; this is the level of refiguration properly speaking.

If emplotment can do this, it is in part because what happens in the plot takes time, although this is the time of the work, not of the objective world. To put it another way, at its deepest level emplotment configures time itself in that it ties together the episodic aspect of the story (the then and then and then) and the configurational unity that makes it a whole. In the final analysis, it is this tensive unity of the plot that we understand when we read or hear a narrative. It follows, therefore, that if we are to attempt to make explicit how we understand a narrative we have to attend to both its episodic and its configurational aspects, and particularly how they relate to each other. This unity is not that of an eternal now. It has a temporal dimension, and that temporal dimension is the discordant concordance spoken of earlier.

Finally, the plot is the basis for presenting the characters in the story. Here it is clear that Ricoeur is an Aristotelian who believes that the characters are always subordinate to the plot; which is not to say, as Frank Kermode has shown, that developing the characters is not a means of furthering the development of the plot, in that all character development calls for more narration; nor is it to deny that the development of the plot itself may not also lead to the enriching of a character or many characters.[6] As regards Atwood's story this seems to me to imply that we must attend as much to Joseph the therapist as we do to the first person narrator who was his client. We must do this if we are to see what mimesis of action underlies their interactions, which for Ricoeur is what narrative is finally about. To get to that question, however, we must first say something about time in "The Sin Eater."

Although Atwood makes use of a quite sophisticated narrative technique as regards temporality in her story, it should not be construed as what Ricoeur, following A. A. Mendilow, calls a tale about time.[7] That is, while every narrative has a temporal dimension just because it has a plot, not every narrative deliberately sets out to emphasize this dimension or to explore it, as, say, Proust does in his *Remembrances of Things Past*. In other words, while Atwood makes use of what Dorrit Cohn describes as the techniques of narrated monologue as well as what we might call the present of presentation, which is particularly striking in the opening of her story ("This is Joseph . . ."), it is not so much time itself that is at stake here as it is this narrator's sense of self as influenced by this unusual man and, if we may dare say so, her identity.[8]   In fact, the time of the world of this text is quite everyday and even linear. We cannot say exactly when (or where) it takes place, except that it is after the Forties, at a time when black mourning dress is out of fashion and when some women wear Indian-print dresses, but this does not matter.   The implication of something like our own day is sufficient to affect us with a sense of recognition of this world.   Nor do the shifting temporal points of view that go with the narrated monologue really convey a different quality of time so much as they emphasize the narrator's own sense of disorientation and anxious wonder.

CHARACTERS IN TIME

Time, therefore, is more a means to an end, the presentation of character and the mimesis of action, in this text than it is the thematic focal point of Atwood's tale. So what can we say about these characters and this action, particularly as they relate to identity and religious identity? To answer this question we need to take a closer look at the two main characters and their interactions, then to see how this interaction draws the reader into the plot.

The female narrator is, at least on the surface, the easier to describe. Middle-aged, in the middle of a divorce, uneasy with her life and looking for meaning, she has been in therapy with Joseph, who tells her life is not fine and dandy; in most ways it is "a big pile of shit," and the only question is deciding how best to cope with it. But are we to believe him? Or is he like many therapists willing to tell his patient many things in order to shake her out of her acquired patterns of behavior and thinking? This possibility, I think, points to one of the loci of ambiguity in this story, particularly if we approach it with the question of religious identity in mind. For Joseph is a strange creature who in many ways recalls the biblical Jesus and his antitype Joseph, yet in other ways inverts them.[9] Like Jesus he has many devoted women patients/followers; he tells parables as in the case of his account of the tradition of sin eating;[10] he has a sense of justice; and he likes to associate with the poor and with outcasts from good society. Also he is seedy looking but talks well. He can be ironic when necessary, and according to his first wife thinks he is God himself. He even claims to have all the time in the world. And as a therapist he makes demands on his patients, confronting the narrator early on in their relationship with the question, "do you like me?" What is more, following his death both Karen, another patient, and the narrator have a difficult time believing he is gone. Karen reports that she had a feeling he was not really there, in the closed coffin, following the funeral; and the narrator, at the wake, looking at the messy office in his house, has the sense that he "refuses to be packed up and put away."

Yet Joseph is also an inversion of many of the values associated with Jesus, if he is meant to recall such a figure (and we only get this image through the narrator's words, even when she reports Joseph's own words). He has been married, three times, and is at least sixty years old. He grew up in a slum and thus comes from a city, not a rural background. He likes to talk, and can be boring when he does so, but he especially wants people to know that "he's a human being too." In short, he is utterly this-worldly. He has no transcendent meaning or message of salvation; one simply must learn to cope. If he is a religious type to the narrator, it is as much Krishna with his milk maids as it is Christ with his women followers. Nor can he forgive an early slight (even when in the narrator's dream after the funeral and wake the offender reappears, struggling to attract his attention). And unlike the biblical Joseph, that precursor and antitype of Jesus, he does not want to interpret dreams. Most of all, however, he dies—and he does so not on but by falling off a tree.

Yet he also comes back, at least in the narrator's dream. Is this the action that underlies the configuration of this story? After all, everything, except for the narrator's refusal to eat the cookies offered her at the wake, has been talk and more talk, interspersed with her observations, even if we allow that she is, within her limits and her anger, an acute observer of herself and others. Or is the action somehow related to her telling us this story along with our response to it? (It is this telling, something like a patient recounting her experience to a therapist, that in part accounts for the heavy but obviously narrative use—"I sit down at one of the tables and Joseph sits opposite me"—of the present tense.) This possibility would allow us to link up with Ricoeur's theory of reading as appropriation. That is, that reading entails at least an imaginative response on our part. But why, someone may ask, should we respond with anything other than the aesthetic pleasure due a striking tale? My own sense is that if we deliberately bring the question of religious identity into our act of reading, we come closer to what is at issue on this level of the act of reading and any consequences it may have. First of all, the tale is quite clearly told to us as the implied reader or audience. This is indicated by the narrator's bemoaning having lost someone to tell things to. "There is no one left in my life who is there only to be told." Hence the rhetoric of her account seems meant to appeal to us and to involve us in some way (where this intention is that of the implied, not the actual author). But, more importantly, as regards any question of a mimesis of action, I think it is important we recognize how little action this story really includes. Having done so, we may then say that it ends strikingly on the threshold of action, just as the narrator "remembers" that Joseph is dead and reaches out for the star and moon-shaped cookies again offered her, as the stars begin to shine.

VERSIONS OF THE EUCHARIST

In this regard we may then see that what we confront here is not so much an exorcism (implied in the therapeutic sessions and the work of mourning) as an inverted—or is it really inverted?—Eucharist. Joseph is dead, and in a world without ultimate meaning/salvation, sins are not removed or forgiven; they are simply passed on, through the act of sin eating. Joseph is dead, so there is no transcendent body and blood to eat in a post-sacrificial meal; there is only what remains, his sins. But what does it mean to eat another person's sins? This is one of the questions we are left with, if with the narrator we imagine the act of taking the cookies. And in terms of the general sense of what it means to be religious that characterizes our modern, pluralist world it is a good one. Yet there may also be another possibility, one indicated first of all by Joseph's hand that is blue (dead) and then not blue, but even more so by those shining star-shaped cookies. They introduce a clearly apocalyptic and eschatological note, especially when linked to the oneiric unworldly time of the narrator's dream, the consideration of which makes present past times. Those shining stars seem especially significant because the day when the stars do not shine will be the Day of Yahweh (see Joel 2:10 and 3:15); in the synoptic gospels the day when the stars begin to fall (Mt 24:29, Mk 13:25, Lk 21:25; see Revelation 6:13).

Yet this day of judgment is countered, at least one religious tradition and community tell us, by the word of hope that shines amidst a "crooked and perverse generation" as the word of life (Phil. 2:15), which seems to be what our angry narrator needs and in her own way grasps by reaching out for the meal of Joseph's sins. This act of initiative recounted in the present tense overlaps one possible meaning of the lived present in general; namely, that it is the untimely moment of initiative situated between the past that is no longer and the future that is not yet (or to use Ricoeur's more spatial imagery, adopted from Reinhart Koselleck: between our space of experience and our horizon of expectation).[11] If this time of initiative, of being able to act, requires and is grounded in the hope the tradition calls faith, this may also be conveyed by the doxology the community says accompanies such hope, a hymnic cry that calls on the stars to shine and praise the lord (Psalm 148:3). This note of hope and meaningfulness, of being able to live and act, then, seems to be another possible implication of the act of taking (and eating) those cookies, which remain while Joseph seems to have disappeared.

Perhaps it is in our recognition of this choice and what it may entail, along with our acting on it, even if only imaginatively, that we as readers[12] discover who we are religiously. The narrator seems to have made her choice, even though we as readers never really know if she ate the shining cookies, or withdrew her hand, or if her dream simply ended at that point leaving her to ponder its meaning by telling it to us. However, from the interpretive perspective we have adopted it seems that we must also say that within this story there is no clear naming of God. There is merely the ambiguity of what Joseph and her relation to Joseph represent for the narrator: acceptance and coping—or something more. The further question, whether how we as individuals or as a community of interpretation respond to this story—including its plot, its shifting sense of time, and its unfinished action— somehow names God, whether affirmatively or negatively, seems left open but not excluded: on the other side of fiction, on the other side of narrative.

NOTES

1. Paul Ricoeur, *Time and Narrative*, Kathleen Blamey and David Pellauer, trs. (Chicago: University of Chicago Press, 1984-88), 3 volumes.

2. See Paul Ricoeur, "Naming God," *Union Seminary Quarterly Review* 34 (1979), 215-27.

3. For Ricoeur's understanding of the nature of religious language, see my essay "Paul Ricoeur on the Specificity of Religious Language," *The Journal of Religion* 61 (1981), 264-84.

4. Atwood is clearly an author who deliberately through her narrative technique sets out to exclude a single, all-encompassing interpretation. In focusing on the religious resonances in her story we may be playing down, but we are not denying, other perspectives, which in this instance would include feminism and psychoanalysis, or the themes of the meaning of death and the meaning of life in general.

5. For Ricoeur's theory of threefold mimesis, see *Time and Narrative*, Vol. I, pp. 52-87; see also Paul Ricoeur, "Mimesis and Representation," *Annals of Scholarship* 2/3 (1981), 15-32, for an earlier version of this theory.

6. See Frank Kermode, *The Genesis of Secrecy* (Cambridge: Harvard University Press, 1979), pp. 75-77.

7. A. A. Mendilow, *Time and the Novel* (London: Peter Nevill, 1952; 2nd. ed, New York: Humanities Press, 1972).

8. Dorrit Cohn, *Transparent Minds: Narrative Modes of Presenting Consciousness in Fiction* (Princeton: Princeton University Press, 1978).

9. In this sense, he is not what Ziolkowski calls a "fictional transformaton" of Jesus but something more complex, particularly since we see him only through the narrator's eyes and through the second-hand comments she gathers and reports following his death. See Theodore Ziolkowski, *Fictional Transformations of Jesus* (Princeton: Princeton University Press, 1972).

10. In rural Wales, he says, when someone is dying or has died, someone, usually an old, destitute woman, is called in to eat a meal which has been placed on the coffin. This is the ritual meal of sin-eating.

11. Reinhart Koselleck, *Futures Past: On the Semantics of Historical Time*, Keith Tribe, tr. (Cambridge: MIT Press, 1985).

12. Or listeners. The acknowledgements to *Dancing Girls* indicate that this story was initially written for the Canadian Broadcasting Corporation.

NARRATIVE HUNGER
Barbara DeConcini

> Here it is, finally, the shape of my bereavement:
> Joseph is no longer around to be told. There is no one
> left in my life who is there only to be told.
> "The Sin Eater"[1]

> Storytelling is always after the fact, and it is always
> constructed over a loss.
> J. Hillis Miller[2]

NARRATIVE AS LOSS

Whatever else it may be, "The Sin Eater" is a story about desertion and bereavement. It traces the contours of a loss and its aftermath. As such, it seems a peculiarly apt choice for a reflection on narrative theory, since it adumbrates thematically something about the nature of narrative itself. For all narrative is more or less explicitly, "un recherche de temps perdu." In its claim to be a repetition of events that have already happened, it presents itself as a re-presentation, summoning "an absent presence into reappearance," in Northrop Frye's words.[3]

Narratologists of all stripes, from New Critics to deconstructionists, affirm this in one manner or another. Most conservatively put, emplotment is seen as the making of events into a story, and the absence or loss is what is overcome at the level of discourse. As a matter of fact, of course, all we have is discourse, but the discourse claims to be a recounting of some prior series of events. Hence, Hillis Miller's evocative phrase used as an epigraph to this essay, as well as Frank Kermode's characterization of plot as "the great mnemonic"[4]—by making events into a story, narrative creates a presence out of the past, asserting memory over forgetfulness.

A deeper suspicion about narrative's capacity to make sense of things would hold that absence and loss invade even the most coherent and closed of plots (as temporal distortion, displacement, transgression of temporality, fractured surface, overdetermination, intermittence of memory, subversion of manifest sense, undecidabilities, and the like). Indeed, a narrative without such fallibilities would be without hermeneutical potential.[5] Such a narrative theory may grant an irreducible impenetrability to narrative, but it will understand even this as at the service of interpretation. As Kermode expresses it, we are in love with the idea of fulfillment, programmed, as it were, to prefer closed to open forms:

> The world is our beloved codex—world and book, it
> may be, are hopelessly plural, endlessly disappointing;
> we stand alone before them, aware of their
> arbitrariness and impenetrability, knowing that they
> may be narratives only because of our impudent
> intervention.[6]

A more radical critique argues that a narrative's gaps and opacities do not simply grant it hermeneutical potential. Rather, thanks to what Jacques Derrida calls the logic of the sign, not even narrative offers a way out of the mixture of presence and absence. While deconstruction does not deny that we tell stories to make sense of things, it does assert that any unitary sense we make is undercut by the narrative itself.

Atwood's story thematizes these issues of interpretation and our desire to make sense of things. Its making present of absence is nowhere more explicit than in its oneiric conclusion. Because, as we have long since learned from Frank Kermode's *The Sense of an Ending*,[7] endings retrospectively grant order and significance to narrative beginnings and middles, it is this recounting of the narrator's dream that I want to focus on here. In the first part of my essay I offer a reading of the story which might be characterized as narrative consolation. In the second, I confront certain challenges, from both within and without the text, to this reading. In part three, these dissonances prompt a brief hermeneutical excursus.

NARRATIVE CONSOLATION

In *Reading for the Plot*, Peter Brooks correlates the nineteenth century's loss of belief in the sacred masterplot with its predilection for life histories and well-plotted novels of realism. As anxious efforts to recover some explanatory force in a world with diminishing symbolic resonances, consoling fictions of any era may well function as secular analogues to providential plots.[8] It is inviting to read the dream ending of Atwood's story in these terms.

The story's psychotherapeutic context urges on us a Freudian interpretation of the dream as wish fulfillment and disguised remembrance. Many of its manifest elements, of course, suggest that it is a revision of Joseph's funeral earlier that day. I call it revision because in the psychic event—unlike the material event— the narrator's alienation is overcome by Joseph's singling her out ("'I'm glad you got the invitation,' he says," 223) for participation in a symbiotic sacramental table ritual, with resonances of both Penance and Eucharist, in which each ministers to the other. By eating Joseph's proffered sins, despite her resistance, she absolves him from his greatest sin: his desertion and the consequent end of therapy. It is her he selects for this service, her he makes fat (pregnant?) with his sins, and thus protects from death. This last, with strong hints of transcendence, gets conveyed in the story's final transmogrifications: childish cookies—sins—thousands of stars and moons.

If we go with the Freudian critique a bit further, we can, thanks to the analysand's compulsion to repeat and the concomitant phenomenon of transference, understand the analysand's forgiveness of the analyst as her forgiveness of the other(s) for whom he stands—perhaps the husband who has left her, perhaps the father whose loss is the infantile source of her adult anger. This last gets some warrant in the text from the sunflower episode whose lesson, that "the earliest ones are the hardest to forgive," seems at the time lost on the obtuse narrator who is never sure whether Joseph's stories are parables.

This reading of the dream, at least on the face of it, seems to satisfy our narrative hunger for closure, offering us as readers both therapeutic and narrative resolution. We complete our reading as contented as we take the narrator to be, each having overcome our losses in a burst of clarity.

HINDRANCES TO CLOSURE

It is, however, precisely the transcendental ring of the story's final rhetorical flourish—"There are thousands of stars, thousands of moons, and as I reach out for one they begin to shine" (224)—which sets up uneasy reverberations in the reader's ear. For this is the narrator who characterizes the issue which led her into therapy as her anger at reality, "so unfinished, so sloppy, so pointless, so endless" (215). And this is the therapist whose interpretive suggestions are coachings in the reality principle: "This world is all we have. It's all you have to work with. It's not too much for you. You will not be rescued" (222). Is the reader who is struck by her dream's rescue motif and its finished, neat, pointed, and conclusive character being unduly suspicious of its therapeutic resolution?

There are other dissonant notes sounded by the reading of the ending as a consoling fiction of closure. What are we to make, for instance, of the story's ambiguities, ambivalences, and reversals concerning both the sin eater's gender and the therapeutic roles of analyst and analysand? What are we to make of Joseph?

At first, we are told that sin eaters are old women who engage in the practice out of the sheer desperation of hunger and poverty. Geriatric spiritual whores, they are afflicted with an extraordinary sort of eating disorder in which, presumably, long periods of fasting are punctuated by funereal food orgies which leave them social outcasts, flatulent with sins. But there is a second version of the sin eater, for Joseph casts himself in the role: the unconventional analyst with the liberal credentials and wolfish grin who specializes in smart women with detachable husbands. Therapy itself is sin eating in modern dress. And finally, in the dream, the narrator switches roles with Joseph to become his sin eater.

This role reversal is prepared for in the text by Joseph's unconventional version of the therapeutic session which, in its turn, is not unrelated to a set of suggestions concerning Joseph's sexuality and professional ethics. Is Joseph, in fact, a dirty old man, a panderer in the playground which is the therapeutic situation? Is he a totemic figure around whom are clustered these neurotic women, hovering, motherly, making him cookies when he falls out of trees, passing him from hand to hand like a talisman? Satyr, Krishna, old fart, analyst who unlike his biblical namesake is no interpreter of dreams: Joseph's very multivalence may be a clue to his potency in the therapeutic transference, the re-enacted memory of the narrator's apparently dead desires.

Taken together, these shifts in identity from beginning through middle raise questions not easily or completely resolved by the ending. Crassly put, what are these motifs doing in the discourse if the ending does not grant them retrospective significance? What is the hermeneutical potential of these opacities in the text? In the light of them, how else might we interpret the narrator's final willingness to become Joseph's sin eater? Is she, after all, succumbing to his winning ways with his female patients? Does it represent her hunger for him, her willingness to play gopi to his Krishna?[9] Or is the dream a symbolic recognition on her part that Joseph's therapeutic practice is a self-serving version of the talking cure, a con game in which he gets his smart women to pay him money to listen to his own problems? In eating Joseph's sins, does she in fact transgress the taboo against eating the totem animal and thus bring on herself the fate of the outcast? Or does it perhaps suggest that she can resolve his "act of desertion" openly at the expense of becoming a destitute old woman? Is eating Joseph's sins worth the cost? Is it believable that all these tensions which the narrative generates in the nexus of sin eater/therapist/patient/man/woman/sex are so readily resolvable by the romanticized conclusion?

Reference to Atwood's other work bolsters the wager that these sorts of suspicions are appropriately addressed to my original reading of the story's ending. Indeed, they lift up a set of concerns central enough and frequent enough in her fiction to be considered an abiding part of her novelistic vision. For brevity's sake, let me subsume them here, rather too facilely, under the rubric of feminism and food. Forthwith, a few examples.

In *The Edible Woman*, her first novel, Atwood creates the first in her long series of smart women characters who are divided against themselves. Although Marian seems to acquiesce to society's prescription for her fulfillment, her engagement to be married prompts in her a peculiar eating disorder. Dividing the world into the devourable and the undevourable, she becomes progressively anorectic as she projects her own anxieties about being consumed (by her fiancé, by the institution of marriage, by the wife-role her culture dictates). Her inchoate sense of victimization distorts her psychic boundaries, leading her to personalize animal flesh and vegetables and "vegetablize" women. The novel concludes with a darkly comic, bizarrely inverted Betty Crocker-like gesture. Marian eludes marriage by baking her man a cake in her own image, presenting her confectionery double to him "as though she were carrying something sacred in a procession, an icon." His ritualized consumption of her as object is the only sort of marital consummation consistent with her self-preservation.

The life of the clever but alienated narrator of *Surfacing* has reached such a pitch of derangement that nothing short of a healing madness, an archetypal de-evolutionary regression down through the levels of creation, can offer her hope of returning to a freshly human world. Here, too, her archaeology of the self seeks expression in food strictures, motifs of ingestion and incorporation, empathetic identification with wildlife and plants, and symbolic reversals of personification and "vegetablization." We leave her still in the wilderness, poised on the edge of the decision whether to attempt a reconnection with the man who has come back to find her.

Cat's Eye continues the trope, exploring not only the way cultural assumptions about the proper behavior of women affect women's eating patterns but also the deeply entrenched cultural identification of women and meat as objects of man's consumption. When the narrator is an art student and having the *de rigeur* affair with her philandering professor, she notices in her art history course, without making the link, how naked women are presented in the same painterly manner as plates of meat. Later, as a participant in an all-woman art show (in an alternative space which is metamorphosing from a supermarket into a hamburger heaven), she has become more capable of tracing the contours of this identification in both art and life, as well as a whole complex of associations in the novel linking "the female malady" and food.

Suffice these three examples to suggest that what and how Atwood's women eat is freighted with meanings that criticize certain social and cultural assumptions. It may be because of its inherent nature/culture character that food functions for her as a clue to what the critical theorists of the Frankfurt School call "second nature," i.e., to cultural conventions masking as the nature of things and thus assuming unquestioned status as expressions of what is real and abiding.

In this, Atwood's fiction anticipates issues which have become commonplace in recent theoretical literature concerning women and food. In medical and psychological journals and in more popular works as well as in historical studies in art and religion, contemporary cultural criticism is confronting these latent significances of women's relationship to eating and food.[10] A consensus has emerged that women's longstanding disordered eating patterns express their biological and social identity, their struggle against oppression, their ambivalence concerning certain ranges of behavior and emotion (such as assertiveness and anger) and their hunger for nurture, independence, and equality.

Come at from these perspectives, the eating scene with which "The Sin Eater" concludes—indeed, the sin eating conceit itself—is hardly unambiguous. And this, not simply because it involves eating, but rather a special sort of eating: namely, one that is heightened through ritualization, involves a woman divided against herself, expresses that conflict graphically (in terms of indigestion and regurgitation), and symbolically enacts gender and social conflicts.

In sum, this plethora of opacities and dissonances prompts an uneasiness with any reading of the ending as a providential plot. It seems the dream raises at least as many questions as it purports to resolve. Where does that leave us as readers?

MEMORY AND TRANSFERENCE

It has been my intention not to discount totally the interpretation of the dream I proposed early on, but rather to complicate it and to qualify our satisfaction with it. Too many elements in the story undermine our efforts toward interpretive closure, as if Joseph were reaching back from the grave to tell the reader, no less than the narrator, to forget about the rescue. But if, with Kermode, we are ready to wager on the hermeneutical potential of loose ends, we can take the dream's resistance to univocality as an invitation. Our very problems with finding a satisfying interpretation nudge us further in our musings about links between sin eaters and therapists, between psychoanalytic and narrative situations. This is a path that has been traveled before, and it is hard to imagine a more companionable guide along it than Peter Brooks. In *Reading for the Plot*, Brooks develops a new sort of psychoanalytically informed literary criticism—not a psychoanalytic reading of authors, characters, or readers, but a reading of the text itself as a system of internal energies and tensions, compulsions, resistances, and desires. What psychoanalysis brings to the dynamics of temporality and reading is the requirement that we engage the role of memory and the history of desire as they connect narrative ends and beginnings, shaping the creation of meaning within time.[11]

This essay's epigraphs are meant as one way of demarcating the boundaries of that therapy/narrative connectedness in "The Sin Eater." It is a story about the narrator's loss of her therapist. Yet all stories are about loss. These are processes of remembering, as are dreams, as is therapy itself. Thus there is an intensification and multiplication of rememberings in Atwood's story. As a memorial process, it is structured by anachrony, the term Gérard Genette uses to describe the various types of temporal discordance between the orders of story and discourse.[12] Anachrony, one of the traditional resources of literary narration, witnesses to narrative's function as the making present of an absence.

At the level of story (the implied real-life sequence of events), "The Sin Eater's" chronology can be reconstructed as follows:

(1) The narrator has therapy sessions with Joseph, including those in which he tells the sin eater lore, asks her whom she hates the most, asks her whether she likes him.

(2) Karen notifies the narrator of Joseph's death.

(3) The narrator attends Joseph's funeral and the coffee and refreshments afterwards.

(4) The narrator returns to her apartment alone.

(5) The narrator has the dream about eating Joseph's sins.

(6) The narrator recalls/recounts her dream.

At the level of discourse, the plot occasionally disrupts sequence for the sake of pattern (e.g., the various sessions in #1 above are interspersed throughout the story). But particularly striking is the author's favoring of the present tense over the more conventional past tense of reminiscence. This certainly serves to embody narrative memory's capacity to create a presence out of the past, but it also serves to disorient the reader in relation to the narrative present (i.e., the present of the storytelling). This present, or setting, is especially significant in a first person narrative in which the narrator is the main character.

What, then, is the narrative present of "The Sin Eater"? I believe it is alluded to early on in the story, when the narrator comments, "This conversation is taking place in Joseph's office, which is just as tatty as he is and smells of unemptied ash-trays, feet, misery and twice-breathed air. But it's also taking place in my bedroom, on the day of the funeral" (216).

That is, the conversation originally took place in Joseph's office (#1 in the chronology) and is now being remembered/retold by the narrator after his funeral. She is in her bedroom (#6 in the chronology).

This narrative present is more fully established at the story's conclusion, just before the recounting of the dream, in the piece of text which begins "This is a room at night, a night empty except for me. I'm looking at the ceiling. . . . I've been having a dream about Joseph" (222) and ends with the words which are the epigraph to this study: "Here it is, finally, the shape of my bereavement: Joseph is no longer around to be told. There is no one left in my life who is there only to be told" (223).

Where is the story taking place? After Joseph's funeral . . . at night . . . alone . . . in bed. The narrator awakens from her dream, the dream which concludes the story, and lies there, remembering Joseph, taking the measure of the relationship and of her loss, a loss which for her marks the end of therapy—or does it? The situation is itself reminiscent of classical psychoanalysis: analysand lying on the couch, recounting the dream. At the level of story rather than discourse, her last words are not about reaching out to shining stars and moons. They are, rather, words of mourning: "There is no one left in my life who is there only to be told."

She is mistaken, of course. The night is not empty except for her. There is someone there, and there only to be told; for the phrase defines precisely the identity of the reader. We, like the analyst, listen to the story and make interpretive suggestions, eliciting shape and pattern and meaning from sequence. The structuring operation of plot is a work of listening as much as of telling. "We as readers," writes Brooks, " 'intervene' by the very act of reading, interpreting the text, handling it, shaping it to our ends, making it accessible to our therapies."[13]

There is, then, in "The Sin Eater" another, somewhat disguised, transference and it is at the heart of the story's meaning. Joseph and the narrator's memory-work in therapy, their transferential relationship in the reconstruction of the past, images the relationship we ourselves have with the text. "The Sin Eater's" narrator needs us there to be told—if the hermeneutical potential of her story is ever to be actualized.

I have said above that the narrator is mistaken about being alone. But, smart woman that she is, perhaps I underestimate her. Perhaps the storytelling is not so innocent. For, whether we like it or not, she has seduced us as listeners into a dialogic process, a cross-transference. The dynamics of reading are contractual and memorial. Handling the tar baby, we become implicated—almost before we realize it—in a therapeutic relationship which makes demands upon us. Pass the cookies, please.

NOTES

1. Margaret Atwood, "The Sin Eater," p. 223.

2. J. Hillis Miller, *Fiction and Repetition: Seven English Novels* (Cambridge, MA: Harvard University Press, 1982).

3. The phrase is Northrop Frye's, in an address at the American Academy of Religion annual meeting, Chicago, 1984.

4. Frank Kermode, *The Genesis of Secrecy* (Cambridge, MA: Harvard University Press, 1979), p. 113.

5. Kermode, passim.

6. Kermode, pp. 64, 65, 145.

7. Frank Kermode, *The Sense of an Ending* (London: Oxford University Press, 1966).

8. Peter Brooks, *Reading for the Plot* (New York: Alfred A. Knopf, 1984), p. 6.

9. Just after attending Joseph's funeral and before her dream, the narrator discovers a Hare Krishna magazine among her son's things. The incident provides several details for the manifest imagery and latent sense of the dream, including the blue god surrounded by adoring cowherdesses and the meat/sex link she makes explicit in relation to it.

10. See, for example, Rudolph Bell, *Holy Anorexia* (Chicago: University of Chicago Press, 1985); Caroline Walker Bynum, *Holy Feast and Holy Fast* (Berkeley: University of California Press, 1987); Kim Chernin, *The Hungry Self* (New York: Harper & Row, 1985); Geneen Roth, *Feeding the Hungry Heart and Breaking Free from Compulsive Eating* (New York: New American Library, 1982, 1984); Susie Orbach, *Fat Is a Feminist Issue* (New York: Berkeley Books, 1979); Carol Adams, *The Sexual Politics of Meat* (New York: Continuum, 1990).

11. Brooks, *Reading for the Plot*, xiii-xv. For an alternative use of the dynamics of desire in the reading of narrative texts, see the second

edition of the earlier work by René Girard, *Deceit, Desire, and the Novel* (Baltimore: Johns Hopkins University Press, 1980).

12. Gérard Genette, *Narrative Discourse* (Ithaca: Cornell University Press, 1979), p. 40.

13. Brooks, *Reading for the Plot*, p. 234.

DESTROYING DEATH: JESUS IN MARK AND JOSEPH IN "THE SIN EATER"
Mark McVann, F.S.C.

INTRODUCTION

The episode of the Gerasene demoniac in the Gospel of Mark and Margaret Atwood's "The Sin Eater" are both fascinating stories. They fascinate us because they strike at a primal level of feeling and consciousness. They narrate the possibility of dramatic personal transformation through a mediator who presides over confrontations between life and death. Basic and seemingly immutable boundaries are crossed in these stories. The result of the boundary crossings and confrontations is the possibility of a new beginning, of life transformed. These stories tell against suspicions—even while seeming to affirm them—that, as Joseph puts it, "life in most ways [is] a big pile of shit" from which there is "no rescue." The Gerasene demoniac and "The Sin Eater" are thus stories of gratuitous and paradoxical reversal: boundaries are crossed and new statuses achieved; expectations turned on their heads and new horizons opened. Recognition of the mediators' identity and status as divine or godlike is the pivot around which these stories turn.

I will proceed with my analysis in two sections. The first will concern itself with the episode of the Gerasene demoniac in the context of Mark's 'sea-cycle'; the second will address "The Sin Eater." In both analyses, boundary crossings, status changes, and the mysterious identity of the protagonists will receive attention.

THE SEA-CYCLE IN THE GOSPEL OF MARK

The story of the Gerasene demoniac (Mark 5:1-20) cannot be read in isolation. It is an integral part of the Markan sea-cycle (4:35-5:43), a series of stories which itself needs to be read in the context of the whole gospel. In the sea-cycle, Jesus is revealed as having power over death, no matter how or against whom it manifests itself. Therefore, Jesus' identity as a divine person who saves from death constitutes the sea-cycle's theme and variations.

The sea-cycle consists of four stories: the calming of the storm on the sea; the Gerasene demoniac; the woman with the flow of blood; and the raising of Jairus' daughter. The common topographic element which unites the stories is the Sea of Galilee. This is an important Markan setting because the sea carries connotations of chaos and death. The fact that Mark shows Jesus exercising his power over death on and by the sea indicates that he overcomes the forces it represents.[1]

The sea setting is significant also because it may be read as recalling for Christian readers the waters of baptism; that is, the waters through which they themselves pass in a ritual reenactment of the death-resurrection of Jesus. In the ritual of baptism, death is overcome and life transformed. This pattern of overcoming death and transforming life is repeated four times in the sea-cycle. Although each exposure of the theme is taken from a different angle, the focus is consistently on Jesus as the only one who can save. Jesus' power over the forces of death and the settings on and by the sea combine to unify the cycle not only topographically but structurally and thematically as well.

However, before the sea-cycle and the episode of the Gerasene demoniac itself can be addressed, we need to review very briefly the events in Mark's gospel which precede them.

Mark begins his gospel with the announcement of Jesus' identity as "Christ, the Son of God" (1:1). This is followed by an introduction of John the Baptist, whose principal function is to announce the coming of the great one who follows him. Jesus appears and is baptized in the Jordan River. At this, the sky opens, and Jesus sees a dove descending on him and hears a voice claiming him as the speaker's Son (1:2-9). Immediately afterwards, Jesus faces the devil in a trial in the desert, and because he is God's Son, emerges the victor. Then he bursts into Galilee to announce the Kingdom of God, call disciples, and begin his career of preaching and healing. After a series of episodes, including a number of controversies about his identity (is he a blasphemer? [2:6]; insane? [3:21]; demon possessed? [3:22]; prophet? [6:4]), he delivers a long sermon, consisting largely of parables about seeds. He finishes and instructs his disciples to take him to the other side of the sea, the point at which the sea-cycle proper begins.

Each of the four stories in the sea-cycle shows clearly that the desperate situations described are completely beyond human ability to alter or improve: the power of death seems to triumph everywhere. Only an agent wielding the power of God can intervene to restore things to their proper balance and save life from destruction: the storm has the disciples completely at its mercy; the demoniac cannot be restrained in any way; the woman has suffered for years despite the efforts of physicians; the little girl's death is certain and eventually happens. Mark shows his readers that Jesus is the one who wields God's power to reverse each of these hopeless situations. The sea-cycle, then, is structured along the following lines: it is introduced with the calming of the storm in which Jesus' power to turn death aside is clearly manifested. Stories immediately follow about a living man in the house of the dead (the Gerasene dwells among the tombs); a dead girl in the house of the living (Jairus' daughter dies at home); and, placed between them, a woman who is an example of living death (her impurity makes her permanently outcast, i.e., as good as dead). In each case, Jesus defeats death and restores life.

The Storm on the Sea (4:35-41)

The voyage across the sea is itself a major boundary crossing because the other side is foreign territory, an unclean land belonging to gentiles, not to Jews like Jesus and his disciples. The power of death, represented by the storm, attempts to thwart Jesus' crossing the boundary between Jews and gentiles. It is defeated, however, and Jesus arrives victorious on the other side to confront it a second time.

The Gerasene demoniac (5:1-20)

Jesus and his disciples reach the other shore of the lake, where death now confronts Jesus in the form of a demoniac who dwells among the tombs. Here among the unclean tombs in this unclean land of gentiles, death reigns unchallenged. This point is underscored by Mark's elaborate description of the demoniac's predicament in 5:2-5. No one can do anything for or about this man, despite repeated attempts. Constantly shrieking and bruising himself with stones, he lives his life like a perpetual funeral rite, signifying the triumph of death's powers. The Gerasene's situation is completely hopeless. Like the disciples during the storm, the demoniac can be saved only through the Son of God's power over death.

Readers soon learn why no one has been able to help or restrain this man: he is possessed by a myriad of powerful demons: "Legion, for we are many" (5: 9). Despite his phenomenal power, beyond anyone's ability to control or crush, 'Legion' realizes that he has more than met his match in Jesus: "What have you to do with me, Jesus, Son of the Most High God? I adjure you by God, do not torment me" (5:8). This tomb-inhabiting demon fears his end via death, his source of heretofore unbreakable strength. The emissary of death, 'Legion,' begs Life's ambassador, God's Son, not to be cast out from this land where he has exercised absolute sovereignty.[2]

Then we come to the bizarre episode where 'Legion' asks and receives permission to enter the large herd of swine on the hillside. 'Legion' invades the herd which stampedes down the hill and drowns in the sea (5:12-13).

This is Jesus' most dramatic exorcism in Mark. No where else is the casting out of a demon accompanied by such a spectacular event. Mark has already stressed the demon's strength and power; they are emphasized again in the notice about the size of the herd of swine. Not just a few swine, but *two thousand* of these unclean animals hurtle down the cliff into the sea. This, of course, is the same sea which just a few verses previously had attempted to destroy Jesus and his disciples, to kill Jesus' mission of bringing life and purity to the unclean land of the Gerasenes. Death, the ultimate uncleanness, now banished from the tomb-dwelling demoniac and inhabiting unclean swine (symbolic of its proper place), is itself destroyed in the waters of chaos and death over which Jesus has already triumphed.

Thus, this story prefigures the resurrection of Jesus at the gospel's conclusion in that the Gerasene, like Jesus, comes forth to new life from the tomb:

.... our man [the Gerasene] was obsessed with death, and impersonated (in the contemporary idiom, was possessed by) the ineluctable Lord of the Dead. His behavior was a continuous mourning ritual. . . . He represents death at large amongst men, and Jesus' act is a triumph over death. It is a resurrection scene.[3]

A basic and seemingly immutable boundary has been crossed: the Gerasene has been released from death's grasp. The agent who effects this passage, as he was correctly identified by 'Legion,' is God's Son. This, however, is not the end of the story. The reaction to Jesus' exorcisms is often briefly mentioned (see, e.g., 1:27; 9:26), but in 5:14-20 it is a developed sequel.

The original witnesses, the swineherds, tell their story twice (5:14, 16), and in between we read twice that the man with Jesus and the demoniac are the same person (5:15, 16). By this double repetition, the narrative insists that the demoniac's transformation is not imaginary. That is, Jesus has really defeated death: the boundary between death and life has been crossed.

The sight of the liberated and now clothed demoniac sitting calmly (apparently at the feet of Jesus) is too much for the Gerasenes. It is extremely important to see here that what makes the people afraid (5:15) is the demoniac's transformation, *not* the destruction of the swine. The narrator makes certain to tell us that the people are afraid *before* the mention of the pigs again in 5:16.

Of what are they afraid? Why do they ask Jesus to leave their territory? The reaction of the people makes sense in these terms: if it is true that until the exorcism the man was possessed by death, and the one responsible for liberating him is asked to leave, then the inference that must be drawn is that the Gerasenes prefer death to life precisely because they reject the source of life which has just been disclosed to them: Jesus, whom the demons recognize brings their doom (see 1:24). They fear their loss of power. Apparently 'in league' with them, the Gerasenes choose the *status quo* where death reigns unchallenged.

However, the breach in death's power cannot be shored up: the Gerasene is a living symbol of it. Indeed, the exorcised Gerasene with Jesus by the sea—a baptismal setting—is himself a baptismal image: like candidates for baptism, he was naked and then clothed

(5:15); like the baptized, he preaches what Jesus had done for him (5:19); that is, how Jesus released him from the tomb.

Whatever the actual events of this exorcism may have been—and they cannot be recovered—Mark's interest is to demonstrate Jesus' status as Son of God and his consequent power over death and its envoys: through Jesus, life overcomes death, and the unclean land of the gentiles is purified. Interpretations which focus on the so-called "violence" of the swine's destruction miss the point of the story: with no violence on his part, Jesus ends both the pollution and violence by which death had ruled. The man held in thrall to death has been freed from the tombs and restored to an authentic human status and life. Instead of being a funeral rite, his new life proclaims the victory of life over death.

The Hemorrhaging Woman (5:25-34)

Jesus and his disciples return to the Jewish side of the lake. Upon his arrival, Jesus is asked to save a dying girl, but his progress to the house where she lies sick is interrupted by the episode of the hemorrhaging woman.

This woman is another victim of the powers of death. Her incurable hemorrhage makes her permanently unclean and thus cuts her off from those who are clean and have life and who regard her as dead. Close to the seashore (the baptismal setting), where Jesus has disembarked, the woman's touching Jesus effects her cure—restores her to life, as it were—and Jesus commends her faith.

The Raising of Jairus' Daughter (5:21-24, 35-43)

Just as this victory over death is won, news of a defeat arrives: Jairus' daughter has died during the delay caused by curing the woman. Jesus encourages faith (5:36) and proceeds to the house where he dismisses the mourners who mock his announcement that the girl is sleeping (5:40). For Jesus, and for those who follow him, death is only apparent.

Jesus enters the house and raises the dead girl (5:41-42). The story closes with Jesus giving two commands: first, the witnesses, whose astonishment knows no bounds, are to tell no one about this; second, he tells her parents that the girl is to be given something to eat.

Why not tell people? Perhaps because, like the mourners, they would only mock the belief that Jesus has power over death. Why give the girl something to eat? "One must recall that the resurrection of the daughter of Jairus appears as a baptismal theme in the earliest [Christian] monuments. The eating then would have to be added to complete the baptism-eucharist pair as so often elsewhere."[4]

For the fourth and final time in the sea-cycle, Mark shows that Jesus, God's Son, transforms death into life. Baptismal imagery is close at hand throughout the sea-cycle because Mark reminds his readers that baptism also transforms: through it, death is overthrown and new life given.[5]

Mark continues his story of Jesus, concluding with the narration of Jesus' own passage from death to life. At the story's end, a young man in white robe, symbolic of baptism, announces that Jesus has been raised to life (16: 5-7).[6]

"THE SIN EATER"

In Margaret Atwood's "The Sin Eater," as in the Markan sea-cycle, the power of death seems to be everywhere, surrounding the narrator completely, denying her any rescue. However, at the end of the story, triumph over death surfaces as an astonishing possibility. Furthermore, Joseph's identity, like Jesus', is a mystery, a constant question. Joseph seems to have no past except for vague rumors about his dealings with women, his marriages (into which we have no insight), and his having been thrown out of a mental hospital where he sided with the mentally ill patients ('the possessed', 215). Like Jesus, Joseph specializes in failures and outcasts, in people who can't pay for his services. What explains his phenomenal success with patients whom other therapists wouldn't touch with a "barge pole" (215)?

Relationship with Joseph, as with Jesus, is taxing; he asks embarrassing questions: "Do you like me" (222; see Mark 4:40)? And the narrator, like Jesus' disciples in Mark, is never really sure exactly what Joseph's meanderings about gardening and plants mean: "Sometimes, though, he's really telling you something" (214); "Sometimes Joseph's stories are parables. . . " (220; see Mark 4:3-8, 26-32). Like Jesus', Joseph's parables contain agricultural images; like Jesus, he says scandalous things intended to jolt his patient-disciple into some new awareness (see Mark 4:40-41). This tactic is exemplified in a discussion of Joseph's enduring hatred for another boy who had picked his sunflower many years before:

> ". . . if I ran into the little sod tomorrow I'd stick a knife into him."
> I'm shocked, as Joseph intends me to be. . . .
> Is this Joseph proving yet once more that he's a human being, or am I intended to understand something about myself? (220)

Joseph's death, like Jesus', seems senseless and cruel: he fell from a tree he was pruning because "It was cutting off the light to his flower beds" (216). Jesus also dies on a "tree" (the cross is frequently called a tree in the New Testament, e.g., Acts 5:30), and he dies so that others will have the "light." Though Joseph is clearly a strong and deeply insightful person, the source of his strength, wisdom, and authority is frustratingly obscure. Who is he?

The atmosphere in this story is oppressive, almost claustrophobic. Except for the last scene of the story, where the narrator's transformation occurs, we find ourselves in closed and confining spaces suggesting tombs: the narrator's untidy apartment; Joseph's office ("just as tatty as he is, smelling of. . . misery and twice-breathed air," 216); and at the wake, where Joseph's closed casket looms large. But it is also here at the wake that death, apparently so uncompromising, seems most unreal: "It seems like some joke he's playing. . . that's supposed to make us learn something. . . . *All right, Joseph,* I want to call, *we have the answer, you can come out now.* But nothing happens, the closed coffin remains closed. . . " (217). What is Joseph trying to teach? What are they supposed to learn? What is the joke he's playing?

The story emphasizes again that Joseph's death is somehow not real when, after the wake, the following exchange between the narrator and Karen takes place:

> "I kept having the feeling that he wasn't really there," says Karen as we go up the walk.
> "Really where?" I say.
> "There," says Karen. "In the coffin."
> ". . . don't start that." I can tolerate that kind of sentimental fiction in myself, just barely. . . ."Dead is dead, that's what he'd say. Deal with here and now, remember?" (218)

This same point about Joseph's seeming survival of death is made a third time when we learn that his study ("that rummage sale") will be left the way it was when he died. This makes sense "because Joseph is in this room, unfinished, a huge boxful of loose ends. He refuses to be packed up and put away" (220).

Who is Joseph, really? The answer seems to be that Joseph, like Jesus, because he is a teacher with some kind of a divine identity, is immune to death. As the end of the story shows, he shares this immunity with his disciple-patient, the narrator. Joseph's divinity is clearly suggested by the narrator when she reports that Joseph's first wife says: "Had the idea he was God himself, some of them [his patients]. Not that he minded all that much" (219). The point is made again when Joseph appears in the narrator's dream; his hand is a "bright blue. . . a picture book blue" (223). This color has already been identified with divinity: ". . . there's a picture of Krishna playing the flute, surrounded by adoring maidens. His face is bright blue, which makes me think of corpses" (221). In her dream, Joseph, like Krishna, is surrounded by adoring maidens, his chorus of wives. Then the narrator remembers he is dead—or at least seems to have died.

Joseph, then, is a Christ figure and has the power to release life from the strangle hold of death: "Joseph is an expert on people who try suicide. He's never lost one yet" (218). Equally, he does not deny the harsh realities of living: "Life," Joseph insists, "in most ways [is] a big pile of shit" from which there is no "rescue" (215). Jesus agrees: "Whoever wishes to come after me must deny himself, take up his cross, and follow me. For whoever wishes to save his life will lose it. . . " (8:34-35).

Indeed, there is no rescue from *life*, but rescue from *death* is another matter. Is that not the point, after all, of the ritual of "sin eating" in the first place?

We left Joseph's wake with the narrator's claim that the people at the wake knew the answer. But what was the question? It clearly has to do with eating since the story is structured around eating as a unifying theme. It opens with a discussion of sin eating; eating is very prominent at the wake (which occurs roughly in the middle of the story), and eating appears again at the story's end. In each case, Joseph's teaching something, death, and eating are all combined. This, then, seems to be the question: is eating here a ritual which, like baptism, marks a radical change of status, a passage from death to life?

The white cookies hold the key to this mystery. The cookies brought to the wake by Joseph's first wife "remind me of Christmas, of festivals and celebrations" (219). These cookies, then, are made to celebrate a birth, a new life, and connote happiness and joy. Like the death which occasioned them, the cookies are both ironic and appropriate.

These same cookies appear at the snack-bar in the airport in the narrator's dream. It might be tempting to conclude that the narrator is about to eat Joseph's sins. After all, Joseph says: "My sins." *However*: "His voice sounds wistful, but when I glance up he's smiling at me. Is he making a joke" (224)? The cookies were ironic at the wake, and are so here as well. Additionally, this is the second time the narrator connects Joseph's death with a joke. The first was at the wake where the white cookies are introduced. What are these cookies? What's the joke?

It seems that the joke is death, and the cookies the means of overcoming it. In her dream, Joseph is teaching the narrator that death is overcome in the profound embrace of life—by "sin eating"—which is precisely the purpose of his life as a therapist. The narrator does have a sense of this: "Here it is, finally, the shape of my bereavement: Joseph is no longer around to be told. There is no one left in my life who is there only to be told" (223).

However, the last line of the story indicates that she no longer needs someone who is there only to be told, to eat her "sins." Joseph has done that for her. He of the "truly gross" sweater (214), himself "a kind of syphilitic of the soul" (213), has eaten them all. His death discloses the meaning of his life as a therapist. Sin eaters were needed for only "A couple of hours per patient. . . as opposed to twice a week for years and years, and *with the same result in the end*."[7] And the best part is that there is no talk involved: "'You wouldn't even have to listen to them,' he says. 'Not a blessed word. The sins are transmitted in the food.'" In the final scene there is no conversation; the narrator's transformation takes place in silence.

It is important to see that the narrator's dream is about meeting Joseph in an airport, a setting where journeys, boundary crossings, specifically journeys into "the heavens" begin. The narrator, then, is on the threshold of a significant boundary leap. In this context of an impending journey, Joseph's "sins"— "children's party cookies, white ones. . . decorated with silver balls and colored sugar"—float up towards her. What Joseph ironically calls his sins here become the catalyst for the narrator's entry into a new universe: "There are thousands of stars, thousands of moons, and as I reach for one they begin to shine" (224). Sin and death are no more, having been defeated by Joseph's death and return. He offers her his "sins" and she ascends with him into the heavens ("around us is dark space"). The narrator reaches to take a cookie and they become transformed into symbols of hope, the deathless heavens: thousands of shining stars and moons, a universe where death has been left behind. What happens in this dream is a passage from death to life set in contexts of boundary leaping and ritually eating white cookies, reminiscent of communion wafers: what is to be eaten is the offerer himself transformed, the eating of which transforms the eater.

What the narrator has at last learned about herself, it seems, is that she no longer needs Joseph to eat her sins—to be there to be told—because she is no longer in the desperate situation of failing to make sense of reality as when she first came to him. Through him, reality has been changed radically. She has been healed. Joseph's death is not the "act of desertion" (216) it had seemed, but an act of rescue. The moment of crisis precipitated by Joseph's death does not mean death has closed in on her too. On the contrary, and paradoxically, Joseph's death has brought her into an astonishing universe shining with possibilities of new life, of rescue from death.

TRANSFORMATIONS

The pattern of life overcoming death through a mediator with divine powers is a theme common both to Mark's sea-cycle and "The Sin Eater." In both stories, the power of death, and the boundary between life and death, seem dominant and immutable. However, both make the point that this is only apparent. Another theme common to both is the gradual revelation of the mediators' identity: disciples recognize their teachers' parables about seeds (Jesus) or house plants (Joseph) as teachings that life must be accepted for what it is. They also recognize that death is not finally the triumph of destruction and chaos because the Divine Parabler is stronger than death. Those who have "ears to hear" are the ones to whom the mystery of life overcoming death has been confided (see Mark 4:11). Jesus' disciples in Mark and the narrator in "The Sin Eater" have been initiated into this mystery and experience the transformation which accompanies it.

Both stories also emphasize the change in status of the central characters. Jesus undergoes a status transformation at the end of the story in his crucifixion and resurrection. Those who come to him also undergo similar transformations when he breaks the power death has had over them. This breaking of death's power in the sea-cycle is permeated with allusions to baptism, the ritual passage from death to life.

Joseph's death is also the radical transformation of his status. We learn that, like Jesus, he is more powerful than death and provides passage from death to life for the narrator, a woman who had been in the grasp of chaos, enduring an existence that made no sense. The breaking of death's power in "The Sin Eater" is illuminated with references to eating, because eating here connotes the ritual passage from death to life.

The mystery of the breaking of death's shackles, both stories suggest, is available to the divine teachers' disciples. The hope that life is not finally, utterly, and abjectly subject to death is a theme both universal and powerful. The hope of life's ultimate triumph over death is expressed in Mark's two-thousand year-old gospel, and in Margaret Atwood's modern short story. In both stories, readers experience a glimpse into a fascinating universe where the seemingly immutable boundary between life and death is crossed, and where thousands of stars and moons begin to shine: a new place where all who hear of it marvel (see Mark 5:20).

NOTES

1. See David Rhoads and Donald Michie, *Mark as Story: An Introduction to the Narrative of a Gospel* (Philadelphia: Fortress Press, 1982), p. 66; and Augustine Stock, *The Method and Message of Mark* (Wilmington: Glazier, 1989), p. 160.

2. The demon's name, "Legion" has led many commentators to interpret the story in light of the Roman occupation of the land. For such an approach see Ched Myers, *Binding the Strong Man: A Political Reading of Mark's Story of Jesus* (Maryknoll, NY: Orbis, 1988), pp. 190-94.

3. J. Duncan M. Derrett, "Legend and Event: The Gerasene Demoniac: An Inquest into History and Liturgical Projection," *Studia Biblica* 38, 1969), 202.

5. For a more thorough discussion of Mark's sea-cycle, see my "Markan Ecclesiology: An Anthropological Experiment," *Listening: Journal of Religion and Culture*, 23/2 (Spring, 1988), 95-105; and "Baptism, Miracles, and Boundary Jumping in Mark," *Biblical Theology Bulletin*, (November, 1990).

6. On the young man at the tomb as a baptismal image, see Robin Scroggs and Kent I. Groff, "Baptism in Mark: Dying and Rising with Christ," *Journal of Biblical Literature* 92 (1973), 531-48.

7. Emphasis added.

HIDDEN SINCE THE FOUNDATION OF THE WORLD: GIRARD, TURNER AND TWO MYTHIC READINGS
David Scott Arnold

I believe that the maze can be mapped out; we do not have to describe the same spirals interminably.

René Girard[1]

Stranded in the midst of a vast space which nobody has made sense out of for you, you settle down to mapmaking, charting the territory, the discovery of where things are in relation to each other, the extraction of meaning.

Margaret Atwood[2]

MYTHIC REALITY

Over the past four years, in courses bearing such titles as "Western Religious Thought" and "Religious Dimensions in Literature," I have encouraged my students to read and reread Margaret Atwood and the Gospel of Mark, and without fail such texts have proved to be pedagogical dynamite. I select Mark's gospel not only for its brevity but for its tight, immediate, insistent perplexity: it always challenges the class to view differently their understanding of gospel, narrative, implication of story, closure, sense of ending (or its lack)—all valorized dimensions of the critical winds coursing through and across journals, academic chatauquas, and hallways these past decades. And Atwood has proven to be as profound, exhilarating and disturbing a writer as the other regulars I invite into the seminar room, such as Melville, Joyce, Eliot and Murdoch. All such writers invite us to "dive deeply," as Melville once put it and Carol Christ once rephrased it, for they all engage us with the mythic dimension of reality. Whatever "dycrasia" hovers over discussions of the term "myth" (and such discussions are legion), to the last student we all *know* with Atwood that myth is at hand. We might know it with Mark's gospel, as well, but with Atwood it is a cinch. What does this mean?

The mythic approach to reading a text emerged in this century because of the encounters and discoveries made by those who felt they could get underneath or behind the literal level of meaning in a work of imagination, a cultural artifact, a dream. The encounters were initially anthropological and psychological— Frazer, Harrison, Tyler and Malinowski on the one hand, Freud and Jung on the other—and later adopted or elaborated for the literary critical understanding of texts, a move illustrated especially, I would suggest, by Maud Bodkin's provocative *Archetypal Patterns in Modern Poetry* (1934).

Now this move to get behind or beneath is a confidence held by myth criticism to discover the key that might unlock what seems at first blush to the rational mind to be perplexing or mysterious or riddling. Ordinary "daylight," commonsense thinking seems to be merely the tip of an iceberg lurking or ciphered beneath our conscious awareness. Myth and literature affect us as they do, suggests John Vickery, because they "arouse responses uncircumscribable by rational knowledge or empirical description . . . . [We find that] myth leaves us with the tantalizing mystery and puzzle as to its ultimate or real meaning."[3] It is this unconscious reality, myth critics believe, that dominates our private, individual and indeed collective, racial encounters with life, since it is from such chthonic depths that our dominant archetypes and myths of reality have emerged. The tenet espoused by this view is that *mythos* preceded *logos* and the best criticism ought to take one back to the mystery of experience. The primary aim of many myth critics in both religion and literature is the retrieving of buried meanings presently hidden from view, and we often therefore find such telling phrases as "Girard's enterprise of disclosure"[4] or Hopper's interest in a strategy that might enable us to tack truthfully into "the undisclosed [,into] that which still remains hidden within and behind the manifold expressions of our modern and contemporary arts."[5] Although we are not always put in mind of this perspective, there are imaginative authors out there who depend powerfully on it, and critics among us who make us mindful of its relevance for our understanding of human being. I should like in this brief essay to illustrate the significance of a mythic approach to such texts by drawing upon two contemporary critics versed in myth criticism, René Girard and his concept of mimeticism for Mark's gospel, and Victor Turner and his concept of liminality for Atwood's "The Sin Eater."

GIRARD ON MYTH

Throughout René Girard's career one finds expressed the confidence that myth represents what, at bottom, must be a primal gesture of mimetic desire grounded in violence. The clearest expression of this view may be found in an essay by Tobin Siebers, "Language, Violence and the Sacred":

> [M]yth and ritual exist to ensure the containment of violence. They maintain the false differences that motivated and rationalized originary acts of violence by creating narrative structures that obscure the role of the many in the victimization of the one. Myth and ritual distort the sequence of real events, making it impossible to return to any origin within the logic of the mythical narrative.[6]

Thus, Girard's very definition of myth expresses a triangular linkage among two desiring a third. I have used the word "primal" to suggest that his understanding of myth looks back to an originary scene of cultural violence that is powerfully suggested by the scapegoat mechanism, imperfectly erased by successive stages of cultural history. In an early chapter of *The Scapegoat* entitled "What Is a Myth?" we find the following: "Each time an oral or written testament mentions an act of violence that is directly or indirectly collective we question whether it includes the description of a social and cultural crisis."[7]

This observation, of course, immediately brings to mind Mark's account of the Gerasene demoniac. Because the account contains, indeed revolves around stereotypes of persecution that engender such cultural crisis, Girard sees Mark's narrative as an exemplary text that invites a mythic reading, an interpretive act that will help us to decipher the traces of the sacred imperfectly hidden in the documents before us.

And they *do* need deciphering. "We do not know how to decipher [such] documents."[8] We often find Girard remarking that we are always missing the boat in our interpretations of such texts, somehow unable to see "what they really are," not least because of their beguiling, puzzling, riddling "external trappings."

Girard directs our attention to myths as they relate to the "foundations of the world," our cultural symbol systems of meaning originally spun to foreclose an endless spiral of sacrificial violence. His is an essentializing perspective on myth that some have linked also with Mircea Eliade and Carl Jung. My point is that however long we have been inhibited from a true meaning of myth, Girard would have us believe that we now are able to behold "the only truly radical demystification available to us."[9]

If myth involves anything, it is a lack of differentiation, and Girard cites Lévi-Strauss as the first to note that many myths share a family resemblance (especially in their beginnings) by way of such terms. Girard would maintain that such lack is more than rhetorical—it is grounded in the actual experience of real persecution. Again: the origin of a myth is the real persecution of a scapegoat; such victimization is a reality deeply shaping human identity. This is the dynamic behind Girard's understanding of cultural anthropology and the myths we may hear to make sense of our lives. From such a perspective, one can well anticipate certain applications to the mythic story of the Geresene demoniac. Girard is adamant about its application:

> In historical persecutions the "guilty" remain sufficiently distinct from their "crimes" for there to be no mistake about the nature of the process. The same cannot be said of myth. The guilty person is so much a

part of his offense that one is indistinguishable from the other. His offense seems to be a fantastic essence or ontological attribute. In many myths the wretched person's presence is enough to contaminate everything around him. . . . The definition of victim as sinner or criminal is so absolute in myth, and the causal relationship between crime and collective crisis is so strong, that even perceptive scholars have as yet failed to disassociate these details and to identify the accusatory process. The persecution text, whether medieval or modern, provides the needed Ariadne's thread.[10]

If the scapegoat mechanism embodied in myth can be defused, can be shown for what it actually is—a false or demonic form of transcendence—then one will be free of its power, its "irresistible tendency to mimeticism."[11] This is precisely the demystifying function of the gospels, in Girard's view, and it is powerfully presented in the story of the Gerasene demoniac as a rendering of mimetic crisis. The victim, the one possessed who, having broken the chains of his community, wanders alone howling and stoning himself among the tombs, reminds us of those desperate images of laceration found in Dostoevsky's *The Brothers Karamazov*.

Girard is keen to point out the reciprocity between the possessed and the Gerasenes—they somehow conspire to resist definite expulsion, thereby achieving some communal valence: the mimetic character on both sides is evident, for "the possessed imitates these Gerasenes who stone their victims, but the Gerasenes in return imitate the possessed."[12] The same doubling is found in the attachment of the community to their demons mirrored in the demons' desire not to be expelled from the country of the Gerasenes. Girard's reading enables us to understand why the Gerasenes become anxious about the possessed victim "sitting there, clothed and in his full senses, the very man who had the legion in him before" in response to Jesus' healing.

Girard further unpacks this text by noting the significance of the fall from the high cliff for its collective and ritual connotations in response to the effect of a scapegoat. All differences are polarized onto the victim in a mythic crisis of mimetic conflict. But in the present text, there is a fundamental reversal, for the "miracle at Gerasa reverses the universal schema of violence fundamental to all societies of the world. . . .The drowning of the swine has a definitive character; it is an event without a future, except for the person cured by the miracle."[13]

The system of mimetic reciprocity in this community is threatened by the events leading up to the cure recounted in Mark's text. The demons anticipate this more lucidly than the humans. As Girard writes, "The only hope of the demons in the presence of Jesus is to remain on the edges of the universe where they formerly held sway in its most evil-smelling corners. The demons turn to him willingly for shelter from the abyss that threatens them.[14] But they do not survive. Not only is the demoniac cured, but the demons/Legion are drowned after having fallen from the high cliff. The system of cyclic violence has been utterly unhinged: "the treatment of these themes is extraordinary. It corresponds strictly to what is demanded at this point *by the revelation of the victim's mimeticism.*"[15]

TURNER ON MYTH

Both "The Gerasene Demoniac" and "The Sin Eater" are mythical stories of crisis seeking generative meaning in the face of disorder. Further, they both invite the mythically relevant concept of *limen*, because we feel that "the human cultural order is a kind of pointed veil over a deeper, superhuman order, the mysteries of which begin to be accessible only to those who have been stripped during initiation of profane status and profane rank."[16] But I shall direct the relevance of Turner's understanding of myth only to Atwood's story, in order that the reader might appreciate another perspective on the significance of myth.

The main distinction I wish to note is that Victor Turner is more attentive than Girard to the transitional movement embodied in mythicity, and therefore less willing to grant full ontological weight to the generative moment of origination (of which we are forever blind).[17] Myths for Turner address the transitional, the processive, the *movement* from there to here. They particularly reveal the nature of *liminality*.   Indeed, Turner defines myth in just such terms: "myths are liminal phenomena: they are frequently told at a time or in a sight that is 'betwixt and between.'"[18] This perspective on myth illuminates much of Atwood's "The Sin Eater," a story certainly rich in liminal imagery.

Margaret Atwood's writing has attracted the attention of myth critics for many reasons, one being that much of it is "structured according to the one recurrent narrative archetype, that of the rebirth journey, or quest into the unconscious," as Annis Pratt suggests in *Archetypal Patterns in Women's Fiction*.[19] Atwood is keenly attendant to the contours of our late "time," and much of her narrative power may be seen in her ability to draw us into that mythic space between event and meaning, to implicate us imaginatively by way of her mysterious, gnomic figures, to invite us into our "time between time," when the inherited traditions are no longer able to speak, and when therefore structural closure in our fictions is no longer felt to be at hand. "In myth," notes Turner, "we see nature and spirit" (two dominant mythic tropes in so much of Atwood's poetry and prose) "at their shaping work—and this in the liminal moment in and out of time."[20] One is reminded immediately of "The Sin Eater" closing, that fascinating dream sequence ending with the speaker entering the timeless, from "coming out" of ordinary reality to "going into" events registered in primordial time—beyond measurement, other than clock time. From earth to air, beyond description and thus beyond writing, to a literal *ek-stasis*, a standing outside of the body, we follow this shifting sense into a different medium of mythopoeic experience by way of the story's dreamlike quality. It might reveal the true nature of reality because of the language of this uncertain, exploratory telling, a revelation offered to the reader because of the reader's participation in the "mythic space." This last observation is another way of noting that Atwood is powerful because we are not let go of her narrative significance. How true is Ira Progoff's simple observation, "The subject of dream and myth reaches to the core of the nature of [human being]."[21] And the cultural limits are blurred in myth; boundaries are crossed, particularly in dreams, that mark meaningful moments of transition that signify flashings-forth of the numinous. As Stanley Hopper says elsewhere, "That we live within a symbolic reality . . . Our 'thinking'—religious, philosophical, literary—belongs to 'that prodigious net of numinous creation in which man is captured, although he himself has brought it forth' (Erich Neumann)."[22]

There is no need to rehearse the full narrative of "The Sin Eater" to reveal the relevance of a mythic reading. The teller finds herself presently in a liminal stage, in a dreamlike state of limbo. Her crisis is brought on by the death of her *pharmakon*, her psychic mentor, the gnomic Joseph, by all accounts a figure of mythic potency and perhaps her "cultural hero." He is revealed as lecherous, ironic—indeed, a dominant mark of his being a threshold figure—and *unpredictable*, forever negotiating all the logical moves of the narrator's imprecations, as she tries to fix him into some domesticated pattern of social accommodation.

A mythic reading cannot help but note the portal through which we enter this strange *rite de passage*—the myth of "the sin eater." This myth defines much of the way the narrator's encounter with otherness will be interpreted, for it suggests the power of the marginal figure to absorb disorder, to stay the chaos, by ingesting the threat to the community—the same theme engendering the tension presented in Mark's story of the Gerasene demoniac.

Joseph, in a real sense, has guided the dreamer into this mythical world we read, between the no longer (his life) and the not yet (her life), and so we find her in the process of connecting with the sacred, with those emblems of *numinosum*[23] which cloak and envelope such a liminal encounter. ("Only connect," E. M. Forster says early in our century.) Thus, one might say that the central symbols of "The Sin Eater" are death and rebirth. As an initiand, the teller reviews, hears again the recitation offered by Joseph that assumes a kind of salvific power for her. The rite of the sin eater does not function as a cautionary tale or as a "guide to ordinary life." Rather, it brings the narrator "temporarily into close rapport with the primary or primordial generative powers of the cosmos, the acts of which transcend rather than transgress the norms of human secular society."[24]

As Joseph says, these sin eaters are destitute in order that they can keep "body and soul together." He draws the narrator into a depth where she might learn "to raise calla lilies in [her] cellar," a depth later referred to as Joseph's darkness. Joseph, who "makes you imagine . . . what it's like to be dead," Joseph, who falls out of a tree, an act that becomes an expression of irrationality when used by his first wife ("Are you totally out of your tree?" she cries, in disbelief when hearing a suggestion from his second wife about a possible procedure in performing Joseph's wake)—in such illustrations we see that Joseph's significance provides and pervades the mythic contours of this telling.

It is from her dream-state descent into this subconscious realm, where Joseph's darkness becomes hers, that the possibility of surfacing is revealed by the story's tentative, radically immanental conclusion. She may have discovered that in "seeing things as they are and letting things be as they are [,] a new movement from reality to Reality is possible. Thus, there is not a rejection of the mythological imagination in our time but a new approach to it."[25] We are left with the narrator in the space of this mythicized realm, where we find a freedom symbolizing the teller's need to go beyond the limits of her previous state of being, and so she is enveloped in a suspended time shot through with transcendent images of the *numinosum.* By the end of the story, we participate with the narrator in hints of recovery, in that "liminality," as Turner puts it, which "strains toward universality but never realizes it."[26] Her hand reaches for the stars, and she sees that they begin to shine only when she remembers that Joseph is dead. It is he who has provided the dark space, and from that grounding in his "unfinished room" she emerges beholding a beginning felt to be epiphanous. Atwood has once again fashioned a liminal tale engaging our imagination by way of the stuff of myth, another fiction which might help us "only connect" with a life, as Joseph says, without rescue.

NOTES

1. René Girard, *"To double business bound:" Essays on Literature, Mimesis, and Anthropology* (Baltimore: Johns Hopkins University Press, 1978), p. 224.

2. Margaret Atwood, "Northrop Frye Observed," *Second Words* (Boston: Beacon Press, 1984), p. 405.

3. John B. Vickery, "Literature and Myth," in Jean-Pierre Barricelli and Joseph Gibaldi, eds., *Interrelations of Literature* (New York: The Modern Language Association of America, 1982), p. 72.

4. Burton Mack, "Introduction: Religion and Ritual," in Robert G. Hamilton-Kelly, ed., *Violent Origins: Ritual Killing and Cultural Formation* (Stanford: Stanford University Press, 1987), p. 20.

5. Stanley Romaine Hopper, "Jerusalem's Wall and Other Perimeters," in Howard Hunter, ed., *Humanities, Religion and the Arts Tomorrow* (New York: Holt, Rinehart and Winston, 1972), p. 229.

6. Tobin Siebers, "Language, Violence and the Sacred," in *To Honor René Girard*, Alphonse Juilland, ed. (Saratago, CA: ANMA Libri & Co., 1986), p. 215. This volume, to my knowledge, is the most adequate and helpful to date in showing the relevance of Girard's thought for our time.

7. René Girard, *The Scapegoat* (Baltimore: Johns Hopkins University Press, 1986), p. 24.

8. Girard, *The Scapegoat*, p. 24.

9. Girard, *The Scapegoat*, p. 30.

10. Girard, *The Scapegoat*, p. 36.

11. Girard, *The Scapegoat*, p. 183.

12. Girard, *The Scapegoat*, p. 171.

13. Girard, *The Scapegoat*, p. 179.

14. Girard, *The Scapegoat*, p. 181.

15. Girard, *The Scapegoat*, p. 179. My emphasis.

16. Victor Turner, "Myth and Symbol," in David L. Sills, ed., *International Encyclopedia of the Social Sciences*, Vol. 10 (New York: Macmillan Company & Free Press, 1968), p. 580.

17. For another example illustrating the mutual relevance of Girard and Turner in another medium, see Paisley Livingston, *Ingmar Bergman and the Rituals of Art* (Ithaca and London: Cornell University Press, 1982), pp. 92-97.

18. Turner, "Myth and Symbol," p. 576.

19. Annis Pratt, *Archetypal Patterns in Women's Fiction* (Bloomington: Indiana University Press, 1980), p. 135.

20. Turner, "Myth and Symbol," p. 581.

21. Ira Progoff, "Waking Dream and Living Myth," in Joseph Campbell, ed., *Myths, Dreams, Religion* (New York: E. P. Dutton & Co., 1970), p. 176.

22. Stanley Romaine Hopper, "'*Le Cri de Merlin!*' or Interpretation and the Metalogical," in Joseph P. Strelka, ed., *Anagogic Qualities of Literature* (University Park and London: Pennsylvania State University Press, 1971), p. 15.

23. For a very accessible discussion of this term as it relates to the mythical in experience, see Aniela Jaffe, *The Myth of Meaning* (New York: Penguin Books, 1975), passim.

24. Turner, "Myth and Symbol," p. 577.

25. Lynn Ross-Bryant, "Literature as Mythopoesis," in *Imagination and the Life of the Spirit* (Chico, CA: Scholars Press, 1981), p. 187.

26. Turner, "Myth and Symbol," p. 579. The best comprehensive introduction to myth as it relates to the study of literature might be

Vincent Leitch, "Chapter Five: Myth Criticism," in *American Literary Criticism from the Thirties to the Eighties* (New York: Columbia University Press, 1988).   A more difficult but deeply rewarding work is that of Eric Gould, *Mythical Intentions in Modern Literature* (Princeton: Princeton University Press, 1981).   A fine book on the relevance of myth for the study of religion and modernity is Ivan Strenski, *Four Theories of Myth in Twentieth-Century History: Cassirer, Eliade, Lévi-Strauss and Malinowski* (Iowa City: University of Iowa Press, 1987).

THE REDEMPTIVE TEXT
Dorothy Figueira

EXPLANATION AND INTERPRETATION

We have before us two texts which deal with the theme of exorcism, one consisting of a scriptural passage and the other a fictional retelling of a myth. What are the grounds of interpretation relative to Scripture? Do they differ from those of literature? In other words, if a text is Scripture, does it demand a privileged reading or should Scripture be read and interpreted in the same manner as literature?

Two fundamental approaches can be adopted with respect to a text. They are contained in the verbs "to explain" and "to interpret." In modern criticism, structural, psychoanalytic, and deconstructive analyses serve as possible modes of explanation. As methods, they lack universal application. Certain authors, genres and epochs lend themselves to one method above others. Furthermore, is not the very validity of seeking to explain human existence using ingenuously scientific terminology a questionable endeavor? It is easy to borrow from the sciences models with which we attempt to understand human discourse. Ultimately, however, the reader must question the assumptions that lead to the choice of one model over another. A cogent response to the infraction of scientific methods prevalent in recent criticism can be found in the work of Hans-Georg Gadamer, a philosopher who counters systems based on the assumptions of technology with articulate hermeneutic theories grounded in the historical reality of humanity. Gadamer's method seeks to establish a hermeneutic based on humankind comporting itself in history, presented as the pre-existing loam of life and the human quality underpinning existence. He provides a schema for perceiving the operation of wisdom in history and literature without artificially omitting the factor of application. In other words, Gadamer calls upon the reader to submit to the governing rules of the text. In the following pages, I shall examine the role of literary and biblical hermeneutics within the larger context of general hermeneutics and discuss the texts before us in light of Gadamer's theories.

GADAMER'S HERMENEUTICS

Hermeneutics entails traversing the distance between the text and the present situation. Through Gadamer's basic concept of effective historical consciousness,[1] the individual becomes aware that the tradition of the text affects his situation and seeks to clarify not only the horizon of the present situation but also the horizon of the text. Thus, Gadamer equates understanding with application. We are able to apply a text because, as historical beings, we possess traditions.[2] The hermeneutic task arises when the interpreter, familiar with the subject matter of the text through tradition, recognizes that he is, at the same time, a stranger to it.

Understanding consists in the fusion of the horizons of the text and the interpreter.[3] The continuous tradition of the text bridges the temporal distance between the text and its interpreter by establishing a common prejudicial pre-understanding of the subject matter. Toward belonging historically to a text, the reader must put his prejudices at stake in a confrontation with the text. These prejudices can either be legitimate or illegitimate, true or false.

Once freed from any purely negative connotation, prejudices are seen as the conditions through which we experience. In order to understand the text of a tradition, the interpreter has to engage him in a conversation with the text. The interpretation of art always involves self-understanding as it involves a meeting of worlds (horizon of the work and observer). It is important to realize that, for Gadamer, the experience of art is not subjective because it does not involve a possession of individual consciousness; its truth belongs to both subject and object (the art work). Gadamer, therefore, maintains that the dialectical terms of the question and answer develop the only logical form of being open for truth claims. The text itself asks its question before the interpreter begins to question the text. In Gadamer's system the reader is neither implied nor passive. The individual acts as mediator between history and the future through his being-in-history.

FROM SCHLEIERMACHER TO GADAMER

With his interpretive system, Gadamer serves as both an heir and critic of nineteenth-century hermeneutic thought.[4] Reformation hermeneutics emphasized that the message of Scripture stood in the way of natural pre-understanding of human beings. Faith alone (i.e., faith in God's becoming man and in the resurrection) promised justification. Thus, one's good works were what the interpretation of Scripture demanded. Christian worship became confession, empowerment and a call to faith. It rested as much as possible on the correct interpretation of the Christian message. Once the interpretation of Scripture in a sermon became more prominent in the Christian worship service, the task of theological hermeneutics came to the fore, not serving a scientific understanding so much as the practice of proclamation by which good news was supposed to reach the simple person in such a way that he realized that he was addressed and intended.[5] Consequently, application was not a mere "application" of understanding, but the true core of understanding itself. It represented not only an essential moment in the hermeneutics of religious texts but made the significance of hermeneutic questions as a whole visible; its role surpassed that of a methodological instrument.

In the age of Romanticism, Schleiermacher and his successors developed hermeneutics into a universally applicable teaching skill or technique (*Kunstlehre*) which ostensively legitimized the peculiarity of theological science and its methodology. With Schleiermacher, the modern notion of science brought pressure to bear upon the self-understanding of hermeneutics; that is, it was forced to overcome complete alienation of the subject. The critical imposition of an artificial apparatus intended to open up whatever is alien and make it one's own supplanted the communicative ability through which people mediate themselves along with the tradition in which they stand.

Schleiermacher's contribution to hermeneutics, his introducing of psychological interpretation alongside normally used grammatical interpretation, was further developed by Wilhelm Dilthey, who held that all the traditional methods of hermeneutics (grammatical, historical, aesthetic, psychological) attain a higher realization of the ideal of understanding only insofar as all means and methods serve the comprehension of the individual structure as such. In this manner, Dilthey constructed a precedent for literary criticism's desire to discern the singularly valid structure and to distinguish it from all that does not match its standards.

In *Truth and Method*, Gadamer opens his discussion on theological hermeneutics with the following quotation from Rudolf Bultmann: "The interpretation of the biblical writings are [sic] subject to exactly the same conditions as any other literature."[6] Gadamer reads Bultmann as implying the presupposition of a living relationship between the interpreter and the text that he calls a fore-understanding. He then asks whether this fore-understanding exists innately in humans as beings concerned with the questions of God or whether it comes from God (in the form of faith). In other words, Gadamer questions both the universal validity of fore-understanding as well as its sole derivation from the vantage point of true faith. For Gadamer, Scripture exemplifies a larger hermeneutic problem: what occurs in the confrontation with an alien tradition to which one has never belonged or which one no longer unquestionably accepts?[7]

Gadamer suggests that our relation to the New Testament should be understood both in terms of the self-understanding of faith and the relationship between understanding and play. Gadamer likewise directs us back to the relationship of myth and *logos*, noting that the relation of the Christian theologian to the biblical text is similar to that of the Greek to the myth. Myth like the biblical narrative, we are to assume, must not be defined on the basis of modern science but from the point of view of the acceptance of *kerygma*, in terms of an inner claim of faith.[8] The understanding of a text begins with a dialogue: what is said in a text begins to find expression in the interpreter's own language and is taken up in such a fashion that it speaks and finds an answer in the words of the interpreter's own language.

To the extent that one's self-understanding is dominated by modern science and method, it is difficult to hold fast to theological insight and religious experience. Gadamer represents self-understanding based on scientific procedures as a form of self-possession that precludes the very possibility of transcendence. If understanding and the possibility of self-transcendence demand a loss of self, then the structure of the game supplies an important component to the hermeneutic process.[9] The game and one's absorption in it function as a means to ecstatic self-forgetting, the free buoyancy of an elevation above oneself. What elements comprise the relationship between faith and understanding in terms of the freedom of the game? By "game," Gadamer specifically does not mean an arbitrary and subjective attitude, but rather a dynamic whole, a back and forth movement wherein the subject relinquishes autonomy.[10]

Gadamer concludes, therefore, that the interpretation of Scripture, as opposed to literature, necessitates its acceptance by the believer as valid truth. Religious texts offer valid understanding only for someone accepting the alternative of belief or disbelief. Scripture addresses only those allowing themselves to be addressed. The believer can only understand the text if it speaks directly to him. Moreover, the status of Scripture as proclamation renders its success dependent on the power of the word itself; the proclamation cannot be detached from its fulfillment. In the sermon, the scriptural text receives its full reality (rather than the reality it possesses in commentary or exegesis) when it communicates the understanding of what Scripture says and also bears witness itself.[11] The actual completion of understanding does not take place in the sermon as such, but in its reception as an appeal directed to each person who hears it. The text of the New Testament is already an interpretation of the Christian message; it simultaneously functions as a mediator of this message. The proclamation of the gospel speaks through all earlier mediations in a way comparable to the repetition of a legend or the continual renewal and transformation of a mythical tradition in literature. Thus, the real event of understanding goes beyond what we can bring through methodological effort and critical self-control.

Gadamer, after qualifying the privileged reading of Scripture, notes that it otherwise shares the general interpretive model that he assigns to literature. The primary task of understanding

Scripture, as in the case of literature, rests on the reader's application. The term "application" provides an essential factor in any hermeneutical system, whether it be historical, literary or theological. To understand Scripture demands the establishment of its relation to the present. One has not understood Scripture until it can be applied to the situation at hand. Scripture cannot be understood aesthetically or historically because its claim to be applicable in the present comprises an essential element of its nature.

Thus, Gadamer privileges the reading of Scripture within the general context of historical and literary hermeneutics. Literature, however, does not consist of an arbitrary accumulation of signs. Already in his interpretive system, Gadamer reifies the understanding of literature through the concept of application. Interpretation of Scripture, while privileged, enjoys the elevated status accorded to literature in general.

GADAMER'S HERMENEUTICS, THE DEMONIAC, AND THE SIN EATER

Viewed in this context, Gadamer would apply the same criteria to his interpretation of the myth of the sin eater in the Atwood short story as he would to the tale of the Gerasene demoniac in Mark 5. Our reading of the New Testament passage would, however, be governed by the additional criterion of its status as *kerygma*.

Atwood sets up a relationship between the narrator and her psychiatrist, a dynamic which consists of her needs versus his attempt to convince her to take responsibility for her attitudes, anger and expectations of him. The reader is thus confronted with a situation that foregrounds the necessity of taking responsibility for the totality of one's experience in reality. The narrative poses this question in a dynamic fashion, expressed both mythologically (the sin eater story) and in a modern psychiatric configuration. The psychiatrist's telling of the sin eater story, of a ritualistic custom from the past, functions thus as a metaphor for the contemporary events related in the narrative. The crisis arises with the psychiatrist's death. Here, the focus of tension shifts.

The demands of a broader experience of reality are thrust upon the narrator as a result of her interaction with the other women in the therapist's life. The funeral scene is thematically contiguous with the sin eater tale. While the narrator eats at the wake she is forced, whether she likes it or not, to "eat" the "sins" of her therapist's life beyond the consultation room. He no longer functions merely as the helper and guide in her search for stability, but has become more fully human with the revelation of his sins. These "sins," as the dream metaphor expresses, are too rich. However, the narrator cannot escape the responsibility of "eating" them. Beyond the grave, the psychiatrist performs his last therapeutic act, forcing his patient to abandon her defensive posture and assume a place in the world.

According to Gadamer, the interpretive process involves the dialectic of question and answer. Again, the question which "The Sin Eater" asks concerns the nature of responsibility. The problem of responsibility appears in various guises. The narrator's ambiguous attitude manifests itself in her relationship to the therapist: she is both reluctant to give up her cynicism and in need of rescue. Clearly, the narrator prefers to rely on the therapist and is, predictably, "furious with him" for the act of climbing the tree that led to his death. He was guilty of "risking all our lives," and his death serves as "an act of desertion."

The therapist's wife and ex-wives present different approaches to the question of responsibility. These women also provide information concerning the therapists's "sins." The narrator reacts to these revelations with fear: "I do not need his darkness." The concluding dream sequence brings together all preceding elements of the narrative and foregrounds the narrator's need to "eat the sins" of the therapist as a prerequisite for spiritual growth.

A striking aspect of "The Sin Eater" involves its metaphoric dimension. The narrator's quest can be seen to reflect Gadamer's concept of the movement of hermeneutic understanding: finding one's own in the alien, becoming at home in it, as the fundamental movement of the spirit, whose being is only a return to itself from being otherwise.[12] The narrator's "therapy" replicates the hermeneutic quest with the exception that this woman does not set out upon a quest for self-transcendence, but life and circumstances force it upon her. Her movement toward self-understanding remains essentially on the unconscious level of her dream. Nevertheless, the initial misconception of the narrator in Atwood's story reflects the self-alienation of the subject before the hermeneutic quest. The subject resolves this conflict in recognizing that the alien is, in reality, "part of its true home" in the spiritual sense. Likewise, for the reader, the answer to the question of the text involves the fusion of each reader's own horizon, her relationship to accepting responsibility, and the horizon of the text expressed in the mythological, metaphoric and psychiatric configurations of the narrative.

Gadamer would approach Mark 5 as he would a work of literature. The question of the text can also be perceived as one of recognition. Using Gadamer's concept of application, the reader makes these issues valid for her own experience. However, Gadamer adds another dimension to the literary hermeneutic: Scripture cannot question truth claims; there are no true or false prejudices whose validity we must test. The text's meaning is really Christ's coming as the Word. In Mark 5, hermeneutic recognition implies belief; belief in God as God wields such power that the most pathetic are cured. Hence, belief brings redemption. Thus, the interpretive act is taken to mean exactly what the passage is taken to mean. My interpretation makes sense only as a projection of my belief (or even, doubting belief) in Christ's love for humankind and his sacrifice on the cross to free us from sin. Mark is then both the (con)text and the interpretive system. To the extent to which the psychiatrist takes the sins of others on himself, he functions as Jesus. Just as the patient confronts the experience of the psychiatrist as a total being when he dies, so too must the believer confront Christ as a total being in light of his death. Most importantly, however, both the demoniac in Mark 5, the patient, and the reader must return to their natural environment with greater awareness.

In Gadamer's interpretive system, the reader is called upon to surrender herself in self-interpretation. However, the philosopher suggests that the scriptural text's status as *kerygma* implies not only our applying the text but, to a certain extent, the text appropriating us. Following Aristotle, Gadamer holds that the notion of experience does not allow for the ideal of the nonparticipating observer but endeavors to open our reflective awareness of the community that binds everyone together. Gadamer reiterates this point and stresses the way in which the being of the interpreter pertains intrinsically to the being of what is to be interpreted. Whoever wants to understand something already brings along prejudices that anticipatorily join her with what she wants to understand, a sustaining agreement. Therefore, it is never a simple application of knowledge and methods to an arbitrary object. Only one who stands within a given tradition is in a position to receive the questions that a given text poses. According to Gadamer, in the case of both literature and Scripture, the reader no longer stands alienated and need not function as a pawn in a world without text, value or redemption.

NOTES

1. Hans-Georg Gadamer, "Die Kontinuität der Geschichte und der Augenblick der Existenz," *Geschichte: Element der Zukunft* (Tübingen: J.C.B. Mohr, 1956), p. 41, defines this term in the following manner: "What I mean [by effective historical consciousness] is first that we do not raise ourselves out of the event and, as it were, approach it in such a way that the past becomes an object to us."

2. Hans-Georg Gadamer, *Truth and Method* (New York: Seabury, 1975), p. 257.

3. Gadamer, *Truth and Method*, p. 364: the result of interpretation (*Auslegung*) consists of the fusion of the horizons of the text and the interpreter i.e., the realization (*Vollendungsweise*) of effective historical consciousness.

4. Hans-Georg Gadamer, *Reason in the Age of Science*, Frederick G. Lawrence, tr. (Cambridge, MA: MIT Press, 1982), pp. 126-31.

5. Gadamer, *Reason in the Age of Science*, p. 129.

6. Gadamer, *Truth and Method*, p. 295.

7. In specific instances of our confrontation with the language or discourse of art, another possible hermeneutic problem can occur. What happens when no powerful tradition exists into which one's own attitude may be absorbed?

8. Hans-Georg Gadamer, *Philosophical Hermeneutics* (Berkeley: University of California Press, 1976), p. 53.

9. Gadamer, *Philosophical Hermeneutics*, p. 51.

10. Gadamer, *Truth and Method*, pp. 91-114.

11. Gadamer, *Philosophical Hermeneutics*, pp. 57-58.

12. Gadamer, *Truth and Method*, pp. 14-15.

SIN EATING AND SIN MAKING:
THE POWER AND LIMITS OF LANGUAGE
Martha   Burdette

FORT AND *DA*

Just as Sigmund Freud borrowed from literature to explain his therapy, his model of the mind, and his method, so literary critics have appropriated psychoanalytic theory and method to interpret fictive and nonfictive texts.[1] Such interpretations can focus on character analysis, narrative structure, conflict, the author, or the writing process itself, to name but a few possible topics.   In each case, the critic, using psychoanalysis, this "systematic study of self-deception,"[2] looks beyond what is present in the language of the text, to fill the gap between what is said and what is really meant, between what is intended and what is actually done, and/or between what one wants and what one can truly have. Patterns of textual repetition, traces, and substitutions provide ways of connecting what is present in the text to what is absent.

One of the most engaging and helpful passages in psychoanalytic texts for use in interpreting the Markan passage and Margaret Atwood's "The Sin Eater" is related by Freud in *Beyond the Pleasure Principle,* originally published in 1920.   In one section Freud relates the beginnings of language and narrative development in his eighteen-month-old grandson.   It seems that the child is left alone in his bed for long periods of time while his mother is outside.   During her absence the child plays a game with his favorite toy, a cotton reel attached to a string.   Throwing the reel over the side of the bed while holding on to the string, the baby exclaims, "ooh," which Freud interprets to be the German word *fort*, meaning "gone" or "away."   Then, drawing the reel to himself once again, the young child says joyfully, "a," which, to Freud, sounds like *da*, or "there" in English.

Freud interprets his grandson's activity as the baby's way of representing and coping with the mother's absence, discovering in the process the power of language to express his desire.   The baby can control the object of desire, the mother, by substituting the reel for her, yanking it to and fro to suit his needs. According to the Freudian model, all infants try from the point of separation from the mother to regain her. Indeed, from infancy through adulthood, the individual, unable to have the mother, will substitute one object of desire after another for her. The substituted object of desire in the case of Freud's grandson is the reel.

In pairing the reel's movements with the words *fort* and *da*, the baby has constructed, as the critic Terry Eagleton notes, a primitive narrative in which a lost or absent object is recovered.[3] Such goal-directed action is the basis of narrative, for, as Peter Brooks explains, the drive to restore the lost, changed, or absent object is the momentum for all plots.[4]

The *fort-da* game is also useful in understanding the role of the interpretive community in giving the narrative meaning. The baby assigns order or structure to the mother's actions and uses sounds he has picked up from the language around himself to make his meaning known to others. The baby, in using *fort* and *da*, does not make up his own language for which he alone assigns meaning. Neither does he use words unrelated to the reel's action or his goal. Instead, meanings are based on interpersonal experiences he has had with his interpretive community. This third view of language development is called "dialogism"[5] and is based on the assumption that language evolves out of a dialogue between people. Freud, part of the baby's interpretive community, puts together the baby's sounds, the context, and the movements of the reel and perceives the combination to be a representation of the baby's desire for the mother's presence.

Through the use of words, the baby unites his personal experiential knowledge with the larger experience of knowledge held by his community. This "union experience,"[6] which permits humans to relate through "rented" meanings, however, has limitations and drawbacks in representing experience. The language version of experience and the experience itself may not fit well, leaving what is experienced poorly named or misrepresented entirely. This idea of slippage between "world knowledge" and "word knowledge" has been duly noted by postmodern writers and critics and is particularly striking in the two texts of this study.[7] The drive to restore meaning through language, successfully accomplished in the Markan passage, is thwarted in Atwood's postmodern text.

SANITY THROUGH LANGUAGE

In the Markan text, the Gerasene demoniac's lost sanity is successfully restored through language. The demon-possessed man roams the tombs around Gerasene, crying and babbling in language that his community cannot understand, unlike the babble of Freud's grandson that can be interpreted as a meaningful utterance. Jesus uses language as a tool to name the demons. Jesus first calls for the "unclean spirit" to come out of the Gerasene. When the demoniac recognizes and names his tormentor "Jesus, Son of the Most High God" (5:7), Jesus asks for the demon's name. Once Legion speaks his name to Jesus, the demons are projected into a herd of swine. The Gerasene, cleansed by Jesus' words, desires to follow his interpreter, but is left instead with words, with a miraculous story which he is instructed to tell others. This story of the transference of sin onto the swine, also considered unclean, prepares the Gerasene's audience and others for a later story of transference. The transference of humankind's sins to Christ will be the narrative that all believers will be instructed to repeat to others.

This is the text that Atwood writes over in "The Sin Eater." As with the *fort-da* game and the miracle of the Gerasene demoniac, a marginal figure looks to language and to an interpreter to restore meaning to her life. Instead of a biblical narrative that reflects a deeper master narrative—the Christian message, the Good Word—we find a postmodern narrative that "uses and abuses, installs and then subverts, the very concepts it challenges." [8] Atwood uses language to show how language fails to explain the experiential, how language fails to make meaning. The unnamed narrator is furious that her interpreter Joseph and her own words have deserted her, leaving her without rescue in a world of simulacra.

Joseph, the analyst, is supposed to be the Witness to Truth. He is supposed to hear her stories and interpret her dreams so that the past will open up and shed light on her present.[9] Joseph should remain silent, play dead, while she exposes her neurosis through slips of the tongue, obsessional repetitions, and verbal discrepancies between what she says and what she feels. Like the biblical Joseph, who saved his people, her Joseph must help her reconnect the symbolic reference with the signifiers, that is (á la Freud's grandson), connect the reel with the mother. Since she has already spoken or conceived in language the rejected experience before repressing it, she, the analysand, should be able to re-integrate the signification into discourse with the analyst's help during the analytic process.

The narrator's Joseph, however, does not remain silent. He tells his own stories about flowers and wives, and even complains about his work. He does not care much to hear about her dreams, and he certainly does not care to tell her what the dreams mean. She should tell him. Moreover, he does not set himself up as the Witness to Truth: "Life in most ways was a big pile of shit, he said. That was axiomatic" (215).[10] Instead of just "playing dead" so the psychoanalytic process can reveal the split between the analysand's unconscious and the analysand's conscious, Joseph actually dies.

Like the analysand, Joseph can no longer trust language to say what he wants it to say or use it to find meaning. He distrusts phones, carriers of spoken language, preferring to see the clients in the flesh so that he can pair the verbal with the nonverbal to understand what his patient is really saying. After all, Joseph believes that "most of the message in any act of communication. . . [is] nonverbal" (216). Just as the narrator finds it hard to know when Joseph is "running off at the mouth" (220), so Joseph views so much of what his patients tell him as "fakery or invention" (215). Joseph even proposes a nonverbal approach to analysis: he suggests the eating of a patient's sins at the verge of death, a meal free of words, of sentimental fictions, as the perfect solution for the weary analyst.

NONVERBAL CUES

In the postmodernist's style, however, Atwood shows that nonverbal cues are no more reliable than spoken language. The nonverbal, as well as the verbal, has replicas. Just as the narrator's question *"What am I going to do?"* can always be replaced by *"What am I going to wear?"* (216), so the nonverbal presents substitutions. The wives, "all blondish and vague around the edges" (221), resemble each other; indeed, they seem to run together. One wife wears a replica of a bird's nest that even contains eggs. Like the felt skirts with appliqués of cats and telephones the narrator has worn in high school, replicas are everywhere.

The nonverbal, like the verbal, also misrepresents situations. The narrator expects dark clothes and funereal looking dresses and decorations. Instead, the wives all wear pastels, and the food and flowers bespeak celebration rather than loss. Joseph's office, with all its loose ends, gives every indication that Joseph can walk in at any moment.

Atwood presents the complex, contradictory, and slippery play of nonverbal signifiers best in the narrator's dream. In the essentially nonverbal manifestation of the unconscious, the latent dream-thoughts of the dreamer's suppressed desire find form. The woman's anxiety dream about dinner parties "one plate short" has evolved into a last supper for Joseph's sins. The dream-work distorts and conflates two wishes: "I wish Joseph were alive," and "I must cope with the tragedy of Joseph's death." As a consequence, Joseph first appears alive, then dead, then alive again. Freud suggests that such alternation between life and death in one dream may signify a wish for indifference to a death, which helps the dreamer deny an intense emotional response to the death. An analysis of the first two of the dream's early segments presents the concatenation of the subject's desire, which has only been present in neurotic symptoms to this point.

The first segment presents the dream's milieu, a condensation of the day's residue and ongoing fears. Appropriately, it is a departure scene in an airport terminal, which conflates her fear of heights, her sense of "not going anywhere" in a senseless life, and her need for escape. The sounds of crying women and children and the laughter of other travelers fill her ears. To some degree, both groups symbolize the responses to Joseph's wake—a strange blend of celebrating and mourning that the subject, deeply concerned with proper appearances, has found unsettling. Unlike the avoidance behavior that marked her responses at the wake— she did not want to know any secrets—the woman seeks information at the ticket counter to no avail. The realization that she is without a passport, necessary not only for travel, but also to identify herself, contributes to her anxiety and decision to leave.

In the second dream segment, Joseph spots her and she looks at him. The gaze moves quickly to his clothing, rather heavy for summer. The woman tries, as usual, to make sense of Joseph's appearance and behavior: "I've never seen him in any of these clothes before. Of course, I think, he's cold, but now he's pushed through the people, he's beside me. . . . His own hand is bright blue, a flat tempera-paint blue, a picture-book blue. I hesitate, then I shake the hand but he doesn't let go, he holds me" (217-18).

The selection and presentation of the cold, blue hand conflates death and a deity—a dying, resurrected god. The blue signifies the cold touch of death and her memory of the blue-faced god Krishna appearing on the cover of her son's magazine. Of course, the book belongs to the robin-burying son, who leaves "a sort of bathtub ring of objects"/"a deposit"/ "sandwiches with bites taken out"/ "cigarette butts" (221), much as Joseph leaves a littered, smelly office with dying begonias—unfinished and unwashed. Like Krishna, Joseph is surrounded by "adoring maidens." Unlike Krishna, who represents removal from this world, Joseph signifies coping/deserting for the subject. Either way, there is no rescue.

This image of Joseph as death/resurrection in the dream is but one link in the chain of life/death, light/darkness, male/female, analyst/analysand, up/down, dirty/clean, and fictive/non-fictive, that play of opposites and substitutes ever present behind what the patient has expressed or will express in spoken language. Joseph, the powerful male deity of her dream, associated with the moon, stars, and darkness, and with Dumuzi/Tammuz, the vegetation god of presence/absence mourned especially by women, refuses to stay buried. The death/regeneration motif is overdetermined by Joseph's association with trees and a broken bough, a golden flower and the need to stick "the sod" who picked it, as well as by Joseph's desire to bring new life by listening to people's "sins." Joseph "doesn't let go" (223) but holds the subject's hand "confidingly" as the second segment ends.

DESIRE AND ABSENCE

Like Freud's grandson and the Gerasene demoniac, the narrator of Atwood's text longs for an absent object, a person who can/should understand all, someone "who is there only to be told" (223). In dreaming about Joseph, she yanks the reel toward her to bring closure to her narrative. Just as Freud's grandson and the Gerasene are left with a story to substitute for the missing object of desire, so is the nameless woman.

Atwood's character's story, however, does not have the same neat closure as does the Gerasene's in the biblical text. The dream ending floats into infinity. The dreamer reaches for a cookie, and the shining stars and moons of the sugary cookie coating become "real" stars and moons, but we, the readers, are not sure that she eats it, or if she eats it, what she knows about Joseph's sin. Perhaps it is as she recounts earlier in the narrative after waking from the dream but before recounting it in the secondary elaboration of language: "Joseph is no longer around to be told. There is no one left in my life who is there only to be told." Is this because she now knows his sins? Is this because she has accepted his death? Or is it both or neither?

Atwood's choice of narrator in this postmodern rendering of the psychoanalytic process parodies the women of Freud's studies on hysteria. Anna O., Dora, and Emma von N. tell secrets to the great Witness to Truth, who subsequently leads them, through language, to the source of their problems.[11] Joseph's patient, however, does not connect the signifiers with signifieds to bring sense to her life narrative. Joseph leaves the narrator much as her son leaves his paperback books—"face-down and open in the middle" (221). Language, whether spoken or nonverbal, is like a "bathtub ring of objects" (221) that muddies attempts to explain the world and leads nowhere but around and around. Instead of being able to name the demons and call them out, Atwood's frustrated analyst joins the swine.

A psychoanalytic reading of these nonfictive and fictive narratives thus makes us confront one of the most important discussions of our age: the meaning-making abilities and difficulties inherent in language. Freud's grandson, a twentieth-century Sisyphus, rolls an object and writes in space and with words his story of desire. There is futility in the gesture, for the words and the reel can never be nor adequately replace the mother. The young child, like Sisyphus, is locked into a situation over which he has no control, and yet he must make meaning of his game. The significance seems to come in his persistence, in the goal-directedness of his struggle in the meaning-making process. It is as Joseph says: "You're stuck; . . . now you have to decide how best to cope" (215).

NOTES

1. Examples of psychoanalytic literary criticism are Frederick Crews, *Out of My System: Psychoanalysis, Ideology and Critical Method* (New York: Oxford University Press, 1975); Leo Bersani, *A Future for Astyanax: Character and Desire in Fiction* (Boston: Little, Brown, 1976); and Harold Bloom, *The Anxiety of Influence: A Theory of Poetry* (New York: Oxford University Press, 1973). The texts by Sigmund Freud that I have depended on are *Beyond the Pleasure Principle*, J. Strachey, tr.; International Psycho-Analytical Library; E. Jones, ed., No. 17 (London: Hogarth Press, 1920); and *Inhibitions, Symptoms, and Anxiety*, Alix Strachey, tr.; James Strachey, ed. (New York: W. W. Norton, 1959). I have also profited from the following: Reuben Fine, *A History of Psychoanalysis* (New York: Columbia University Press, 1979); Sarah Kofman, *The Enigma of Woman: Woman in Freud's Writings*, Catherine Porter, tr. (Ithaca: Cornell University Press, 1985); and Jacques Lacan, *Écrits: A Selection*, Alan Sheridan, tr. (New York: W. W. Norton, 1977).

2. Bennett Simon, *Mind and Madness in Ancient Greece: The Classical Roots of Modern Psychiatry* (Ithaca: Cornell University Press, 1987), p. 272.

3. Terry Eagleton, *Literary Theory: An Introduction* (Minneapolis: University of Minnesota Press, 1983), p. 185.

4. Peter Brooks, *Reading for the Plot: Design and Intention in Narrative* (New York: Vintage Books, 1984), p. 12.

5. Michael Holquist, "The Politics of Representation," in Stephen J. Greenblatt, ed., *Allegory and Representation* (Baltimore: Johns Hopkins University Press, 1982).

6. Daniel N. Stern, *The Interpersonal World of the Infant: A View from Psychoanalysis and Developmental Psychology* (New York: Basic Books, 1985), p. 172.

7. Stern, *The Interpersonal World of the Infant*, p. 175.

8. Linda Hutcheon, *A Poetics of Postmodernism: History, Theory, Fiction* (New York: Routledge, 1988), p. 3.

9. Anika Lemaire, *Jacques Lacan*, David Macey, tr. (Boston: Routledge & Kegan Paul, 1977), pp. 217-18.

10. Margaret Atwood, "The Sin Eater."

11. For feminist treatments of Freud's female cases see Charles Bernheimer and Claire Kahan, eds., *In Dora's Case: Freud—Hysteria—Feminism* (New York: Columbia University Press, 1985), and Juliet Mitchell, *Psychoanalysis and Feminism: Freud, Laing, and Women* (New York: Vintage Books, 1975).

THE OLD IN/OUT
Ann-Janine Morey

ON NARRATIVE AND CONTROL

I was asked to write an essay on narrative from a feminist perspective using the Mark 5 account of the Gerasene demoniac (verses 1-20) and Margaret Atwood's short story, "The Sin Eater" as my inspiration. I like the commission, because the structure of the assignment replicates a metaphoric process that can be a helpful tool for literary critics in at least two ways. First, just as metaphor is created by comparing two unlike things, the literal combination of which has no particular significance, I have been asked to compare two unlike things which may produce a meaning beyond the literal identity of the components. Second, using metaphoric process as a tool encourages some literary-critical risk taking we have seen too little of lately. Despite its fascination with hi-tech literary criticism, religion and literature scholarship has done little to explore the androcentrism of its own practices, a sign of just how much narrative control is an essential foundation of our cultural world.

That is, critical narratives, just like the fiction we purport to explore, are invested in control, and this is true even of narratives that eschew conventional literary controls. Any time we tell a story we build a structure and a frame around ourselves, a temporary shelter, to invoke the poignant metaphor Mary Gordon uses to define her 1987 collection of short stories.[1] Every story forms a narrative doorway, a shelter for our efforts to make sense of time and loss and ourselves in that flow. A story cuts into what would otherwise just look like one damn thing after another, and establishes boundaries which we can patrol, resist, reinforce, or dismantle and try again. Putting Mark 5 in contact with "The Sin Eater" highlights issues of fictional and cultural control when we read metaphorically, when we are willing to jeopardize the complacency of familiar stories.

Certainly the Mark 5 narrative is a controlled piece of writing, a slice from a longer and highly stylized piece of propaganda which readily lends itself to the formal and mythic expectations of structural analysis.² The discipline of the narrative is a feature that is quite apparent even when read all by itself, and an outstanding feature when the tale of the Gerasene demoniac is placed next to Atwood's "The Sin Eater." But the Atwood story, if not controlled by the same kind of decisive structure that determines the scriptural event, is also an account about control, authority and transformation. The Markan text describes an ideal cosmos and then mimics that structure in the narrative; the Atwood text describes the actual cosmos and mimics that structure in the narrative.

In "The Sin Eater," a seedy, generous, and opportunistic therapist named Joseph falls out of a tree to his death, leaving his three wives and the narrator, a client, to react to and reflect upon the meaning of the loss. Beginning from the opening "This is Joseph," the narrative is present and circular, weaving a straggly web of past memory and conversations that radiate out from the starting point, Joseph, but trail off in no satisfying conclusion or direction. As with many Atwood texts, food is a central symbol and metaphor, inviting the reader to pursue connections between listening and eating, therapy and spiritual gluttony, loss and consumption, women's minds and the carnivorous appetites of men. In both structure and content, then, "The Sin Eater" would seem to be an ideal choice for reflecting upon feminist and narrative perspectives.

By comparison, the Mark 5 account is as absent of feminist opportunity as "The Sin Eater" is replete. In this brief account, one of a sequence of miracle stories in Mark, a man possessed of many demons is exorcised by Jesus, who permits the legion to enter a herd of pigs. The pigs rush over a cliff and drown. The once crazy man is grateful, but his neighbors are not, and while he tries to persuade them that this event betokens good news, they insist that Jesus leave the neighborhood. A linear narrative which moves from an origin point of chaos to a restoration of order, the story affirms the absolute authority of Jesus over the malignant forces of cosmic darkness.

What first stands out when we put these narratives side by side is how different they are. "The Sin Eater" is filled with detail, so much so that the symbolic and metaphoric clues begin to resemble litter rather than coherent contributions to a planned account. That is, "The Sin Eater" is filled with debris both rich and tawdry; a K-Mart sweater, calla lilies, sunflowers, maroon slippers, begonias, a folktale, a garden, a fall, a vulpine therapist with a heart of gold and a blue hand, cookies, three wives dressed in blue, mauve and beige, a dream about an airport, and through it all: sin, food, and consuming, consumable woman. There is so much to hold in mind that when you try to focus upon one element in the story, you have to let go of numerous other important clues. The Joseph story won't be gathered. Everything in it tends toward disorder and cosmic ambiguity, a narrative strategy that replicates the meaning of "The Sin Eater" by stuffing the reader with the same kind of effluvia that have to be absorbed by the Sin Eater before there can be final peace. There is center to the tale, but no authority, for even when he was alive, Joseph existed to pronounce the fact of no authority, no rescue. "Life in most ways was a big pile of shit, he said. . . .Forget about the rescue" (215). Joseph is dead and the angry, bewildered female narrator finds no positive effect in the transformation. There is no future promised or secured in the Joseph account; there is no one left in her life to whom she may speak and be heard (223).

In contrast, the Jesus account is as stylized and orderly as the Joseph account is disorderly, and only a willful reader will be more than temporarily distracted by the spectacle of the suicidal swine, who clean up any lingering litter by taking all human and cosmic messiness with them over the cliff. Jesus is clearly the central, controlling authority, and the short account of this colorful miracle drives purposefully to that point. Although not everyone in the story is happy about his authority or control, we are left no doubt that even when the authority departs the region, order is secured; a future has been promised and inaugurated. The healed man has an entire regional audience to whom he witnesses about his portentous transformation.

THE IN/OUT TROPE OF CONTROL

Further inspection of these two unlikely pieces reveals the control mechanism they have in common: a structure built upon the very banal metaphoric trope of in/out. In/out is one of the most familiar metaphors we use, so routine and necessary to our speech that virtually any piece of writing can be said to assume an implicit in/out orientation on the world. According to Lakoff and Johnson, "we are physical beings, bounded and set off from the rest of the world by the surface of our skins, and we experience the rest of the world as outside us. Each of us is a container, with a bounding surface and an in-out orientation. We project our own in-out orientation onto other physical objects that are bounded with an inside and an outside."[3] Similarly, we make or designate "containers" even when there is no literal, physical geography to mark boundaries. Thus we can speak of being "out of his mind," "falling in love," "keeping her in sight," being "in trouble " or "out of danger," or simply feeling "out of it." Finally, "into" and "out of" offer an important variation, for they carry the way in which boundaries and territories are transformed and changed: the water turns into wine; courage comes out of despair; cookies are made into the shapes of stars. We conceptualize events, actions, activities, ideas and our bodies in terms of boundaries, for "there are few human instincts more basic than territoriality" (29). Thus, while controlling and patrolling the boundaries of our physical and psychic environment, we push on those "containers" in order to create new ones.

The Mark 5 account of the Gerasene demoniac revolves around a dramatic boundary transformation: out of the man, into the sea, the result of which is nothing less than a sign of a complete renovation of human boundaries by the in-breaking of the kingdom. The first half of the narrative is built on "out;" the second half is built upon "in." While paraphrasing from the Revised Standard Version, I've reproduced and italicized all the actual in/outs that are used in the text. Jesus, coming *out* of the boat is met by the demoniac coming *out* of the tombs, a man so tormented by demons he can break fetters in pieces. He cries *out* and hurts himself with stones, and then he cries *out* when he sees Jesus because Jesus has commanded the evil spirits to come *out* of the man. The spirits, however, do not want to be sent *out* of the country. They ask to enter (an implied "in") the pigs, and having done so, the narrative indicates the essential transformation that has occurred by shifting to *in*. That is, once the legion enter (go *into*) the swine, who rush *into* the sea and drown *in* the sea, the action proceeds from within normal boundaries. The herdsmen tell the story *in* the city and *in* the country, the demoniac is clothed and *in* his right mind, and Jesus gets *into* his boat, while the healed man does as he is told and proclaims the news *in* the Decapolis. The only problem with all this "in-ness" is that as a result of his own power, Jesus is "out." Having terrified the inhabitants with his transgression of natural boundaries in order to restore divine boundaries, he gets into his boat because he has been asked to depart from (an implied "out") the neighborhood. Being in control may put you out.

While the Gerasene demoniac narrative is an orderly account of control, authority and transformation, "The Sin Eater"—using the same in/out—is, like Joseph, a seemingly messy, disorderly, and exasperating entity of control, authority and transformation. The narrative evokes not a definitive and dramatic transformation, but flux, uncertainty and shifting boundaries with no clear conclusion. Indeed, the narrator's reminiscences take place in an astonishing number of locations, including, it seems, no place at all. In terms of physical location, the narrative shifts relentlessly. The narrator thinks about or talks to Joseph "in Joseph's office," "in my bedroom," "in an airport terminal." Joseph falls "out of a tree . . . in his garden," an unexpected boundary breach which moves him to new territory "in his coffin," leaving the narrator to consider whether sins are "in the food" and whether she is responsible for ingesting ("in") the "cookies cut into the shapes of moons and stars."

All these geographical location shifts have something to do with states of mind, if not essential states of being: witness the change in Joseph's estate when he falls out of a tree and into a coffin. When alive, Joseph would not sit "in indulgent silence," if you "ran out of things to say," although he claimed he had "all the time in the world." This falsehood becomes transparent to the narrator although she still hopes he is faking, and imagines calling to the closed coffin, "you can come out now." But Joseph's sins hover "in the air," and while she struggles to combat the "fiction in myself," without doing it "out loud," she is waging a battle of crucial hordes wondering if she is "out of my mind," or "out of your tree," trying to keep some essential center "in mind," trying to get "everything straightened out." The last line of the story leaves her with a floating plate of cookies "cut into shapes of moons and stars," and as she "reach[es] out for one they begin to shine." Some sort of kingdom seems to be at hand.

AN EARLY SIN EATER

As I noted earlier, "in" and "out" are so common that it would be impossible to write a story without them, so lest the reader begin to feel that I am abusing the privilege of literary criticism and theory I add to my demonstration a further item. "The Sin Eater" is not Atwood's first essay at a Joseph narrative. A revealing earlier version is embedded in her first novel, *The Edible Woman*, a narrative that is also built upon eating as basic in/out activity.[4] Marian, the heroine of *The Edible Woman*, responds to her engagement and upcoming marriage to Peter by hiding and burrowing in bizarre places. She is a demoniac in training, looking for a suitable cave or tomb, and she becomes so detached from herself that the narrative shifts from first to third person and stays there throughout the long middle section of the novel. Not only is she frightened of captivity by marriage; she associates that captivity with a repulsive kind of female body. At the office Christmas party she observes the women around her, seeing them as grotesque porous blobs: "What peculiar creatures they were; and the continual influx between the outside and the inside, taking things in, giving them out, chewing, words, potato chips, burps, grease, hair, babies, milk, excrement, cookies, vomit, coffee. . ." (171). Feeling "suffocated by this thick sargasso-sea of femininity," she looks to Peter as a refuge, "something solid, clear: a man," so she can "hold onto him to keep from being sucked down" by this messy female future. Yet as her marriage looms closer, she is more and more repelled by the entrance and exit capacity of her own body, until she is finally unable to eat.

There are two male rescuers in the novel. Her fiancé, Peter, is the orderly, authoritative Jesus to whom she clings as a certainty against her fate as a reproducing female body. Yet when he encourages her to exploit her desirability as a female body (a different object from the reproducing female body), she feels like a devourable commodity or a hunting trophy. Peter with a camera becomes, in her eyes, a "homicidal maniac with a lethal weapon in his hands" (253). Duncan, the skinny, sallow student type she meets at a launderette, serves as the disorderly, enigmatic Joseph figure, and she uses him as an excuse for fleeing the authoritative controlling Peter/Jesus. But neither male figure can save her from the in/out dilemma, and she is forced into enacting her own ritual destruction and reclamation. She bakes and eats herself in effigy as a pink cake. She performs an in/out operation upon herself as an ambiguously weighted means of regaining control.

Finally, there is Marian's roommate Ainsley, who has determined to have a child without the nuisance of a husband. She does need, however, a suitable donor for her immaculate project. Ainsley selects a victim, a man who is known for seducing women but who is outraged when Ainsley's plan is revealed. A scene follows in which Ainsley and Marian commit the unforgivable sin of laughing at his indignation. Wrathfully, the young male chauvinist pig plunges down the apartment stairs, followed by Ainsley and Marian. Marian knows she can't really help, but since "everyone else was leaping over the cliff, she might as well go too" (220).

Atwood refers to lemmings and herd instinct in this passage, and you can see why I like the episode. It tells the same kind of story as the Mark 5 pigs, but in *The Edible Woman* there is no clean sweep of messiness. Even though the indignant pig and his adversaries all go over the cliff, no one is reclothed or restored to his/her right mind. Ainsley still has to find an agreeable father; Marian has yet to ponder fully all these things in her heart in order to escape her containment by Jesus/Peter.

By referring to this prior text—a respectable literary method, I believe—we see that "The Sin Eater" is a revisitation of *The Edible Woman*. Sadly enough, "The Sin Eater" shows a regress for the female narrator. She has no name in the short story, and the Jesus figure has disappeared, leaving only the enigmatic, ungatherable and unpalatable Joseph. We leave the nameless female narrator at some point of transformation, but we have no idea if, in reaching for the cookies, she enacts a triumph or a further loss. In fact, we are forced to ask, has this been a narrative about the loss of a therapist, or the loss of a self who never has a chance to appear?

READING ATWOOD VIA MARK

Putting the Mark 5 account of madness, healing and divine authority next to these collected Atwood narratives helps us read Atwood. The mythic dimension of the Atwood text is more fully opened to us as a narrative about madness and control, and we see how much an ordinary and even trivial metaphoric manner of communication carries a narrative beyond ordinary significations. *The Edible Woman* and "The Sin Eater" are based upon an essential act of control and boundary transformation: eating, a literal in/out which claims connections with another basic in/out activity, sex, which in turn leads to therapy/salvation (he's in control, she's out of her mind).

Furthermore, the analogy between sex, eating, therapy, and salvation that extends from Mark 5 to Atwood has a darkly fascinating implication for women. In certain kinds of mental illness—schizophrenia, for example—the person lacks the usual screening mechanisms for sensory, external information that healthy persons assume to help them ignore some things and concentrate on others. But in some kinds of mental illness, there are no normal boundaries, and the self is virtually unprotected from a bombardment of unprioritized sights, sounds and smells. Without the usual filtering grids, the person is an easy prey for "demons," for s/he has no way to contain and mark what should be "in" the mind and what should be "out." What social psychologist Nancy Chodorow says about women sounds horribly the same. We have, in her words, a "permeable ego membrane," which makes us more porous and more responsive to others. "There is a tendency in women toward boundary confusion and a lack of sense of separateness from the world."[5] According to Chodorow's work, women are less able to define or defend our own "in" and "out." That is, of course, why the sin eater as Joseph tells the story is a woman. The three activities of the story—eating, sex, and getting saved—seem to be areas of perpetual trauma for women, who historically and contemporaneously have difficulty defining, defending, or sustaining a healthy identity relative to food, sex and salvation. One acceptable way to conclude the comparison is to develop further appreciation of the orderliness of salvation offered through the figure of the authoritative savior. Some kinds of soul-sickness may require divine intervention.

READING MARK VIA ATWOOD

But as with all metaphoric methods, the reading can take another direction. Using Atwood to read Mark 5 helps us see another implication of the scriptural text. Women may be more vulnerable to attack by demons, but the gruesome irony is that for a woman living under patriarchal rule, the cure may be no better than the sickness. Mark 5 may answer a need for rescue, but Atwood may be telling the truth about that rescue. The marauding demons could be the rescuer himself, or, perhaps, simply, there is no rescue for women. In other words, we all experience in/out but we don't all experience in/out from the same position.[6] The authority, control and transformation that seem to be so satisfactory in a patriarchal narrative may look a lot different from a feminist perspective.

The Joseph narrative describes the way the world is for women, promising no rescue, not even for the savior. Of Marian's marriage crisis and desire for rescue, the first Joseph prototype, Duncan of *The Edible Woman*, says, "it's your own personal *cul de sac*, you invented it, you'll have to think your way out of it" (272). In "The Sin Eater" the women visit the tomb but the Joseph savior is still dead in his coffin. But unlike the Jesus, the Joseph was tolerably honest when he lived. "The world is all we have, says Joseph. It's all you have to work with. It is not too much for you. You will not be rescued" (222). On the other hand, the Jesus narrative in the gospel promises a restoration of order, a transformation of all temporal ambiguity and mess, a miraculous normalization and perfection through the word and activity of an authoritative male figure. Read against Atwood, all this amounts to for women is the old in/out. And considering how often women have been demonized as crazy when they refuse to honor sexist boundaries about themselves, we know metaphorically that the Gerasene demoniac, like the sin eater, was a woman.

FAIRY TALES AND FICTION

The last story of Mary Gordon's *Temporary Shelter* is a story called "The Writing Lesson." Gordon begins: "Fairy tales, we have been told, have within them the content of all fiction. As an exercise, write the same story as a fairy tale, and then as the kind of fiction we are more used to."[7] Gordon then traces a theoretical story line in both fairy tale and fictional form. Fairy tales begin with a secure, sturdy center structure—perhaps a house with thick walls in the middle of the woods. In fairy tales, even unspoken feelings are understood, and in fairy tales something definite must happen. In fairy tales there is loss, quest, and transformation, and they will usually involve a hero and a happy ending.

Fiction may do many of the same things, yet every parallel step is entangled and complicated by the complex of the real, or for Gordon, what is the moral dimension of human life—the novelist's imperative to tell the truth about human existence. Only after we've understood the compromised and compromising development of fictional narrative relative to the world of fairy tale are we ready to go back to the beginning and "describe the house" of fiction, as she charges the reader in the last sentence of the story. Feminist analysis of in/out in the Gerasene demoniac shows us this: the Mark 5 narrative with its secure, authoritative boundaries and tidied-up world is a fairy tale; "The Sin Eater" is the "true" story—temporary shelter.

NOTES

1. Mary Gordon, *Temporary Shelter* (New York: Random House, 1987).

2. For example, Elizabeth Struthers Malbon, *Narrative Space and Mythic Meaning in Mark* (San Francisco: Harper & Row, 1986).

3. George Lakoff and Mark Johnson, *Metaphors We Live By* (Chicago: University of Chicago Press, 1980), p. 29. Subsequent page references will appear parenthetically immediately following the quoted text.

4. Margaret Atwood, *The Edible Woman* (New York: Warner, 1969). Page references to this paperback edition appear parenthetically immediately following the quoted text.

5. Nancy Chodorow, *The Reproduction of Mothering: Psychoanalysis and the Sociology of Gender* (Berkeley: University of California Press, 1978), p. 110.

6. Indeed, if there is a difference between the way women and men observe boundaries (and I do mean to pose this as a question), Lakoff and Johnson's definition of in/out may be too androcentric. See, for example, Luce Irigaray, "When Our Lips Speak Together," *Signs* 6 (Autumn, 1980): "Between us the movement from inside to outside, outside to inside knows no limits. . . . Between us the house has no walls, the clearing no enclosure, language no circularity" (73), or Hélène Cixous' call to write from the female body, "with its thousand and one thresholds of ardor" which "will make the old single-grooved mother tongue reverberate with more than one language." In "Laugh of the Medusa," *Signs* 1 (Summer, 1976), 885.

7. Gordon, *Temporary Shelter*, p. 208.

MARGARET ATWOOD AND ST. MARK:
THE SHAPE OF THE GAPS
Terence R. Wright

ISER AND THE READER'S TASK

My concern in this study is with the role of the reader in these two stories, not any particular reader in a specific place and time but with Wolfgang Iser's "implied reader," who is not so much a person as "a textual structure" or "a network of response-inviting structures" brought into being by the interaction of the text (the marks on the page) with an historical reader.[1] Iser's theory is phenomenological, describing an aesthetic object which can only exist in the mind; it is a contribution to *Wirkungstheorie*, the theoretical attempt to describe what always takes place in the process of reading a text, rather than *Rezeptionstheorie*, the study of the reception of certain texts by actual readers in particular periods of history. "No one's afraid of Wolfgang Iser," as Stanley Fish observed, because he offers such an inoffensive compromise between the poles of objectivity (placing all authority in the text) and subjectivity (allowing readers to interpret in any way that they choose).[2] Everyone ought to be grateful to Iser, I want to argue more positively, for constructing a framework and a terminology within which to discuss both the power which texts exercise over their readers and the freedom readers have to interpret texts in the light of their own beliefs.

The danger of the piscine position as of other critical theories on the subjective end of the reader-response spectrum is that they give all power to the reader and none to the text. Reading is reduced to a form of therapy, pursuing well-worn personal identity themes without the reader ever learning anything new or being changed by a text.[3] Iser, on the contrary, offers the possibility of conversion, which lies at the heart of both these stories. For in filling the gaps in these narratives modern readers are forced to question their secular assumptions about life and to shape for themselves a set of answers to spiritual questions. The gaps in Margaret Atwood's "The Sin Eater" may be less clearly-shaped than those in Mark's gospel (in which the implicit answers are relatively obvious as well as being reinforced by explicit statements), but they function in similar ways to stretch their readers' horizons.

Iser himself lays great emphasis upon the capacity of literary texts to change their readers, stimulating latent faculties and enabling them to "discover a new reality," to reshape their perceptual world.[4] Iser's model for reading and criticism is not the first-person narrator of Henry James' short story, "The Figure in the Carpet," who claims definitively to have interpreted Vereker's last novel, spelling out its meaning and thereby depriving it of all mystery and power. It is rather one of the characters of that story who provides the model for Iser's implied reader by experiencing the meaning of his friend's work and allowing his whole life to be changed by it. Meaning, Iser insists, is not "an object to be defined" but "an effect to be experienced" (AR 10). Reading is an "astonishing process" through which we are enabled "to experience things that no longer exist and to understand things that are totally unfamiliar" (AR 19). The text manages, through a complex set of "strategies," to undermine the "repertoire" of familiar ideas that constitutes our reality, making our ideological assumptions visible to ourselves, forcing us to revalue them and thus to reshape our world (AR 68-85). It performs the miracle of making us see "with new eyes" (AR 181).

The secret of such textual power, according to Iser, lies not so much in what is explicitly formulated as in what is left implicit, to be supplied by the reader: the gaps, blanks, indeterminacies, vacancies and negations of the text. Iser uses all these terms to describe the various methods by which the reader is stimulated to supply meanings, to make connections and to resolve ideological contradictions in ways which are shaped and guided but not spelled out by the text. Any withholding of information (even as trivial as the color of a character's hair) counts as an indeterminacy which readers will tend to resolve. The "blanks" between opposed perspectives in a novel, whether of characters, narrators or ideological norms, positively demand to be filled. The reader of Fielding's *Joseph Andrews*, for example, must supply the "virtual morality" of that novel, which lies between the impractical idealism of Parson Adams and the worldliness of his opponents (IR 40-4). The reader of Thackeray's *Vanity Fair* also cannot "fail to resolve" the gulf between "illusion" and "reality" in the minds of the day-dreaming Amelia and her scheming friend, Becky. But that reality is conveyed not through an omniscient but through an unreliable narrator whose very untrustworthiness serves to "compel the reader to view things for himself and discover his own reality" (IR 120).

There is an historical dimension to Iser's theory, an increasing indeterminacy in literature culminating in modern fiction in Beckett's self-contradictory narrators. Unlike Roman Ingarden, who distinguishes between "adequate" and "inadequate," true and false actualizations of a text, Iser expresses a decided preference for texts which can be "concretised in different equally valid ways" over didactic propagandist works which impose narrow limits on their readers' freedom (AR 170-78). Yet some of his metaphors suggest that the text exercises a great deal of control over the reader, who follows its "instructions" (AR ix) and fills its "hollow form" with "mental images" (AR 216). Literary strategies are described as "laying down the lines along which the interpretation is to run" (AR 92), as if to deviate were to be derailed. Iser struggles sometimes to escape from New Critical assumptions which reveal themselves in spatial metaphors of texts as containers holding meaning within them.[5] At other times, however, he warns readers against trying to fit a single "plug" into Murphy's many "verbal sockets" (IR 263) and, in a metaphor which finds resonance at the end of Margaret Atwood's story, sees the reader as "interpreting" the stars, drawing lines between them in order to construct "the plough" or "the dipper" (IR 282). No one would deny that the stars are "there" and, after some discussion, we can often reach intersubjective agreement on the shape of the gaps between them. But Iser does not insist that this is their meaning.

THE GAPS OF MARK 5:1-20

All this is particularly relevant to Mark's gospel, which is riddled with gaps, the most famous of which is the ending. The second-century church, dissatisfied with the frightened women apparently failing to pass on the angel's message, supplied a more explicit ending detailing a number of resurrection appearances. More recent scholars, however, argue that readers are constrained to supply an ending of their own, guided by expectations stimulated but not spelled out by the text.[6] Another massive gap in Mark's gospel is created by the seemingly opposed depiction of Jesus as both human, easily moved both to pity and to anger, and divine, his identity being confirmed by heavenly voices at key moments such as his baptism, transfiguration, crucifixion and resurrection. This gap, of course, was given theological recognition at the Council of Chalcedon when the limits of orthodox interpretation were articulated: to emphasize either his humanity or his divinity at the expense of the other became heresy. Yet another "structured blank" is created by the depiction of the disciples as utterly blind and stupid in spite of their election by the divine Jesus, a contradiction which can, given a number of historical assumptions about the pragmatic context of the message, be interpreted as polemic against the Jerusalem church.[7] The text as it stands provides shapes of prestructures as an encouragement to future followers of Jesus similarly afflicted by a sense of their own weakness.[8] Do not despair, runs the implicit message: discipleship has always been difficult.

These are all massive gaps which any reader of the gospel is compelled to fill (and given fairly clear instructions how to do so). Their resolution comprises what Iser calls the "horizon" or background against which the particular "theme" of the Gerasene swine must be understood. The more immediate context, of course, is another example of divine power which precedes it in the narrative, the stilling of the storm, which gives rise to the question, still ringing in the mind of any reader of this passage, "Who is this, that even wind and sea obey him?" (4:41, Revised Standard Version). It is the question, repeated in various forms throughout the gospel, to which readers are invited to respond with faith. Its answer is sometimes made explicit, for instance in the opening verse of the gospel (although this, like the ending, may well be a late addition supplanting "literary" implicitness with didactic explicitness). It is certainly more interesting, Iser would argue with Paul Ricoeur and Frank Kermode, when revelation comes in the form of a secret, in narratives like Jesus' own parables, whose continuing capacity to redescribe life lies in their meaning not being fixed but open, to be entered into in creative faith.[9] What excites literary critics about Mark's gospel is the way in which "the narrative defines the implied reader as a faithful follower of Jesus" without denying his/her freedom, laying down the potential lines which his/her imagination must actualize.[10]

The account of the healing of the demoniac, then, depends on horizons of expectation which the reader is stimulated to supply. Even the seemingly straightforward report of the arrival of Jesus and his disciples on "the other side of the sea" (5:1) locates the action symbolically as an extension of the kingdom to the gentiles. Jesus, who began his ministry in Galilee with an act of exorcism, is made repeatedly to act in parallel fashion on either side of the Sea of Galilee, indicating that his mission is to Jews and gentiles alike.[11]   The point is given further symbolic emphasis by the cleansing not only of the "unclean spirits" but of the unclean animals they enter. This also prestructures the implied reader's understanding of a later indeterminacy in the narrative: the refusal by Jesus to grant the demoniac's request to remain with him. In a sense, this is the big surprise of the story, for once making Mark relinquish "and" for "but." In contrast to earlier injunctions to secrecy (1:34,44; 3:12), Jesus here instructs the cured man to proclaim the good news, which quickly spreads among the gentile cities on the east bank of the Jordan.

Another major element in this story also relies on the prestructuring of the reader's response. For the Markan Jesus has clearly come not only to cross geographical and cultural boundaries but to redraw sociological "maps of purity." He has already cured a leper (1:40-2), eaten with sinners and tax-collectors (2:14-16) and broken Jewish dietary law (2:18-28). So the fact that he displays his power by a miracle involving unclean animals and so many unclean spirits in an unclean person whose worship he later accepts assumes additional significance; it invites the reader to question traditional Jewish concepts of purity.[12] The narrative goes on, of course, to mingle the healing of the woman with a hemorrhage, as unclean a person as it was possible to imagine, with the raising of the daughter of a ruler of the synagogue (5:21-43).

There are a number of more problematic gaps in this particular narrative, one about thirty miles wide, which is the distance between Gerasa and the Sea of Galilee, another indication that Mark's landscape is more symbolic than realistic. There is also the question of the demoniac's name, which serves not only to indicate the size of his problem but to link him with unclean Romans. He is given unusually sustained and sympathetic treatment, more than is necessary for a straightforward healing narrative indicative of Jesus' power. The poetic inversion of v. 5 emphasizes the severity of the demoniac's suffering while the implication of the repeated assertion that "no one could bind him" or "subdue" him (5:3-4) must be that Jesus is no ordinary one. He has a special status which the demoniac immediately recognises even "from afar" (5:6). The second part of the narrative, after the spectacular destruction of the swine, broadens the perspective, as so often in this gospel, to take in the amazed and frightened response of the crowd. That they should beg such a great healer and miracle worker to leave their region stretches still further the gap between Jesus and ordinary mortals.

It does not, of course, require a sophisticated narrative theory to discover that the main point of this story is to celebrate a particularly dramatic example of Jesus' divine power. Iser's theoretical framework, however, does enable critics to discover and to describe the resonance and range of meanings running through this small segment of narrative, illustrating the power of a seemingly simple text to communicate complex theological ideas not so much explicitly, as in the demoniac's naming of Jesus as the Son of God, as implicitly, stimulating the reader to construct a complex network of symbolic codes which give the story additional layers of meaning. The narrator, technically, is omniscient, able to intervene at will to exert firm control over the reader's response in the manner of all propagandist literature. But, in Ernest Best's words, "he appears to have kept his omniscience to himself,"[13] rarely daring to enter the mind of his principal character, leaving much of his meaning unspoken and forcing the readers to build their own response of faith.

THE GAPS OF "THE SIN EATER"

Margaret Atwood's first-person narrator, in contrast, is not even technically omniscient, being limited to her own somewhat cynical consciousness. But she likes to think that she knows everything, complaining that she finds "reality so unsatisfactory . . . So unfinished, so sloppy, so pointless, so endless." It does not, according to her standards, "make sense" (215). Most of the perspectives provided in the story are similarly cynical, particularly that of Joseph, who sees life as "a big pile of shit" from which there is no hope of rescue (215). His wives too harbor few illusions, the first laughing at the devotedness of his patients and the second suggesting that he committed suicide. Nevertheless, the possibility of spiritual awareness is implied by the narrative: firstly in the practice of sin-eating, however ridiculous Joseph himself may find it; secondly through the interest in Krishna shown by the narrator's son, however absurd and adolescent she may find it; and finally through the dream sequence with which the story ends.

There is, then, a massive gap between the cynical secular assumption of all the perspectives voiced by the characters (including the narrator) and the spiritual possibilities adumbrated (if not substantiated) by the text. The narrator herself may not recognize the language of "sin," but the fact that she feels reality "unfinished" and in need of "rescue" adds weight to the implied spirituality of the text. This, it would seem, is the whole point of the dream sequence. Joseph, unlike his biblical namesake and seedier in his attire, may not have shown any interest in dreams, refusing to "say what they meant" and preferring the waking to the sleeping world (222). But it is a commonplace of our contemporary repertoire, to use Iser's term, a product of the popularization of Freud, that dreams reveal what the conscious mind refuses to accept. So the dream here takes on added significance, demanding to be read in subversive relation to the secular values of the waking world.

A number of potential links between the dream and the everyday world encourage such a reading. In the dream, for example, Joseph's hands are bright blue, the color of Krishna's face in the religious magazine brought home by the narrator's son. In the dream too a deaf-mute holds out a huge yellow flower, recalling the sunflower whose spiteful plucking by the boy next door first taught Joseph to hate. As in the dream Joseph calls the cookies offered by his first wife (as at the funeral) "my sins," though there is indeterminacy here in the narrator's inability to gauge his tone (224). The dream ends mystically with the plate of cookies cut into the shapes of moons and stars floating towards the narrator against a background of dark space and her memory that Joseph is dead: "There are thousands of stars, thousands of moons, and as I reach out for one they begin to shine" (224).

The role of the implied reader in "The Sin Eater" is to draw the lines between these stars, to recognize the shape of the gaps in the narrative and so to construct the "meaning" of the story (which cannot, of course, be spelled out explicitly). There is less guidance here than in the Gospel of Mark. But the secular assumptions of all the characters are clearly to be distrusted. The apparent certainties of the narrator's world are all suspended by Joseph's death. She wants, for example, to tell him that he can come out of his closed coffin and hear "the answer," as if death were a kind of game of which resurrection was the goal (217). She feels his sins "hover around us, in the air" at the funeral party, undermining the relative's confident assertion "what a fine man he was" (217). The comfortably solid if somewhat seedy doctor has lost all the coherence invested in him by the narrator, becoming "a huge boxful of loose ends" (220). And when the second wife whispers that his fall was no accident, the gaps in the narrator's repertoire of secular norms loom even larger. "I want Joseph to remain as he appeared," she confides: "solid, capable, wise and sane. I do not need his darkness" (221). A further flashback, however, confirms her suspicion of the doctor's insecurity, revealing him as desperate to be liked.

There are no positive assertions in Margaret Atwood's story, no voices from heaven confirming the truth of the reader's construction of meaning. The word "Christ" is used only to swear, while God is merely what Joseph's patients thought he was. There is no suggestion that the tradition of sin-eating should be restored or that Krishna provides all the answers. But that even such cynical secularists as Joseph and the narrator continue to suffer from a sense of sin, a fear of death and an eternal longing unsatisfied by the world is clearly one implied meaning of the story. The ideological repertoire of secularism is very much called into question by the literary strategies of the narrative.

Iser's terminology, as I hope to have shown, is capable of revealing and describing some aspects of the reader's construction of meaning in both of these stories. This is a relatively modest claim, always open to the objection that it has revealed nothing new. And if this is what takes place in reading, then all readers will feel that they knew it all along (even if they had not attempted to describe the process in the same detail). Such modesty about the role of criticism, however, seems to me well-placed, recognizing as it does that the "meaning" of a literary work, the experience of its reading, is the product of the dynamic interaction of a reader with a text. To emphasize one of these two aspects at the expense of the other is to commit literary heresy.

NOTES

1. Wolfgang Iser, *The Act of Reading: A Theory of Aesthetic Response* (London: Routledge, 1978), pp. 34-35. Subsequent references are in parentheses (AR).

2. Stanley Fish, "Why No One's Afraid of Wolfgang Iser," *Diacritics* 11/1 (1981), 2-13.

3. See similar complaints in Robert Scholes, *Textual Power: Literary Theory and the Teaching of English* (New Haven and London: Yale University Press, 1985).

4. Wolfgang Iser, *The Implied Reader: Patterns of Communication in Prose Fiction from Bunyan to Beckett* (Baltimore and London: Johns Hopkins University Press, 1974), xiii. Subsequent references are in parentheses (IR).

5. Robert M. Fowler, "Who Is 'the Reader' in Reader-Response Criticism?", *Semeia* 31 (1985), 5-23. Compare Robert C. Holub, *Reception Theory: A Critical Introduction* (London: Methuen, 1984), pp. 100-101.

6. See, for example, Norman Petersen, "When Is the End Not the End? Literary Reflections on the Ending of Mark's Narrative," *Interpretation* 34 (1980), 151-66.

7. Werner Kelber, *Mark's Story of Jesus* (Philadelphia: Fortress Press, 1979).

8. Robert C. Tannehill, "The Disciples in Mark: The Function of a Narrative Role," *Journal of Religion* 57 (1977), 386-405.

9. This is, of course, the central point of Frank Kermode's *The Genesis of Secrecy* (Cambridge, MA: Harvard University Press, 1979). See especially p. 44, where Kermode quotes Ricoeur on the subject.

10. David Rhoads and Donald Michie, *Mark as Story: An Introduction to the Narrative of a Gospel* (Philadelphia: Fortress Press, 1982), p. 140.

11. Kelber, *Mark's Story of Jesus*, pp. 31-42.

12. Jerome H. Neyrey, "The Idea of Purity in Mark's Gospel," *Semeia* 35 (1986), 91-128.

13. Ernest Best, *Mark: The Gospel as Story* (Edinburgh: T & T Clark, 1983), p. 118.

SACRED PIGS AND SECULAR COOKIES: MARK AND ATWOOD GO POSTMODERN
William G. Doty

> You create out of what you lack. Not what you have.
>
> John Fowles[1]

Bell Hooks, speaking at a Dia Art Foundation "Critical Fictions" conference in New York, about the imagination as a subversive force: "It disrupts, subverts, decenters, challenges hegemonic discourse." "Critical fiction deconstructs conventional ways of knowing." But, reflects reporter Stacey D'Erasmo, "what is critical fiction'? I wonder. Did I miss a term somewhere? I begin to feel worried. I'm already behind on postmodernism and now it's too late—the discourse has gone on without me. Disconsolate, I begin to eat my Oreos, trying not to chew too loudly."[2]

POSTMODERNIST INTERPRETATION

Given the conclusion of Margaret Atwood's story and especially that of Barbara DeConcini's paper ("Pass the cookies, please," accompanied in the consultation that gave rise to these papers by a real plate of cookies), I'll stress that I did not commission D'Erasmo's remarks! Nor did I come to the Fowles headnote from Barbara's citation of Miller ("Storytelling is always after the fact, and it is always constructured over a loss"); since both Fowles and Miller are speaking of the fabulator's world and process, the congruence is simply serendipitous.

But then few things are truly serendipitous, and one might worry about all these narrative conjunctions, and complain with George Stroup about the bewilderingly diverse proposals that today invoke "narrative."[3] Certainly narrativity as a *point de appui* to the syntactical dimensions of texts and traditions of many stripes has brought out dimensions easily lost to the deep-semantics approaches that so readily reinscribed stories within rationalistic frames and theologies: "what the story is really all

191

about is xxx;" exit story.   Hermeneutics of deceit have
maneuvered more of our century than hermeneutics of the
imaginative revisioning of the traditional, the reconstructive
prolepses that have metaphored into language just what was
being experienced, poetically; but I am encouraged to find in these
essays that the story is *not* being replaced but revisited in
imaginative replays.

I want here to move through some of the themes represented in
the consultation and these subsequent essays (including some not
given in Boston 1987).   That I am partly commenting on patterns
in the essays rather than simply reproducing all of my own
conference paper represents appreciation for the papers of the
other conferees as well as reflective attention to the overall issue
they raise: namely, just how we interpret important texts of our
culture in a postmodernist era.

I've avoided stipulating a list of what makes the postmodern
postmodern, agreeing with Robert Fowler that "trying to define
the postmodern is like trying to define the Tao."[4] It includes in our
case points such as LaHurd's notice of how Mark challenges
reader expectations, and of course precisely the reader-response
emphasis upon the performing of meaning which she and Arnold
stress; Jasper's note about Paul de Man's correction of the reader-
response "father," Wolfgang Iser, with respect to re-emphasizing
the problematizing of the text itself—no simple messages
anymore, anywhere; even the development of various codes in
which a narrative's meanings are arrayed—for instance
DeConcini and Morey developing an analysis from what Roland
Barthes refers to as the alimentary code of narrative, the
language of and about food and its incorporation or rejection, its
semiotics of desire or repulsion.

Or we could point to the mythic analysis associated with René
Girard, that Arnold talks about, or the post-Freudian
psychoanalytic criticism represented in Burdette and DeConcini,
or the way in which various contributors speak of the existential
dimension of these texts—Figueira, for instance, developing
Ricoeur's insight that understanding is already application.
Hence Wright and Arnold can speak of the intention of criticism to
change readers (as can, of course, the preacher Lowry) in a

manner that would have shocked a previous generation of secular critics.

Part of the argument for change was carried by James Wiggins' seminar paper (not included here) wherein he spoke of the "symptoms of atrophied imagination" in our culture, and challenged those of us working with stories to attend more fully to their world-altering imaginal power, their power respecting tradition that continues to be innovative as it brings our rememberings of the past into the present for the projective work of ethical reflection on the future. Yes, the volume is about story, and about interpreting story, and about how significances are forged today, collocations of meanings by which we confront the exhausted Master Narratives to see if our wordsmiths can yet sing together a songline whose rhythms will encode survival for this generation.

Only Pellauer and Detweiler name the problem of finding the appropriate interpretive *community*, a problem postmodernists are no readier to resolve than were modernists, and a problem—in the guise of religious fundamentalism—that novelist Atwood addresses so painfully in *The Handmaid's Tale*.

THE MULTIPLE FORMS OF CRITICISM AND THE CONTROL OF DISCOURSE

A simple listing of the interpretive approaches represented here is quite impressive, and suggests that contemporary approaches to both biblical texts and secular stories are rich beyond the imagining of any previous period in which one or another methodology usually predominated. Although few are fully voiced here, in this small book we have feminist analysis, rhetorical criticism, close-textual-analysis, psychoanalytic criticism, emplotment-narratological analysis, reader response criticism, deconstruction (intertextuality; the suggestion that the text itself is powerful in its own enactment as well as dissolution), philosophical-hermeneutical reflections, theologizing, and symbolic-metaphoric charting. Side-glances at mythic analysis, insights from ritual studies perspectives, and archetypal analysis are also present.

Part of a life-long dream is realized here for me in having a single text (in this case a pair of texts) approached simultaneously from a number of different methodological perspectives. But perhaps I've always been a postmodernist, since multiplicity of approach is frequently named as a characteristic of postmodernist positioning. A raft of options has always been available, of course; what is striking here is that the options simply lie side-by-side, without worrying issues of dominance or singularity or control—although Morey's paper does indeed raise the important question of the control of the discourse.

One approach that has helped critics understand the control and contexting of discourse and hence its very makeup, is that found in Edward Said's *Orientalism*. This work is, along with Hayden White's *Metahistory*, one of the works of our generation that breaches Nietzsche's, Freud's, sometimes Foucault's leadership toward the sorts of hermeneutics of deceit and sophisticated secondary naïveté I keep hoping Paul Ricoeur will develop yet further.

Said's own political involvement in Palestinianism leaves him alert, sensitive, and receptive to many of the subtle overtones of the discourses under which the Near East has been storied and read as a Western tale. Said leads one to conceive of a new "near/far-East/West" seen from a global, not a Europeanistic perspective, much the way Walter William's own empathic identification with cross-sexual berdaches in Native American culture led him to learn more about them than any other contemporary Westerner had yet known, and to share his findings in *The Spirit and the Flesh*.[5] Each of these three approaches leaves one disturbed, displaced, even temporarily destoried, as we learn how cataractically our vision has excluded systemically the Others we found less than Suburban American.

Said's analytic, much like that of Foucault (with whom Said is sympathetic), bares the nastiness of Western-White views of what was never in actuality, although it was so considered, fully Christian-European. Repeatedly Said shows how cultural and linguistic paradigms become the reality frames through which the noematic (what is being perceived) is permitted to show itself.[6] From Genesis onwards, it is asserted that it is by *naming* that one dominates; the signs of the discourse pronounced by authorities become the textbook or databank descriptors and enforce the pragmatic or political dimensions—hence our concern in Alabama when Judge W. Brevard Hand ruled that social science textbooks should be burned because they advocated "secular humanism" as a religion (the action was revoked by the Southeast Regional Court in the following September 1987).

Tillich's "ultimate concern" was cited by Judge Hand, but as usual in Trivializing Amerika, without the qualifiers that such concern must reflect a lasting quality, an eternality, and that the religious object would involve a sense of otherness, sacredness, or holiness (which is why Tillich's stipulations must be seen in close association with Rudolph Otto's understanding of the religious object as being *mysterium tremendum et fascinans*). Except for the judge's brother, no professional witnesses from academic religious studies or theology were considered important or competent enough to testify alongside the right wing fundamentalists to whom a transcendental deity—no doubt masculine, white and upper-middle-class—must have hinted that Deconstruction, Derrida, and the Devil all begin with the same letter of the alphabet. Hardly a postmodernist freedom of methodological choice!

To be sure, the "choice of story itself" is already a hermeneutical determination,[7] as well as the readings that constitute audiences trained by familiarity with one or another set of materials and types of "literature," and that is true for the Alabama school system no less than for the AAR consultation that gave rise to this book, and that begins with a tensional opposition between a biblical pericope (Mk. 5:1-20) broken in Funk's *New Gospel Parallels* into two "scenes" (Vol. 1, p. 200, pericopes K23.1 & 2) and a Margaret Atwood story, "The Sin Eater," whose "scenes" oh so obviously play between the realms of reality, dream, fantasy, and remembrance. Precisely the juxtaposition of texts by the chair of the consultation, Robert Detweiler, asked us to read each in light of its mate: which fantasies rule the Gerasene pericope? and what swine need cathartic relief in Atwood's story?

INTERTEXTUALITY AND READER-RESPONSE THEORY

Again I refer to Morey's feminist reading of the paired texts, but also to the issue of intertextuality, the situation in which Atwood can be said by Burdette to "write over" the Markan text, DeConcini can draw in Atwood's *other* fictions, Jasper points to Genesis 45 "behind" Mark's story, and both LaHurd and McVann develop the redactional contexts of our passage within Mark's overall literary structures. There is even a more widely-conceived intertextuality, an intertextuality of image, when Burdette compares Atwood's Joseph to Osiris, or when McVann and Pellauer conjure up symbolic resonances in the Markan text derived from early Christian (post-Markan) interpretations of the Eucharist and baptism.[8]

Reader-response criticism appears repeatedly in this volume, either explicitly or as part of the informing-posture of the critics, although I noted less emphasis upon it as the papers were being revised. Robert Fowler considers such criticism one of the indices of postmodernist scrutiny: he means by it first a concentration upon the reader and the reading experience, and second the development of a critical model of reading that concentrates upon the syntactic or temporal experience of reading and emphasizes a dynamic, temporal meaning, rather than a static abstract meaning. Hence "reader-response criticism regards meaning as event, not as content," part of what strikes me as a more materialistic or socio-historically-grounded approach than that which ruled form and other earlier modes of biblical and religious criticism.

CANON AND NARRATIVITY

And it certainly reflects the question of canon that has so exercised literary and biblical critics in recent years, because one cannot stipulate a canonical "event" in its relational framework nearly as easily as a canon of particular writings. Canons are not usually, as was true in the case of this consultation, determined by those who know: I've had to give up teaching anthro/psych of religion, critical biblical studies, and Native American religions not because of any authority in the administration "over" me, but because the culture (read: undergraduate students bent on completing a trade major that will immediately provide a high-paying job) perceives such topics as useless. When they must consider Egyptian hieroglyphic myths attributing world creation to male masturbation, Navajo stories of emergence from a series of previous levels of evolution, and many other narrative patterns of Beginnings, slipped into my endless repetitions of Religious Studies 100, what is most often called forth is not so much derision that "they" (the Other, the narratives) are wrong, as sympathy that the instructor hasn't learned how wrong everyone but (name your brand) Conservative Protestantism is.

Hence I'm not just "abstractly" or "intellectually" concerned with the issues of narrativity: it rules our careers daily as we learn never to let students know that we're actually still interested in ([{<"myth">}]), lest our core curriculum status be yet further reduced (a while back our departmental courses on The Jewish Experience, The Christian Experience, and Twentieth-Century Religious Thought were ruled "too narrow" to be approved for the general education listings). My sympathy, then with an Atwood character in another venue (*The Handmaid's Tale*) whom "it hurts" to tell her account yet again:

> But I keep on going with this sad and hungry and sordid, this limping and mutilated story, because after all I want you to hear it, as I will hear yours too if I ever get the chance. . . . By telling you anything at all I'm at least believing in you, I believe you're there, I believe you into being. Because I'm telling you this story I will your existence. I tell, therefore you are.[9]

Certainly there's a compulsive quality behind our fascination with narrativity—why telling makes something, someone real—and much of the debate among narratologists has concerned whether or not there is indeed some deeply archetypal drive-to-narrate, whether we count narrative as in important ways conservative over against the postmodernist decenterings.[10] Arguments in this volume, however, point to the use of narrative as a political change-agent: Frieden's careful demonstration of the parallels between the "foreign agents" of both the occupying Romans and the language in which Mark writes; LaHurd's analysis of the social coping mechanism by which the rhetorical/ritual aspects of the Markan passage operate; Jasper's emphasis upon Mark's interpolations that modify and change the information he is transmitting; and Lowry's sermonic reflection that becomes an implicit metanarrative constructed in parallel to Mark's.

Girard's movement toward finding an ultimate "realistic" referent for the mythic narrative, or his argument that mythic texts cloak and hide their historical "sources," seems to represent a turn away from the imaginative, away from narrative as open-ended play and revisioning of the given toward a one-to-one equation of historical referent and fictional transformation that simply cannot be upheld any longer.[11] This model is the conservative one, the explication of a single "historical" meaning the text must ultimately represent. It is that referred to by Donald Eastman: "The hermetically sealed story, the all-sufficient text, the *canon*, is an ancient dream, a beloved illusion."[12]

The conclusion of "The Sin Eater" gives us a means of graphing our critics' cloture or openness in terms of the self-contained nature of the narrative text: McVann interprets it positively; DeConcini finds it not at all positive but troublesome; Morey suggests that it looks initially positive but that it cannot be *within the intertextuality of the story's own totality*. And Pellauer considers it not like the Markan text an exorcism, but an inverted Eucharist, the stars a reference to the eschatogical Day of Yahweh.

OPEN AND CLOSED TEXTS

References outside the text are highlighted by B. H. Smith and by Eastman with respect to the impossibility of speaking today of "the original version": "no story is told *de novo*; each story is in varying degrees, a revision, a revisiting, a reinterpretation, a rearrangement, a reenactment, a resurrection and a commentary on stories which have been told before."[13] Readers do not read naively but with a historically-contexted set of frames for comprehension and signifying. As Frieden shows here, the very language selected indicates to the wide-awake reader that there are no "mere stories."

When I see the Gerasene story quickly use the Septuagintal name for God, *ho kyrios* (Mk 5:19), then I cannot but feel some political resonance in terms of the determination of frames: Mark was hardly ignorant of the vast appeal of the stories of Jesus' miraculous powers, as well as of the consequently associated stories that suggested that his followers would become empowered to accomplish just such miracles as the *theioi andres* of the hellenistic world were doing. (Any recent study of the Gospel of Mark will provide discussion of the *theios anēr* or Divine Man figure and the evangelist's apparent rejection of it in favor of an ideological model—a servant christology—based on the tragedy of Jesus' Path: those who have found no glorified Divine Man at the tomb are presented as the substitutionary carriers of the Markan conclusion, but precisely [and literally translated] "they said nothing to no one, being afraid, for. . .", an ending that begins an ellipsis that the implied reader is to fill by discipleship.)

Mark's story has the sort of dramatic scenery that led in the last generation to Mark being considered "the most realistic evangelist": a narrative analyst has to love its dialogic interaction and the documentation of the actual number of pigs, even the capping phrase at the end that so neatly provides the folk-cloture, "And the man who had been possessed. . .went away *and began to proclaim*," just as many African tales end with something like "If you found this story sweet, take some of it and share it elsewhere."[14]

Tension is caused by the followers' expectations when Jesus is confronted by an uncouth person (the generic *anthrōpos* is used) whose spirit was *en pneumati akathartoi*, non- (alpha-privative) pure (*katharos*, catharized)—the figure who becomes in the parallel, Mt 8:28, "so fierce that no one could pass that way" (which is remarkable because Matthew tends to downplay such a scene when he excises and condenses the synoptic materials). The excision/relating here comes at the end of Scene One, after the legionnaires have addressed the magician as *Iesou hyie tou theou tou hypistou*—Holy *Jesus-Son*, indeed Son of the sole/highest deity.

This is a marvelously realistic ecstasy, not a Dionysian ekstasis of the worshipper emotionally indwellt, but of the lemming-like pigs, whom we—but not their owners!—are delighted to see carousing drunkenly (the wrong "spirit") into the sea, to the tune of 2000-fold (a periphrasis in Matthew to replace such obvious hyperbole, "the whole herd," and in Luke, "a large herd"). It reminds me of Walter Benjamin's view of Bertolt Brecht's belief in a deplotted theater focused upon situations brought about by those incredible songs I heard Helene Weigle sing in Berlin, song-narratives that interruptingly arrest the seemingly realistic action and disclose it as illusion[15]

The ecstasy of the witnesses, who ought to have found this Jesus rather handy to have around for crowd control, is present only by its absence, which is marked in turn by its antithesis: "those who had seen it. . .began"—not "to worship Jesus," as Mark's narrative foil does when he seeks to climb with Jesus into the boat (Mk 5:18)—but "to beg him [Jesus] to depart from their neighborhood," a motif that will have Apocryphal echoes when the neighbors of Mary and Joseph try to get them to move elsewhere when the boy Jesus bullies his playmates and smashes their brains out when they cross him.

FOUNDING AND EXCLUDING

Look at the *length* of the story in Mark (and Luke)! It is most striking in the context of the Gospel of Mark, which can spare no room, strangely enough, for a resurrection appearance, let alone birth legends; and yet this story that *is* included is so transitory that its very locale vacillates in the manuscript traditions between Gerasenes/Gadarenes/Gergesenes. Suddenly the narrative recognition of the legionnaires ("You are the Son," Mk 3:11, etc.) looms frame-like, it appears less realistic than arbitrarily-scene-setting, and we begin to recognize in action Foucault's "discourse" or "episteme," Said's "orientalizing"—well before the later monological theologies began to construct a medieval safety net for the One True Etcetera.

The duplex power of a discourse consists both in founding traditions of inquiry and exploration and in excluding what does not immediately fall within its paradigmatic markers ("what is truthful' for the archaic poet is not so much what is factually exact as what successfully resists the corrosive darkness of forgetting").[16]   Such ideological perspectives as must be transmitted by schools of theology likewise establish frames, and in my own secular teaching I stress the political power-plays at work as the later gospels seek to replace those considered inferior—Mark and Q and perhaps Thomas. "Inferior" in terms of not representing the politics of the Lukan, Matthean, Johannine branches of Christianity, imbued with Pauline christological corrections to the sheerly-biographical framing of Mark that ends so distressingly with a call to suffering that even the actor Peter, to the pious reader's dismay, could not accept.

When we regard the question of genre, we ought to ask not only what is *added* to the archetype, but also why its authorial tradition did not choose to include materials (if known) that subsequent versions "add." The ideology of Matthew and Luke is evident as they confront the etherealizing applications of Jesus as Revealer-figure (i.e., Q's Jesus) with Mark's own rootedness in Jesus' biostory—a rootedness that was no doubt offensive, initially, to those who held to the pure transcendence of the deity, and hence rejected any virtual incarnation (does the Gospel of John hover?).

Such "saves" as were the work of Patristic-period Christianity have never charmed me about institutionalized religions, aware though I am that only such anal retentiveness keeps alive the inspiration of the originary in societal forms that have both sufficient elasticity and yet structural cohesion—somewhat like sugarfree chewing gum, perduring but cloying. Said's suggestion that "In the system of knowledge about the Orient, the Orient is less a place than a *topos*, a set of references" (p. 177) leads me to recall once again the dominance of frames. The modernist hope was that of narratively respeaking the fragmented world back together, but what has now come at least obliquely into view is the striking possibility that the search in our own time for a simple, single, unified mythological home is itself only a topos that functions as an orientalizing discourse.

But of course what I have just suggested is a postmodernist point of some strength. And Arnold suggests that Atwood does indeed draw us precisely into such a time between the times, in which structural closure is totally lacking for those who face frontally the philosophical-theological questions of our day. Likewise Burdette treats Atwood as a postmodernist narrator who pushes up against the edges of meaning-making; and in the sort of postmodernist jumbling and over-layering of images that Fredric Jameson calls *pastiche*, we have seen Figueira refer to Jesus as a psychiatrist, McVann to Joseph as a Christ figure. Whatever sort of criticism we have in this volume, much of it overcomes traditional historical-critical categories—yet it also has Jasper correcting the ahistorical procedures of postmodernist tendencies at the same time!

BEGINNINGS AND ENDINGS

Let's turn back to beginnings: Atwood's "The Sin Eater" begins: "This is Joseph, in maroon leather bedroom slippers," and his dumb K-Mart acrylic yellow cardigan, probably woven in Taiwan, and we are no less thrust into "realistic narrative" than we were in the Markan story. Narrative skill here leads the apparently realistic description of Joseph immediately (second paragraph) into the legendary-mythological: the Sin Eater's legend captures the reader so quickly, it's uncanny or somehow mythic-beyond-the-usual.[17]

And Atwood's *ending* will be similarly uncanny, yet on an oneiric plane ("This is a room at night. . . .I have been having a dream") that will only now at last allow us to resolve the concatenation of all those *blues*:

a) the (implied) blues of the narrator facing the narrated death of a therapeutic sin eater (in turn implying the implied author's or reader's blues?);

b) the fabulous blue skin of Krishna playing with the gopis—that blue integument that strikes Westerners as so exotic and forbidding, and in Atwater's story is *immediately* followed by the "Do you like me?" by which Joseph and Krishna assemble their various milkmaids (earlier: "I remember certain stories I've heard about him, him and women");

c) and the blue of the sky (presumably) below which Joseph sought to trim his tree (colors feature repeatedly throughout this story, as marked also by the narrator's concern with the appropriate pastel funeral garments);

d) blue as the traditional color of a dead person's flesh in the West—the refusal to let Joseph die because the narrator ennarrates his death;

e) and finally Joseph's waving, gloved-and-bared "picture-book blue" hands at the end, and the large plate of cookies—"My sins," chants Joseph—that can't but recall the blue-plate specials featured at any downtown American diner.[18] Clearly William Gass caught the metaphoric polyphony well: "the worship of the word [blue] must be pagan and polytheistic."[19]

And it was such an ecstatic cookie-plate: "it's too much for me, I might get sick." Yet we know that the *therapy* (the fundamental underlying metaphor of the Atwood story—its Greek root means "to carry something for someone") *must* begin with the moon and star cookies of our own nurseries: we know that no narrative escape may easily replace the journey of struggles with our own Joseph-fathers, anymore than they could for Thomas Mann (the Joseph cycle) or the Northern European folk tale that collated attention to the sin eater scapegoat. And each journey remains paradigmatic as we learn to escape our own desert islands, eat our sins, and face it when *our* "Joseph is dead" ("'Weg-von-hier,' das ist mein Ziel"—Kafka, in the story entitled "Das Ziel"). "Fortunately it is a truly immense journey."[20]

The journey/the story/the storyteller: what we come to *know* through *narratives* lies only briefly upon the blue plate. It is the *connoisseur's* special of the day, it gathers for only momentary delectation the *kennings* of *couth notions* by which we *connote* the *recognitions* of our lives. *Gnostic knowings: cunning cognitions* we dare not *ignore, noble gnomons* that *acquaint* us with the *norms* of future *prognoses*. These last references in italics have been the sorts of word plays to which narratives of knowing lead: see the derivative/cognate words from which "narrative" derives, related to the ProtoIndoEuropean **gno-*, in *The American Heritage Dictionary* (appendix to the historic first edition).[21]

"I've been having a dream about Joseph": we tell people about our dreams of them, and they listen because they know the dreams are about the dreamer; the knowing of the difference leads to narrative, as to how we ask questions into the ellipsis, into, as Wiggins put it, the gap between forgetting and remembering. How we now deal with a crumbled-cookie-plate, a shattering of centralizing discourses that prohibits new emplotments in science or logic; how we begin to uncover the suppressed Other that has been left unvoiced/unnarrated by the act of substituting consistently and monotonously the dominant culture's discourse; how we find a sin eater who cannot be frightened away by the intensity of our nuclear hates . . .[22] or by the wrong heaps of stories; Ralph Norman notes that "those undone at Dachau, or at Johannesburg, or on sundry other killing fields of our century have suffered perhaps not a lack of Sacred Story but a surfeit of it."[23]

Fortunately there's the constant rediscovery of the story, the plunging down into narrative that allows it to "know" you are this or that; it helps you "narrate" all that "gnosis," caught charmingly enough in an account of a grown-up hippie's adventure on the Amazon:

> Realizing you're part of a story gives things meaning. Realizing you're in the story with someone else who's got his own story with threads leading up to your shared story, just the way you do, then even more than meaning, there seems to be fate. Then, when you get meaning and fate happening together, and you see your story and how it is knotted with someone else's, and you see where some of the threads begin, and you are sitting there thinking there is meaning and maybe fate in the way things happen, then, when something from the outside, which maybe was not so outside, comes and ties it up together for both of you, as if that something on the outside had been watching all along and you were right in thinking you were part of a story that had meaning and fate, then, even if you died the next second, it would be OK. You had found a treasure.[24]

NOTES

1. John Fowles, *Daniel Martin* (Boston: Little, Brown, 1987), p. 268.

2. Stacey D'Erasmo, "Yo! Soho PoMo!" *The Village Voice* (26 June, 1990), 71.

3. George Stroup, *The Promise of Narrative Theology* (Atlanta: John Knox Press, 1981), p. 71.

4. Robert M. Fowler, "Post-Modern Biblical Criticism: The Criticism of Pre-Modern Texts in a Post-Critical, Post-Modern, Post-Literate Era," cited from a preprint for the Westar Institute meetings of March 1989. Although we have now an overwhelming bookshelf of books introducing postmodernism—so many that I've just sworn never again to read another!—it is sometimes still the case that unanticipated sites are the most useful: I have in mind the splendid résumé of eight characteristics of postmodernist philosophy in its oppositions to Enlightenment perspectives in Jane Flax, "Postmodernism and Gender Relations in Feminist Theory," *Signs* 12/4 (1987), 621-43, at 624-25. Flax essentially moves to show why historico-social context rather than abstracted and universalized "reason" is now the predominating highest court of appeal, but her description of the sea change that marks contemporary theory is useful, and doubtless would be subscribed to by many of the contributors to this volume. A similar challenge to widely established narratologies is summarized by Barbara Herrnstein Smith, "Narrative Versions, Narrative Theories," in W. J. T. Mitchell, ed., *On Narrative* (Chicago: University of Chicago Press, 1981), pp. 209-32.

5. The works referred to in this paragraph are: Edward W. Said, *Orientalism* (New York: Random House, 1978); Hayden White, *Metahistory: The Historical Imagination in Nineteenth-Century Europe* (Baltimore: Johns Hopkins University Press, 1973); and Walter L. Williams, *The Spirit and the Flesh: Sexual Diversity in American Indian Culture* (Boston: Beacon Press, 1986).

6. On Said's own framings, see now the criticisms of Paul A. Bové, *Intellectuals in Power: A Genealogy of Critical Humanism* (New York: Columbia University Press, 1986); and a graphic exposition of French postcards that demonstrates how tourism is yet another form of hegemonic perspective, by Malek Alloula, *The Colonial Harem,*

Myrna Godzich and Wlad Godzich, trs. (Minneapolis: University of Minnesota Press, 1986; Theory and History of Literature, 21).

7.　As noted by George Aichele, Jr., *The Limits of Story* (Philadelphia: Fortress Press, and Chico, CA: Scholars Press, 1985).

8.　Fowler, "Post-Modern Biblical Criticism," summarizes his earlier work that argued that the Markan Feeding of the 5,000 was actually a Markan creation, as opposed to the Feeding of 4,000 that Mark simply transmits. My impression is that once biblical critics overcame the earliest-is-normative position, the treatment of such internal intertextuality was greatly facilitated, and rationalistic arguments about "derivation" ceased.

9.　Margaret Atwood, *The Handmaid's Tale* (New York: Fawcett Crest, 1985), p. 344.

10.　See the striking debates in Mitchell, *On Narrative*. According to Mitchell, viii, Hayden White and Robert Scholes represent the view I have presented.

11.　René Girard, *The Scapegoat* (Baltimore: Johns Hopkins University Press, 1986), pp. 32, 80. See the excellent treatment of the history:fiction issue by Terry Eagleton, *Criticism and Ideology: A Study in Marxist Literary Theory* (London: Verso, 1976).

12.　Donald Eastman, "Teaching Stories," *Soundings—An Interdisciplinary Journal* 71/4 (1988), 555-66, at 555.

13.　Eastman, "Teaching Stories."

14.　Jasper notes the tension of such an ending with Mark's messianic secret motif, according to which Jesus usually says "keep it close."

15.　Walter Benjamin, "The Author as Producer." In Brian Wallis, ed., *Art After Modernism: Rethinking Representation* (New York: New Museum of Contemporary Art, and Boston: Godine, 1984. (Original publication of the essay was 1984), pp. 297-309.

16.　Charles Segal, "Naming, Truth, and Creation in the Poetics of Pindar," *Diacritics* 16/2 (1986), 65-83, at 65.

17. Segal, "Naming," p. 82, my emphasis: Pindar, "like other archaic poets, *relies on an underlying armature of myth* that he turns to different purposes and clothes with fresh embellishments as particular circumstances demand."

18. In my native New Mexico, "the blue-plate special" was strictly for locals, and it meant hotter-than-hell blue-cornmeal dishes that left one, upon tasting the salsa piccante, so aware of their spiritual hotness that Atwood's words could easily be applied: "the plate floats up toward me, there is no table. . .".

19. William Gass, *On Being Blue: A Philosophical Inquiry* (Boston: Godine, 1976), p. 20.

20. This meaning comes through in the translation by Ernest Kaiser and Eithne Wilkins, who title the story "Das Ziel/My Destination" (in Franz Kafka, *Parables and Paradoxes in German and English*, Nathan Glatzer, ed. [New York: Schocken, 1958], pp 188-89), more clearly than in the Tania and James Stern translation entitled "The Departure" (in Franz Kafka, *The Complete Stories*, Nathan Glatzer, ed. [New York: Schocken, 1971], p. 449). In the latter the story is inexplicably truncated at the "Weg-von-hier" declaration.

21. Subsequent to writing these remarks, I found that in the Mitchell volume *On Narrative*, both Hayden White (1, n. 2) and Victor Turner (163) play through aspects of this word trajectory.

22. I am referring to the powerful essay by Christine Downing, "What Use Are Poets in a Time of Need?" *Soundings—An Interdisciplinary Journal* 68/3 (1985), 301-17.

23. Ralph V. Norman, "Editor's Notes: Managing the Story Where You Are," *Soundings—An Interdisciplinary Journal* 68/4 (1985), 427-34, at 430.

24. Paul Zallis, *Who Is the River: Getting Lost and Found in the Amazon and Other Places* (New York: Atheneum, 1986), pp. 366-67.

THE SIN EATER
Margaret Atwood

This is Joseph, in maroon leather bedroom slippers, flattened at the heels, scuffed at the toes, wearing also a seedy cardigan of muddy off-yellow that reeks of bargain basements, sucking at his pipe, his hair greying and stringy, his articulation as beautiful and precise and English as ever:

"In Wales," he says, "mostly in the rural areas, there was a personage known as the Sin Eater. When someone was dying the Sin Eater would be sent for. The people of the house would prepare a meal and place it on the coffin. They would have the coffin all ready, of course: once they'd decided you were going off, you had scarcely any choice in the matter. According to other versions, the meal would be placed on the dead person's body, which must have made for some sloppy eating one would have thought. In any case the Sin Eater would devour this meal and would also be given a sum of money. It was believed that all the sins the dying person had accumulated during his lifetime would be removed from him and transmitted to the Sin Eater. The Sin Eater thus became absolutely bloated with other people's sins. She'd accumulate such a heavy load of them that nobody wanted to have anything to do with her; a kind of syphilitic of the soul, you might say. They'd even avoid speaking to her, except of course when it was time to summon her to another meal."

"Her?" I say.

The numbers in brackets at the bottom of each page of "The Sin Eater" correspond to the pagination in *The Dancing Girls* . These are the numbers cited by the authors in our volume.

Joseph smiles, that lopsided grin that shows the teeth in one side of his mouth, the side not engaged with the stem of his pipe. An ironic grin, wolvish, picking up on what? What have I given away this time?

"I think of them as old women," he says, "though there's no reason why they shouldn't have been men, I suppose. They could be anything as long as they were willing to eat the sins. Destitute old creatures who had no other way of keeping body and soul together, wouldn't you think? A sort of geriatric spiritual whoring."

He gazes at me, grinning away, and I remember certain stories I've heard about him, him and women. He's had three wives, to begin with. Nothing with me though, ever, though he does try to help me on with my coat a bit too lingeringly. Why should I worry? It's not as though I'm susceptible. Besides which he's at least sixty, and the cardigan is truly gross, as my sons would say.

"It was bad luck to kill one of them, though," he says, "and there must have been other perks. In point of fact I think Sin Eating has a lot to be said for it."

Joseph's not one of the kind who'll wait in sensitive, indulgent silence when you've frozen on him or run out of things to say. If you won't talk to him, he'll bloody well talk to you, about the most boring things he can think of, usually. I've heard all about his flower beds and his three wives and how to raise calla lilies in your cellar; I've heard all about the cellar too, I could give guided tours. He says he thinks it's healthy for his patients—he won't call them "clients," no pussyfooting around, with Joseph—to know he's a human being too, and God do we know it. He'll drone on and on until you figure out that you aren't paying him so you can listen to him talk about his house plants, you're paying him so he can listen to you talk about yours.

Sometimes, though, he's really telling you something. I pick up my coffee cup, wondering whether this is one of those occasions.

"Okay," I say, "I'll bite. Why?"

"It's obvious," he says, lighting his pipe again, spewing out fumes. "First, the patients have to wait until they're dying. A true life crisis, no fakery and invention. They aren't permitted to bother you until then, until they can demonstrate that they're serious, you might say. Second, somebody gets a good square meal out of it." He laughs ruefully. We both know that half his patients don't bother to pay him, not even the money the government pays them. Joseph has a habit of taking on people nobody else will touch with a barge pole, not because they're too sick but because they're too poor. Mothers on welfare and so on; bad credit risks, like Joseph himself. He once got fired from a loony bin for trying to institute worker control.

"And think of the time saving," he goes on. "A couple of hours per patient, sum total, as opposed to twice a week for years and years, with the same result in the end."

"That's pretty cynical," I say disapprovingly. I'm supposed to be the cynical one, but maybe he's outflanking me, to force me to give up this corner. Cynicism is a defence, according to Joseph.

"You wouldn't even have to listen to them," he says. "Not a blessed word. The sins are transmitted in the food."

Suddenly he looks sad and tired. "You're telling me I'm wasting your time?" I say.

"Not mine, my dear," he says. "I've got all the time in the world."

I interpret this as condescension, the one thing above all that I can't stand. I don't throw my coffee cup at him, however. I'm not as angry as I would have been once.

We've spent a lot of time on it, this anger of mine. It was only because I found reality so unsatisfactory; that was my story. So unfinished, so sloppy, so pointless, so endless. I wanted things to make sense.

I thought Joseph would try to convince me that reality was actually fine and dandy and then try to adjust me to it, but he didn't do that. Instead he agreed with me, cheerfully and at once. Life in most ways was a big pile of shit, he said. That was axiomatic. "Think of it as a desert island," he said. "You're stuck on it, now you have to decide how best to cope."

"Until rescued?" I said.

"Forget about the rescue," he said.

"I can't," I said.

This conversation is taking place in Joseph's office, which is just as tatty as he is and smells of unemptied ashtrays, feet, misery and twice-breathed air. But it's also taking place in my bedroom, on the day of the funeral. Joseph's, who didn't have all the time in the world.

"He fell out of a tree," said Karen, notifying me. She'd come to do this in person, rather than using the phone. Joseph didn't trust phones. Most of the message in any act of communication, he said, was non-verbal.

Karen stood in my doorway, oozing tears. She was one of his too, one of us; it was through her I'd got him. By now there's a network of us, it's like recommending a hairdresser, we've passed him from hand to hand like the proverbial eye or tooth. Smart women with detachable husbands or genius-afflicted children with nervous tics, smart women with deranged lives, overjoyed to find someone who wouldn't tell us we were too smart for our own good and should all have frontal lobotomies. Smartness was an asset, Joseph maintained. We should only see what happened to the dumb ones.

"Out of a *tree*?" I said, almost screaming.

"Sixty feet, onto his head," said Karen. She began weeping again. I wanted to shake her.

"What the bloody hell was he doing up at the top of a sixty-foot *tree*?" I said.

"Pruning it," said Karen. "It was in his garden. It was cutting off the light to his flower beds."

"The old fart," I said. I was furious with him. It was an act of desertion. What made him think he had the right to go climbing up to the top of a sixty-foot tree, risking all our lives? Did his flower beds mean more to him than we did?

"What are we going to do?" said Karen.

What am I going to do? is one question. It can always be replaced by *What am I going to wear?* For some people it's the same thing. I go through the cupboard, looking for the blackest things I can find. What I wear will be the non-verbal part of the communication. Joseph will notice. I have a horrible feeling I'll turn up at the funeral home and find they've laid him out in his awful yellow cardigan and those tacky maroon leather bedroom slippers.

I needn't have bothered with the black. It's no longer demanded. The three wives are in pastels, the first in blue, the second in mauve, the third, the current one, in beige. I know a lot about the three wives, from those off-days of mine when I didn't feel like talking.

Karen is here too, in an Indian-print dress, snivelling softly to herself. I envy her. I want to feel grief, but I can't quite believe Joseph is dead. It seems like some joke he's playing, some anecdote that's supposed to make us learn something. Fakery and invention. *All right, Joseph,* I want to call, *we have the answer, you can come out now.* But nothing happens, the closed coffin remains closed, no wisps of smoke issue from it to show there's life.

The closed coffin is the third wife's idea. She thinks it's more dignified, says the grapevine, and it probably is. The coffin is of dark wood, in good taste, no showy trim. No one has made a meal and placed it on this coffin, no one has eaten from it. No destitute old creature, gobbling down the turnips and mash and the heavy secrecies of Joseph's life along with them. I have no idea what Joseph might have had on his conscience. Nevertheless I feel this as an omission: what then have become of Joseph's sins? They hover around us, in the air, over the bowed heads, while a male relative of Joseph's, unknown to me, tells us all what a fine man he was.

After the funeral we go back to Joseph's house, to the third wife's house, for what used to be called the wake. Not any more: now it's coffee and refreshments.

The flower beds are tidy, gladioli at this time of year, already fading and a little ragged. The tree branch, the one that broke, is still on the lawn.

[217]

"I kept having the feeling he wasn't really there," says Karen as we go up the walk.

"Really where?" I say.

"There," says Karen. "In the coffin."

"For Christ's sake," I say, "don't start that." I can tolerate that kind of sentimental fiction in myself, just barely, as long as I don't do it out loud. "Dead is dead, that's what he'd say. Deal with here and now, remember?"

Karen, who'd once tried suicide, nodded and started to cry again. Joseph is an expert on people who try suicide. He's never lost one yet.

"How does he do it?" I asked Karen once. Suicide wasn't one of my addictions, so I didn't know.

"He makes it sound so *boring*," she said.

"That can't be all," I said.

"He makes you imagine" she said, "what it's like to be dead."

There are people moving around quietly, in the living room and in the dining room, where the table stands, arranged by the third wife with a silver tea urn and a vase of chrysanthemums, pink and yellow. Nothing too funereal, you can hear her thinking. On the white tablecloth there are cups, plates, cookies, coffee, cakes. I don't know why funerals are supposed to make people hungry, but they do. If you can still chew you know you're alive.

Karen is beside me, stuffing down a piece of chocolate cake. On the other side is the first wife.

"I hope you aren't one of the loonies," she says to me abruptly. I've never really met her before, she's just been pointed out to me, by Karen, at the funeral. She's wiping her fingers on a paper napkin. On her powder-blue lapel is a gold brooch in the shape of a bird's nest, complete with the eggs. It reminds me of high school: felt skirts with appliqués of cats and telephones, a world of replicas.

I ponder my reply. Does she mean *client*, or is she asking whether I am by chance genuinely out of my mind?

"No," I say.

"Didn't think so," says the first wife. "You don't look like it. A lot of them were, the place was crawling with them. I was afraid there might be an *incident*. When I lived with Joseph there were always these *incidents*, phone calls at two in the morning, always killing themselves, throwing themselves all over him, you couldn't believe what went on. Some of them were *devoted* to him. If he'd told them to shoot the Pope or something, they'd have done it just like that."

"He was very highly thought of," I say carefully.

"You're telling *me*," says the first wife. "Had the idea he was God himself, some of them. Not that he minded all that much."

The paper napkin isn't adequate, she's licking her fingers. "Too rich," she says. "*Hers*." She jerks her head in the direction of the second wife, who is wispier than the first wife and is walking past us, somewhat aimlessly, in the direction of the living room. "You can have it, I told him finally. I just want some peace and quiet before I have to start pushing up the daisies." Despite the richness, she helps herself to another piece of chocolate cake. "*She* had this nutty idea that we should have some of them stand up and give little testimonies about him, right at the ceremony. Are you totally out of your tree? I told her. It's your funeral, but if I was you I'd try to keep it in mind that some of the people there are going to be a whole lot saner than others. Luckily she listened to me."

"Yes," I say. There's chocolate icing on her cheek: I wonder if I should tell her.

"I did what I could," she says, "which wasn't that much, but still. I was fond of him in a way. You can't just wipe out ten years of your life. I brought the cookies," she adds, rather smugly. "Least I could do."

I look down at the cookies. They're white, cut into the shapes of stars and moons and decorated with coloured sugar and little silver balls. They remind me of Christmas, of festivals and celebrations. They're the kind of cookies you make to please someone; to please a child.

I've been here long enough. I look around for the third wife, the one in charge, to say goodbye. I finally locate her, standing in an open doorway. She's crying, something she didn't do at the funeral. The first wife is beside her, holding her hand.

"I'm keeping it just like this," says the first wife, to no one in particular. Past her shoulder I can see into the room, Joseph's study evidently. It would take a lot of strength to leave that rummage sale untouched, untidied. Not to mention the begonias withering on the sill. But for her it will take no strength at all, because Joseph is in this room, unfinished, a huge boxful of loose ends. He refuses to be packed up and put away.

"Who do you hate the most?" says Joseph. This, in the middle of a lecture he's been giving me about the proper kind of birdbath for one's garden. He knows of course that I don't have a garden.

"I have absolutely no idea," I say.

"Then you should find out," says Joseph. "I myself cherish an abiding hatred for the boy who lived next door to me when I was eight."

"Why is that?" I ask, pleased to be let off the hook.

"He picked my sunflower," he says. "I grew up in a slum, you know. We had an area of sorts at the front, but it was solid cinders. However I did manage to grow this one stunted little sunflower, God knows how. I used to get up early every morning just to look at it. And the little bugger picked it. Pure bloody malice. I've forgiven a lot of later transgressions but if I ran into the little sod tomorrow I'd stick a knife into him."

I'm shocked, as Joseph intends me to be. "He was only a child," I say.

"So was I," he says. "The early ones are the hardest to forgive. Children have no charity; it has to be learned."

Is this Joseph proving yet once more that he's a human being, or am I intended to understand something about myself? Maybe, maybe not. Sometimes Joseph's stories are parables, but sometimes they're just running off at the mouth.

In the front hall the second wife, she of the mauve wisps, ambushes me. "He didn't fall," she whispers.

"Pardon?" I say.

The three wives have a family resemblance—they're all blondish and vague around the edges—but there's something else about this one, a glittering of the eyes. Maybe it's grief; or maybe Joseph didn't always draw a totally firm line between his personal and his professional lives. The second wife has a faint aroma of client.

"He wasn't happy," she says. "I could tell. We were still very close, you know."

What she wants me to infer is that he jumped. "He seemed all right to me," I say.

"He was good at keeping up a front," she says. She takes a breath, she's about to confide in me, but whatever these revelations are I don't want to hear them. I want Joseph to remain as he appeared: solid, capable, wise and sane. I do not need his darkness.

I go back to the apartment. My sons are away for the weekend. I wonder whether I should bother making dinner just for myself. It's hardly worth it. I wander around the too-small living room, picking things up. No longer my husband's: as befits the half-divorced, he lives elsewhere.

One of my sons has just reached the shower-and-shave phase, the other hasn't, but both of them leave a deposit every time they pass through a room. A sort of bathtub ring of objects—socks, paperback books left face-down and open in the middle, sandwiches with bites taken out of them, and, lately, cigarette butts.

Under a dirty T-shirt I discover the Hare Krishna magazine my younger son brought home a week ago. I was worried that it was a spate of adolescent religious mania, but no, he'd given them a quarter because he felt sorry for them. He was a dead-robin-burier as a child. I take the magazine into the kitchen to put it in the trash. On the front there's a picture of Krishna playing the flute, surrounded by adoring maidens. His face is bright blue, which makes me think of corpses: some things are not cross-cultural. If I read on I could find out why meat and sex are bad for you. Not such a poor idea when you think about it: no more terrified cows, no more divorces. A life of abstinence and prayer. I think of myself, standing on a street corner, ringing a bell, swathed in flowing garments. Selfless and removed, free from sin. Sin is this world, says Krishna. This world is all we have, says Joseph. It's all you have to work with. It is not too much for you. You will not be rescued.

I could walk to the corner for a hamburger or I could phone out for pizza. I decide on pizza.

"Do you like me?" Joseph says from his armchair.

"What do you mean, do I *like* you?" I say. It's early on; I haven't given any thought to whether or not I like Joseph.

"Well, do you?" he says.

"Look," I say. I'm speaking calmly but in fact I'm outraged. This is a demand, and Joseph is not supposed to make demands of me. There are too many demands being made of me already. That's why I'm here, isn't it? Because the demands exceed the supply. "You're like my dentist," I say. "I don't think about whether or not I like my dentist. I don't *have* to like him. I'm paying him to fix my teeth. You and my dentist are the only people in the whole world that I don't *have* to *like*."

"But if you met me under other circumstances," Joseph persists, "would you like me?"

"I have no idea," I say. "I can't imagine any other circumstances."

This is a room at night, a night empty except for me. I'm looking at the ceiling, across which the light from a car passing outside is slowly moving. My apartment is on the first floor: I don't like heights. Before this I always lived in a house.

I've been having a dream about Joseph. Joseph was never much interested in dreams. At the beginning I used to save them up for him and tell them to him, the ones I thought were of interest, but he would always refuse to say what they meant. He'd make me tell him, instead. Being awake, according to Joseph, was more important than being asleep. He wanted me to prefer it.

Nevertheless, there was Joseph in my dream. It's the first time he's made an appearance. I think that it will please him to have made it, finally, after all those other dreams about preparations for dinner parties, always one plate short. But then I remember that he's no longer around to be told. Here it is, finally, the shape of my bereavement: Joseph is no longer around to be told. There is no one left in my life who is there only to be told.

I'm in an airport terminal. The plane's been delayed, all the planes have been delayed, perhaps there's a strike, and people are crammed in and milling around. Some of them are upset, there are children crying, some of the women are crying too, they've lost people, they push through the crowd calling out names, but elsewhere there are clumps of men and women laughing and singing, they've had the foresight to bring cases of beer with them to the airport and they're passing the bottles around. I try to get some information but there's no one at any of the ticket counters. Then I realize I've forgotten my passport. I decide to take a taxi home to get it, and by the time I make it back maybe they'll have everything straightened out.

I push towards the exit doors, but someone is waving to me across the heads of the crowd. It's Joseph. I'm not at all surprised to see him, though I do wonder about the winter overcoat he's wearing, since it's still summer. He also has a yellow muffler around his neck, and a hat. I've never seen him in any of these clothes before. Of course, I think, he's cold, but now he's pushed through the people, he's beside me. He's wearing a pair of heavy leather gloves and he takes the right one off to shake my hand. His own hand is bright blue, a flat tempera-paint blue, a picture-book blue. I hesitate, then I shake the hand, but he doesn't let go, he holds my hand, confidingly, like a child, smiling at me as if we haven't met for a long time.

"I'm glad you got the invitation," he says.

Now he's leading me towards a doorway. There are fewer people now. To one side there's a stand selling orange juice. Joseph's three wives are behind the counter, all in identical costumes, white hats and frilly aprons, like waitresses of the forties. We go through the doorway; inside, people are sitting at small round tables, though there's nothing on the tables in front of them, they appear to be waiting.

I sit down at one of the tables and Joseph sits opposite me. He doesn't take off his hat or his coat, but his hands are on the table, no gloves, they're the normal colour again. There's a man standing beside us, trying to attract our attention. He's holding out a small white card covered with symbols, hands and fingers. A deaf-mute, I decide, and sure enough when I look his mouth is sewn shut. Now he's tugging at Joseph's arm, he's holding out something else, it's a large yellow flower. Joseph doesn't see him.

"Look," I say to Joseph, but the man is already gone and one of the waitresses has come instead. I resent the interruption, I have so much to tell Joseph and there's so little time, the plane will go in a minute, in the other room I can already hear the crackle of announcements, but the woman pushes in between us, smiling officiously. It's the first wife; behind her, the other two wives stand in attendance. She sets a large plate in front of us on the table.

"Will that be all?" she says, before she retreats.

The plate is filled with cookies, children's-party cookies, white ones, cut into the shapes of moons and stars, decorated with silver balls and coloured sugar. They look too rich.

"My sins," Joseph says. His voice sounds wistful but when I glance up he's smiling at me. Is he making a joke?

I look down at the plate again. I have a moment of panic: this is not what I ordered, it's too much for me, I might get sick. Maybe I could send it back; but I know this isn't possible.

I remember now that Joseph is dead. The plate floats up towards me, there is no table, around us is dark space. There are thousands of stars, thousands of moons, and as I reach out for one they begin to shine.

GLOSSARY

Apocalypse. The Book of Revelation. Small **a**: revelatory, prophetic message.

apocalyptic. Noun or adjective referring to the study of prophetic texts often projecting and describing the cataclysmic end of the world.

audience. In reader response and rhetorical criticism distinctions are often made among the *actual* audience (the historical, real-life readers of the text), the *narrative* audience (the hypothetical readers addressed by a story's narrator), and the *implied* audience (the hypothetical readers addressed by the author who is apparent or implicit in the text itself).

concatenation. In psychology and psychological/psychoanalytical criticism, a psychic chain or constellation.

Council of Chalcedon. 451 CE, declared that Christ had two natures in one person—that he was both fully divine and fully human, and that the denial of either of these involved heresy.

demoniac. Someone thought to be possessed by a demon or demons, as evidenced by irrational and often violent behavior.

diachronic. In linguistics, having to do with the modification of syntax and semantics over a period of time.

dream-work. In psychoanalytic theory, the processes that transform the latent dream-thought into the manifest dream, or what we remember of a dream.

dualism. In theological contexts of late antiquity, having to do with the metaphysical opposition between good and evil or God and Satan.

221

emplotment. The dynamic process that unites the episodic and configurational dimensions of a narrative into a discordant concordance for the reader. Emplotment gives rise to the plot that the reader can follow but not necessarily predict—although one can look back and see, from the perspective of the ending, that it fits what preceded it. The inherent temporal complexity of emplotment means that understanding of a plot is also temporally complex and never a point-like moment of perfect comprehension.

entelechy. In Aristotelian thought and some other philosophical systems, a force that moves the universe toward self-realization.

eschatological. Refers to teachings about "last things," about the end of the world, and/or about the expected return of Christ.

exorcism. The use of formulaic words and actions to remove a demon or unclean spirit from a person believed possessed.

hermeneutics. The art, theory, and methodology of interpretation, often focusing on how an older text is made meaningful to later readers.

horizon of expectations. A phrase coined by the "School of Constance" critic Hans-Robert Jauss to describe the cultural, social, moral, and literary expectations brought to a literary work by the original historical audience, which expectations influence that audience's interpretation of the work.

implicature. Implied meaning which is counter to, or not immediately obvious in, the grammatical structure of a text, and which requires a "reading between the lines."

implied reader. Wolfgang Iser's term for the ideal reader preconditioned by the text's "virtuality"—by the gaps and indeterminacies which engage the actual reader's imagination.

key-word analysis. The examination of a recurring word either synchronically, in a given context, or diachronically, over the course of time.

liminality. A term used by anthropologists to designate a person's "threshold" condition during a ritual or life-passage experience—a condition characterized by temporary separation from the normal social structures and roles, such as people grouped together for a religious pilgrimage.

master narrative. One of the dominating systems or "stories" of a culture, such as Christianity, or Marxism, or psychoanalysis, according to which its members organize and understand their lives.

mimesis. In Aristotelian thought, a creative representation of an action, not merely an imitation.

postmodernism. A cultural movement, said to have begun around 1965, which can be construed as "beyond" modernism in its acceptance of relativism and plurisignificance and its parodic use of tradition, or as a nostalgic attempt to regain the forms and values of a premodern time.

reader response criticism. An umbrella term for a number of literary critical approaches which analyze the interaction of a narrative text with its readers.

rhetorical criticism. In biblical studies, literary analysis of a text by applying classical (e.g., Aristotelian) categories and methods of persuasive language in order to assess meaning and potential impact on the reader/listener.

ritual. Originally used to refer to religious ceremonies, now more broadly applied to actions and words (that may or may not be repeated or formalized) that have a meaning and impact beyond their ordinary significance.

secondary revision or *elaboration*. In Freudian theory, the mechanism of the dream work that creates a semblance of coherence out of incoherent materials.

semiotic. Having to do with the science of signs, especially in linguistics dealing with signs and symbols as they relate to meaning.

Septuagint. The influential Alexandrian Greek translation of the Hebrew Bible.

signified. In the structural linguistics of Ferdinand de Saussure, the concept that the sound-image evokes.

signifier. In Saussurian linguistics, a meaningful form or sound-image of a sign. Signified and signifier together constitute a sign.

synchronic. In linguistics, having to do with the systematic, stable features of language at a given time.

NOTES ON CONTRIBUTORS

DAVID SCOTT ARNOLD was Chair of the Department of Black Religion at Paul Quinn College, and taught literature and religion at the University of North Carolina at Chapel Hill. He is Assistant Professor of Religious Studies at Oregon State University in Corvallis and author of the forthcoming *Liminal Tellings: Otherness in Melville, Joyce and Murdoch.*

MARGARET ATWOOD, who lives in Ontario, is the author of highly regarded novels such as *Surfacing, Bodily Harm, The Handmaid's Tale,* and *Cat's Eye;* story collections such as *Bluebeard's Egg;* poetry collections such as *Interlunar;* and criticism such as *Survival* and *Second Words.* She has been the recipient of many awards, among them the Canadian Governor-General's Award and the Molson Prize.

MARTHA BRUNER BURDETTE earned the Ph.D. in The Graduate Institute of the Liberal Arts at Emory University, where she conducted research on literary theory and narrative competence in normal and dyslexic students. She teaches at Ben Franklin Academy, an alternative secondary school in Atlanta.

BARBARA DECONCINI is Academic Dean and Professor of Humanities at the Atlanta College of Art. She is the author of *Narrative Remembering,* published by University Press of America. In 1991 she will become Executive Director of the American Academy of Religion and Professor of Religion and Culture at Emory University.

ROBERT DETWEILER is Professor of Comparative Literature at Emory University. His most recent book is *Breaking the Fall: Religious Readings of Contemporary Fiction,* published by Harper & Row and by The Macmillan Press in London.

WILLIAM G. DOTY, Professor of Religious Studies at the University of Alabama in Tuscaloosa, is the author of a number of books and many essays and reviews. A volume of essays he has co-edited with William J. Hynes will appear as *Tricksters: Mythical Figures of Metaplay*, and one co-edited with Julie Thompson Klein as *Interdisciplinary Resources*.

DOROTHY FIGUEIRA is Assistant Professor in Comparative Studies at the State University of New York at Stony Brook. She is the author of *Translating the Orient*, published by SUNY Press, and of numerous articles on French and German literatures, exoticism, and East-West literary reception.

KEN FRIEDEN is Associate Professor in the Department of Near Eastern Languages and Literatures and the Graduate Program in Comparative Literature at Emory University. He is the author of *Genius and Monlogue*, published by Cornell University Press, and *Freud's Dream of Interpretation*, published by SUNY Press.

RENÉ GIRARD, one of our most influential contemporary critics, is Andrew B. Hammond Professor of French Language, Literature and Civilization at Stanford University. Books of his available in English are *Deceit, Desire, and the Novel, Violence and the Sacred, The Scapegoat, Things Hidden since the Foundation of the World, Job: the Victim of His People,* and (forthcoming) *A Theater of Envy: William Shakespeare*.

DAVID JASPER is Principal of St. Chad's College and Director of the Centre for the Study of Literature and Theology in Durham, England, and Editor of the journal *Literature and Theology*. Among his books are *Coleridge as Poet and Religious Thinker, The New Testament and the Literary Imagination,* and *The Study of Literature and Religion: An Introduction*.

CAROL SCHERSTEN LAHURD, who received the M.A. in English from the University of Chicago and the Ph.D. in Religious Studies from the University of Pittsburgh, is Assistant Professor of Theology at the University of St. Thomas in St. Paul, Minnnesota. She currently teaches courses in biblical studies and Islam.

EUGENE L. LOWRY is the William K. McElvaney Professor of Preaching at St. Paul School of Theology in Kansas City,

Missouri, has been on the faculty of St. Paul for over twenty years, and preaches extensively across the country. He is the author of *The Homiletical Plot, Doing Time in the Pulpit,* and *How to Preach a Parable.*

"MARK" is the unknown author of the New Testament gospel—probably the first one written—that bears his name. Perhaps he was a companion of Peter and recorded that disciple's preaching in Rome, yet he (or someone) must have depended on older oral sources as well. The strong apocalyptic tone of that gospel is explained in part by the turmoil and violence of his era.

MARK MCVANN, F. S. C., received the Ph.D. from the Graduate Institute of the Liberal Arts at Emory University. He is Associate Professor of Religious Studies at Lewis University in Romeoville, Illinois and Executive Editor of *Listening: Journal of Religion and Culture.* He is the author of a number of articles and reviews on biblical interpretation.

ANN-JANINE MOREY taught religious studies for ten years before moving to the English Department of Southern Illinois University, where she teaches American fiction and religion and literature. She is the author of *Apples and Ashes: Culture, Metaphor and Reality in the American Dream,* and of the forthcoming *Body Language.*

DAVID PELLAUER is Associate Professor of Philosophy at DePaul University in Chicago and editor of *Philosophy Today.* He is the co-translator, with Kathleen Blamey, of Paul Ricoeur's three-volume *Time and Narrative,* published by The University of Chicago Press.

TERENCE R. WRIGHT is a Senior Lecturer in English at the University of Newcastle upon Tyne in England and Associate Editor of the journal *Literature and Theology.* He is the author of *John Henry Newman, The Religion of Humanity, Theology and Literature,* and *Hardy and the Erotic.*

INDEX